Lone Parents' Experiences as Higher Education Students

Learning to Juggle

For Simon, Juliet, Reuben, Laila and Vincent.

Lone Parents' Experiences as Higher Education Students

Learning to Juggle

Tamsin Hinton-Smith

Published by

© 2012 National Institute of Adult Continuing Education
(England and Wales)

21 De Montfort Street
Leicester
LE1 7GE

Company registration no. 2603322
Charity registration no. 1002775

NIACE has a broad remit to promote lifelong learning opportunities for
adults. NIACE works to develop increased participation in education and
training, particularly for those who do not have easy access because of class,
gender, age, race, language and culture, learning difficulties or disabilities,
or insufficient financial resources.

You can find NIACE online at www.niace.org.uk

Cataloguing in Publications Data
A CIP record for this title is available from the British Library

ISBN 978-1-86201-461-9 (print)
ISBN 978-1-86201-502-9 (PDF)
ISBN 978-1-86201-501-2 (ePub)
ISBN 978-1-86201-503-6 (online)
ISBN 978-1-86201-598-2 (Kindle)

Cover design by Book Production Services.
Designed and typeset by Avon DataSet Ltd, Bidford on Avon, Warwickshire, UK.
Printed and bound in the UK.
Cover photo: Simon Pates

Contents

Glossary of acronyms and abbreviations

ADHD	Attention Deficit Hyperactivity Disorder
ALF	Access to Learning Fund
BA	Bachelor of Arts
B Ed	Bachelor of Education
BBC	British Broadcasting Corporation
BME	Black and minority ethnic
BSc	Bachelor of Science
BVC	Bar Vocational Course
CAB	Citizens Advice Bureau
CB	Child Benefit
CESI	Centre for Economic and Social Inclusion
CFS	Chronic Fatigue Syndrome
CBI	Confederation of British Industry
CESI	Centre for Economic and Social Exclusion
CSA	Child Support Agency
DfES	Department for Education and Skills
DIUS	Department for Innovation, Universities and Skills
DLA	Disability Living Allowance
DPhil	Doctor of Philosophy
DSS	Department for Social Security (now DWP)
DTI	Department for Trade and Industry
DWP	Department for Work and Pensions (formerly DSS)
ESF	European Social Fund
FE	Further Education
FT	Full-time
GCSE	General Certificate of Secondary Education

Gingerbread	Organisation for One Parent Families, now merged with One Parent Families
GTP	Graduate Teacher Programme
HE	Higher Education
HEA	Higher Education Academy
HEFCE	Higher Education Funding Council of England
HEI	Higher Education Institution
HEPI	Higher Education Policy Institute
HESA	Higher Education Statistics Agency
HND	Higher National Diploma
JSA	Job Seeker's Allowance
LEA	Local Education Authority
LGBTQ	Lesbian, gay, bisexual, transgender and queer
LLB	Bachelor of Laws
LPC	Legal Practice Course
LSC	Learning and Skills Council
MA	Master of Arts
MPhil	Master of Philosophy
MSc	Master of Sciences
MS	Multiple Sclerosis
NIACE	National Institute of Adult Continuing Education
NDLP	New Deal for Lone Parents
NSS	National Student Survey
NUS	National Union of Students
NVQ	National Vocational Qualification
OECD	Organisation for Economic Cooperation and Development
OFFA	Office for Fair Access
ONS	Office for National Statistics
One Parent Families	Formerly National Council for One Parent Families (NCOPF). Now merged with Gingerbread.
OU	Open University
PGCE	Postgraduate Certificate in Education
PG	Postgraduate
PT	Part-time
QTS	Qualified Teacher Status
SLC	Student Loans Company

SPAN	Single Parents' Action Network
UCAS	Universities and Colleges Admissions Service
UG	Undergraduate
Universities UK	Umbrella group for Higher-Education Institutions
WP	Widening participation
Work Directions	UK public/private organisation delivering welfare-to-work for the Government
WFTC	Working Families Tax Credits
Working Links	UK public/private organisation delivering welfare-to-work for the Government
VSO	Voluntary Service Overseas

Acknowledgements

This book is the product of the contributions of the lone parents balancing caring for their families with working to improve their prospects through completing their university education, who gave so generously of time they had so little of. Thank you also to Gingerbread for helping in facilitating access to those lone parents. I am grateful to the teachers from school days through to university who have encouraged me educationally, representing the same vital positive influences as lone mothers in this book describe being encouraged by. Through the years, Ruth Mapes, Gary Matthews, Jenny Shaw, Richard Whatmore and Ruth Woodfield all made me believe that I was capable of succeeding as a student, so thank you! Thank you also to mum for never-ending support, and of course to Simon, Juliet, Reuben, Laila and Vincent, for tolerance and time spent without me while I worked.

CHAPTER ONE

Introduction: lone parents and widening participation in Higher Education

This book explores in depth the experiences of 77 lone mothers studying in UK Higher Education (HE). In doing so the insights presented benefit from contributions from a larger number of individuals than many comparative qualitative studies, while also providing greater depth than larger-scale quantitative studies. The scope of the research includes the broadness of HE experience in its increasing diversity. Alongside lone mothers following traditional university routes as full-time students on BA or BSc first degree courses, are included the experiences of those studying part-time, postgraduate, distance-learning, vocational and professional courses. The learning trajectories of lone mothers who contributed insights to this book also represent the increasing blurring of boundaries between Further Education (FE) and HE, through including lone mothers studying for HE qualifications franchised from universities to FE colleges, and those studying for pre-entry level, or open courses at Higher Education *Institutions* (HEIs). These shed light on positive and negative impacts of this increasing complexity. The study originally aimed also to include the experiences of lone fathers, who represent one in ten lone parents in the UK. Despite multiple attempts at recruitment, it was not however ultimately possible to secure perspectives from lone fathers in sufficient numbers to allow meaningful comparisons (only two lone fathers contributed insights during the life of the study). The focus of this book is therefore restricted to lone mothers; much of the discussion however refers to lone parents, indicating the relevance of notable policy developments, insights from existing literature, or trends

1

in experience, that are relevant to both lone mothers and lone fathers.

Lone mothers participated in the research longitudinally over the course of twelve months beginning at the commencement of a new academic year, and providing fortnightly updates throughout this period. These updates both responded to particular topics and reported on general progress and on-going experience. This longitudinal perspective contributed greatly to the richness of insights gained, highlighting the different priorities and problems that dominate the lives of lone-parent students at various points during the academic year. Building relationships with lone-parent students over the course of a year provided valuable insight in locating learning experiences against the backdrop of everyday lives and personal history.

It is important to understand lone mothers' motivations to pursue personal and professional development through Higher Education, and the challenges and benefits they encounter. Much research on lone mothers comes from a Social Policy background, focusing on lone parents as welfare recipients, and problematising this persistent social trend of late modernity. This has led to an increase in much relevant work towards tackling dependency through lone mothers' participation in work and training (Klett-Davies, 2007, Millar and Rowlingson, 2001; Bradshaw and Millar, 1999; Duncan and Edwards, 1999; Kiernan, Land and Lewis, 1999; Land and Lewis, 1998; Ford, 1996). This agenda sits alongside wider social discourses that have vilified lone mothers as lazy, feckless and responsible for wide-ranging social ills, from draining public resources to providing a flawed moral example to their children. Lone mothers' narratives in this book provide evidence that is far from this caricature; many are highly motivated to improve the lives of themselves and their children, within the confines of substantial structural constraints (see Zachry, 2005: 2, 582; Hyatt and Parry, 1990: 6). For many, this includes building on educational qualifications, including through HE participation.

Developing understanding of the hard work lone mothers undertake in participating in Higher Education, and the personal, family, and societal benefits of their achievements in doing so is essential both in justifying adequate support for lone mothers' HE participation, and responding to perceptions that they are lazy and responsible for their own frequently impoverished circumstances.

The second area of relevant existing work focuses on mature women learners' experiences as HE and FE learners. While some lone mothers studying in Higher Education are traditional entry age, most are mature students. Similarly, while some mature women students do not have children (Scott *et al.*, 1996: 235), they are, nevertheless, more likely to compared to students of traditional entry age (Merrill, 1999: 159). HE students who are lone mothers therefore share many important facets of experience with the broader group of mature women students, which has been researched much more fully (see Jackson, 2004; Parr, 2000; Merrill, 1999; Wisker, 1996; Davies, Lubelska, and Quinn, 1994; Pascall and Cox, 1993; Edwards, 1993; Hyatt and Parry, 1990). Much of this work also identifies the importance of social class in informing the learning experiences and wider lives of mature women students. This is also relevant to lone mothers, and the salience and limitations of social class as an indicator of experience for this group are examined throughout this book. Research on mature women students' experiences of HE participation inevitably focuses on the challenges they encounter in simultaneously managing the demands of the worlds of family and university, and often also paid work (see Yorke, 2004: 106). This juggling act represents a key area of shared experience between lone and partnered mothers studying at university. Students who are lone mothers share further important aspects of experience with mature students as a whole; these include increased risk of financial hardship (Jackson, 2004: 52), lack of geographical mobility (Yorke, 2004: 106), and problems integrating into university life, both academically and socially (Christie *et al.*, 2005: 3,13).

There are, however, important aspects in which lone mothers' experiences are amplified or redirected by their status as sole rather than primary carers for children; and these areas indicate the need for targeted research. In comparing the insights of lone-mother HE students with literature on mature women students, one of the contributions of this book is to identify the ways that lone parents' circumstances can represent differences in degree, rather than in kind, from those experienced by all parents. For example, lone parents' sole responsibility can exacerbate the pressure of increasing demands on all parents to participate in both paid work and increasingly 'intensive parenting' – devoting ever-increasing energy to nurturing children's emotional, creative, intellectual and social potential, as well as meeting their physical needs.

Despite the wealth of literature addressing mature students' HE learning experiences, it has been suggested that investigation of students' backgrounds and successes has frequently been prioritised

3

over increasing understanding of personal experiences (Wisker, 1996: 6). Such a focus risks downplaying the strong impact of family responsibilities on educational participation, and, indeed, the family responsibilities of mature students in HE have been seen as receiving insufficient interest from commentators (Leonard, 1994: 164). In the case of lone mothers, this deficit continues today, and it is this gap that this book primarily addresses. Some valuable insights have contributed to highlighting particular aspects of lone parents' experiences in education (e.g. Shaw and Woolhead, 2006; Duckworth, 2005; Lipman and Boyle, 2005; Horne and Hardie, 2002; Scott, Burns and Cooney, 1996, 1998; Nelson, Niemann and Van Stone, 1994; Burns and Scott, 1993). This book builds on these insights by extending the focus of data collection, scope of enquiry, and discussion.

There is an identified need for more consistent and up to date statistical data around participation and characteristics of lone parents in Higher Education, and NUS have recommended that: 'The Higher Education Statistics Agency (HESA) and Learning and Skills Council (LSC) should make it a requirement for universities and colleges to collect data on the parental status of a student' (NUS, 2009: 4). The most recent and comprehensive findings have been compiled by the NUS, indicating that between 5 and 8 per cent of full-time undergraduates are student parents, compared to just over a third of part-time students. Further, 35 per cent of women learning full-time are indicated to have dependents under 16, compared to inconsistent, but nevertheless much lower, recorded participation rates amongst men who are fathers, ranging from 1 to 13 per cent (2009: 12). While these statistics do not directly address lone mothers' participation in HE learning, they do indicate the substantial numbers of individuals involved that render increasing understanding of the challenges faced essential. The statistics further attest to the gendered nature of experiences of managing HE learning with parenting responsibilities, contributing to the rationale for this book's focus.

The issues explored in this book are located most centrally in discourses around widening participation (WP) in Higher Education. This book highlights that, despite lone mothers' unique, particularised experience, many key factors in facilitating their HE participation have broader relevance to other WP target groups of non-traditional students. The book will hence be of interest to those with much broader interest in HE participation, beyond lone parents per se. Through the lens of lone mothers as WP HE students, many key aspects of concrete experience are highlighted that problematise the rhetoric of widening participation. The challenges faced by individual learners in their lived experiences of managing HE participation within the complex webs of their wider lives must be addressed and the learners supported if the expansion of HE participation to disenfranchised groups is to be realised in significant numbers.

Chapter 2 locates lone mothers' HE participation in the context of policy trends and developments, spanning key relevant features of the areas of welfare policy and student financing. The chapter considers the implications for lone parents' HE participation of the UK's progressive lowering of the age at which a child entitles a lone parent to Income Support, the child's age at which a lone parent is obliged to seek employment, and the way in which policy discourse around this taps into the stigmatised 'scrounger' status outlined in this chapter. Discussion addresses the limitations of delivery of this policy through the New Deal for Lone Parents (NDLP), with its relatively low levels of support for educational participation, and documents the way in which UK lone mothers can be seen as doubly disadvantaged in their labour force participation by particularly low levels of education and high childcare costs compared to other European countries. The chapter presents evidence that UK lone mothers wishing to engage with Higher Education are further hindered by contradictions between the operation of welfare provision and student support. It explores the position of lone mothers as HE students within the policy discourses of promoting social inclusion through supporting lifelong learning, and competing discourses of widening participation for social equity and achieving a competitive workforce in a global knowledge economy. The far-reaching impact of the introduction of fees and loans is addressed alongside the demise of Aimhigher, and the drive to maximise returns on investment in Higher Education through targeting retention and graduate employment destinations.

Chapter 3 introduces the lone mothers who participated in the research contributing to the book, examining their profile in terms of factors including age, ethnicity, social class and subject area of study, alongside defining and understanding the complexity of single parent status. The chapter further discusses the process and challenges of recruiting lone mothers to contribute their perspectives, and carrying out the research, identifying areas that presented practical problems. Such problems included accurately monitoring participants' characteristics, including for example insight into the relevance of institutional type being hampered by individuals often not knowing whether their university was a pre- or post-1992 institution, and sometimes not wanting to identify it by name for fear of compromising their anonymity. Lone mothers' instrumental and intrinsic motivations for HE participation are explored alongside identification of decisive trigger moments, and the long reverberating effects of educational support and encouragement, or lack of such, during childhood. The chapter explores the way in which family attitudes to learning and wider life are identified as particularly important to informing individuals' HE participation, with a strong value on deferred gratification emerging as particularly significant.

In Chapter 4, lone mothers' experiences as university students are located in the context of the first of three major themes identified through the research: time, money, and childcare. This chapter focuses in depth on the centrality to lone mothers' lives of, invariably, lack of time, and how this manifests as a constant balancing or juggling act of managing inadequate resources. Compared to the double shift of work and home identified by feminism as being carried out by women, lone parent HE students are shown to face a triple or frequently even quadruple burden of playing the roles of both mother and father, as well as student, and often employee as well. Demographic differences in time-scarcity are explored in terms of factors including mode of study (part time or full time, and distance learning or traditional contact), as well as number and ages of children. The chapter further identifies particular crisis times for managing the tightrope between the demands of home and university, including, for instance, school holidays and times of children's illness. Impacts of such a time deficit are demonstrated to include adverse health effects, exhaustion and guilt. Lone mothers' narratives further demonstrate the need to prioritise engendered by the time deficit they experience in participating in HE, manifesting in creative 'needs must' solutions from skimping on housework to sending children to 'play out'. The chapter illuminates the pivotal role of staff and institutions in exacerbating or mediating the stresses of stretched time for lone parents. This is demonstrated to stand in contrast to the rhetoric perpetuated by institutions of individual responsibility for managing home and university life, obscuring institutional responsibility for facilitating manageability for non-traditional students.

The compounding of lone parent HE students' time poverty by a simultaneous deficit of financial resources is explored in Chapter 5.

Research participants discuss their earnings from employment, and entitlement to state benefits, often revealing complex patterns of financial support. Factors including level of financial support provided by non-custodial parents (NCPs) are shown to have a strong impact on financial experience as a lone-parent student. The chapter further explores financial implications of relevant policy developments for lone-parent students and experiences of debt, as well as widespread experiences of difficulty sourcing accurate information about financial entitlements. The struggle to manage overstretched finances is shown as frequently dominating the lives of lone-parent students, informing further knock-on effects on areas including housing, ability to travel to university, and to provide a healthy diet for oneself and children. Particular problems are explored, including the often stigmatising experience of applying to Access to Learning Funds (ALFs), and the way in which lone parent graduates are disadvantaged by being subject to the same income threshold for student loan repayment, despite their sole responsibility for dependents, including high UK childcare costs.

Chapter 6 explores the way in which issues around apportioning scant resources of time and money for lone-mother HE students are crystallised in the issue of childcare, showing how more than any other area, negotiation of reconciling childcare needs and resources draws together the dual defining constraints of access to time and money. The chapter explores lone-parent students' use of different types of childcare, covering both the preschool years, and so-called wrap-around childcare for school-age children. It also examines the often prohibitive constraints of childcare costs, and both parents' and children's wider dissatisfactions with childcare, relied on by lone-parent students to facilitate access to university study, paid work and social activity. The chapter shows that lone parents rely on complex webs of formal and informal childcare, particularly struggling to secure childcare to meet the out-of-hours requirements frequently demanded by Higher Education, with its implicit 'Bachelor Boy' heritage. Such requirements are shown by lone parents' experiences to include vital aspects of the academic experience, including participating in group-project assignments and independent study groups, and for postgraduate students, monitoring science experiments out of nursery hours, or completing residential fieldwork away from home. The chapter also considers the barriers to full engagement with studies caused for lone-parent students by childcare problems, and the role and responsibility of HEIs in providing childcare and acknowledging its limiting effect on the participation of students with dependent children.

In Chapter 7, understanding lone parents' experiences as Higher Education students is located in the context of their wider lives. This includes exploring how their HE participation is integrated into the nexus of home life, paid work, and wider patchworks of responsibilities, relationships and routine activities. This discussion shows how lone mothers' identities as university students and their wider lives variously overlap, clash, enrich, and mutually inform one another, depending on individual and changing interplays of personal circumstances and particular situations encountered. The barriers lone mothers face in participating in Higher Education are investigated, from unsympathetic institutional policies and practices, through to health and illness. This chapter examines the pivotal impact of level of support received from individual staff and HEIs as a whole, to informing lone mothers' potential for positive HE experiences and successful outcomes. The discussion is concluded by exploring the effects of HE participation for lone mothers, including employment and personal development outcomes, alongside wider long-term benefits to children's lives and prospects.

Chapter 8 concludes the volume by summarising the most salient findings evidenced by the research, and identifying key recommendations for supporting lone parents' HE participation. The chapter asks in particular, *what are the material conditions and institutional assurances needed to make a lone parent's successful HE participation a realistic opportunity?* It puts forward fully and relatively cost-neutral recommendations alongside inevitable identification of areas in need of increased financial investment. Identified needs include improved avenues of accurate information and advice, and better monitoring of students' characteristics, as well as specific recommendations targeted at aspects of institutional policy and provision, welfare bureaucracy, and student financing. Areas identified as particularly important include increased provision of pastoral support, counselling, peer mentoring, and support for peer-operated networking initiatives. The chapter further acknowledges the relevance of the future of increasing remote provision for university student groups including lone parents. The book concludes by surveying key relevant aspects of the developing policy context in terms of student finance and lone parent welfare policy, and emerging and projected impacts for lone parents' HE participation in the UK. These include emergent developments, trends and wider ideology that represent features of UK policy post-2010 regime change from a Labour to a Conservative–Liberal Democrat coalition government, and in the aftermath of global recession and its ensuing anxieties. Many of these developments also have broader cross-cultural relevance given major trends in public policy.

CHAPTER TWO

The policy context

It has been argued that mature learners 'make exceptional students who are very motivated and who perform well academically' (Scott *et al.*, 1996: 233). Further, students who are mothers (both partnered and single) have been shown to achieve grades higher than both school-leaver students and mature students as a whole. They also report higher gains in confidence, ability, intelligence and competence than mature students generally. (Scott *et al.*, 1996: 234; Burns and Scott, 1993: 40). This consistent evidence of such pervasive benefits leads to the question of why student parents, as such highly motivated learners with so much to gain, also have a disproportionately high incidence of non-completion, representing a loss, not only for the individuals affected, but also for society (Scott *et al.*, 1996: 234).

Opportunities and constraints affecting lone mothers' successful HE participation must be explored in the context of major changes to both lone-parent policy and student financing over recent years. The increasing extension of the welfare to work agenda to lone parents that began in 1998 has, under consecutive governments between 2008 and 2011, lowered the age of youngest child at which lone parents must be available for work from 16 down to 5. This has huge implications for lone parents' educational participation: both limiting educational opportunities for those lone parents who would like to return to learning but must instead return to employment, and yet also increasing the impetus for lone parents' educational engagement. Re-engaging with paid work requires many lone parents to develop their educational capital for a number of cumulative reasons. These include the comparatively low educational levels of UK lone parents, the high cost of UK childcare (OECD, 2011), and the fact that lone parents must meet such high childcare costs from only one wage. For many lone parents, building on their current level of educational qualification is the only means of accessing sufficiently well remunerated work to afford childcare costs alone.

In addition to these changes, lone-parent HE students are affected by the vast changes encompassed in several rounds of progressive cuts to student financing that have impacted on all students since the introduction of fees in 1998. Lone parents are particularly disadvantaged by the replacement of grants and Income Support entitlement by repayable loans to cover spiralling fee costs. This is compounded both in the short term by the constraints placed by childcare commitments upon ability to finance HE participation through part-time paid employment, and in the long term after graduation by having to manage student loan repayment alongside meeting household and childcare costs alone from what is frequently also a comparatively lower graduate income, given the constraints placed on career opportunities by childcare responsibilities.

Lifelong learning has been promoted as a recognised means of social inclusion (Jones, 2006: 487), and HE participation acknowledged to be 'a critical determinant of life chances' (Naidoo and Callender, 2000: 235). It has been suggested that, as educational qualifications are known to be a key route out of poverty for lone parents and their children, if governments want to meet their commitments to widening and increasing participation in Higher Education, lone parents are an obvious target group. (Callender, 2001). Further, organisations including the National Union of Students (NUS), One Parent Families, 4 Children, The Daycare Trust and Save the Children, have petitioned the government that 'the participation of lone parents in Higher and Further Education is vital to the success of both widening participation in Higher Education and the up-skilling of groups at risk of unemployment' (Gingerbread, 2007b).

Widening participation in HE has been a central aspect of UK educational policy in recent decades. This reflects similar trends in all economically developed societies, in an increasingly competitive, globalised marketplace. There is a history of disagreement at policy level as to the purpose and benefits of promoting HE participation. For example, in 2003, then Labour Education Secretary Charles Clarke suggested that 'Education for education's sake is a bit dodgy', while the following year, Labour Higher Education Minister Kim Howells opined in contrast that government policies on Higher Education had become unduly utilitarian and that enjoying learning for its own sake should be encouraged, rather than the taking of degrees being restricted to a route to a well-paid job (Smithers, 2004). HE policy developments in the intervening years, most notably in terms of the vastly escalated fee levels announced in 2010, render it increasingly unlikely that students beyond the most privileged minority will feel able to indulge in the luxury of pursuing learning fundamentally for its own sake and enjoyment. The prevalence of assumptions around the value and purpose of education centrally inform provision of learning opportunities for groups including lone parents. Against the backdrop of such dominant sociocultural attitudes embodied in policy, the relationship between individual learners' construct understandings and rationales underpinning their own instrumental (financial) and intrinsic (satisfaction) motivations for HE participation.

Lifelong learning and widening participation are frequently justified in terms of social equity. However, they have been more often seen as being driven by the changing labour force needs of postmodern knowledge economies (Naidoo and Callender, 2000: 227; Wain, 2000: 39), as increasing proportions of society are expected to enter skilled employment in the growth areas of finance, business, transport and communications, in place of the declining manufacturing industry (Skills and Enterprise Network, 2001). Unlike previous pressure to expand Higher Education in the 1950s and 1960s, the current drive that began in the late 1980s has included a substantial focus on widening participation through promoting older adult continuing education alongside traditional entry-age students. This development is attributed to the demographic shift toward decreasing numbers of school leavers, resulting in the necessity for institutions to look to non-traditional students to meet their intake targets (Gallagher, Richards and Locke, 1993: 2; Edwards, 1993: 5). 'Non-traditional' students are defined as being those from groups that have been historically underrepresented within the system (Laing, Chao and Robinson, 2005: 169), and recent policy aims to widen participation amongst such underrepresented groups, including both younger and older students.

In the 2003 White Paper, *The Future of Higher Education*, the UK Government stated aims that included a vision of a sector in which we would see 'all HEIs excelling in teaching and reaching out to low-participation groups' (Department for Education and Skills, 2003: 22).

There has been hope that allocation of special funds for widening participation projects would encourage universities to implement high quality schemes to recruit traditionally excluded students (Callender, 2000: 239). But despite increasing student numbers over recent decades, and the efforts to 'ensure that all those with the potential to benefit from HE have the opportunity to do so whatever their background and whenever they need it' (Higher Education Funding Council for England, 2004: 4), levels of participation have remained stubbornly low amongst disadvantaged social groups (Christie, Munro and Wager, 2005: 4). Concern over these low levels of participation has formed an important element of widening participation debates (Callender, 2000: 228). The UK has been far from unique in this failure. For example, the drive to expand HE participation in France is perceived to have failed to deliver hopes of democratisation of access (Deer, 2005). In contrast, in the Scandinavian countries, education is perceived as having been successful in acting as an instrument of equalisation of social status and experience, rather than one of selection (Komulainen, 2000: 452). This, however, takes place against a backdrop of wider social equality of income and life chances (Wilkinson and Pickett, 2011), illustrating the complex mutual causality between material resources and educational opportunity.

From 2001, the UK Government's Aimhigher programme (initially launched as Excellence Challenge), was commissioned to widen participation in Higher Education by raising awareness, aspirations and attainment amongst underrepresented groups (Aimhigher, 2007). It has been suggested that the perceived failure of Aimhigher to deliver on these targets results from too many other government policies working against 'a more just and equitable distribution of educational goods across society' (Brown, 2007). For lone parents, such relevant factors include aspects of student financing and welfare entitlement, the New Deal for Lone Parents (NDLP) agenda, and features of UK childcare provision and support. Nevertheless, whatever the shortcomings of Aimhigher in redressing the inequalities of broader policy, the potential to reach out to disenfranchised groups including lone parents is likely to be substantially further compromised by the replacement of Aimhigher with the National Scholarship Programme (NSP) in 2012, which unlike Aimhigher, includes no funding for recruitment outreach work.

Critics have expressed concern that the UK drive to widen HE participation has concentrated on 'how many' as an indicator of equal opportunities in access, at the expense of exploring inequalities in the qualitative experience of underprivileged student groups (Taylor, 2007: 35; Kingston, 2006; Laing *et al.*, 2005: 170; Reay, 2003: 301; Edwards, 1993: 6, 149). HEIs are charged with recruiting the easiest students first, then searching for the rest; invariably favouring students with high A-level results who need the least 'top up' to get up to good university standard (Watson, 2007). That university students from A-level routes are far more likely to complete their degrees clashes significantly with the documented drive to widen participation to include more women, working-class and black and minority ethnic (BME) students through establishing non-traditional routes to Higher Education in the form of Access courses (Leonard, 1994: 163). Many of the students drawn into Higher Education through Access courses are indeed mature women students with families (Edwards, 1993: 9), including lone parents.

A 2007 report from the National Audit Office revealed that although the UK ranked fifth in the world in terms of student retention, ahead of Germany and the US, one in five students still dropped out of their course. The report recommended that 'more support is needed for all students, especially those studying part-time, who face particular challenges and are more likely to drop out' (Lipsett, 2007). Mature students have lower completion rates, as do working-class students (Yorke, 2001: 148), and those supporting children are identified as being particularly susceptible to dropping out (Hands, Mackay, Ormiston-Smith, Perryman and Wright-Anderson, 2007: 25). It is suggested that HE participation has been encouraged by emphasising individual economic benefits, but that when widening participation students are attracted to Higher Education by such promises, this informs low completion rates (Murphy and Roopchand, 2003: 256). It is perhaps inevitable that issues of retention and completion have risen up various nations' political agendas as governments seek to maximise the return on their HE investment through limiting the financial consequences of student withdrawal (Yorke, 2001: 1, 147; Weil, 1986: 707). Assessments of cost and benefit include also the employability of graduates (Yorke, 2001: 147). This is particularly relevant to students with children, who, it is claimed, often return to semi-professional employment upon completion of their HE studies (Egerton, 2000: 7).

The UK Government has been criticised for an 'ambivalent attitude towards mature students' (Woodley and Wilson, 2002: 329), and for not valuing the non-traditional students they seek to attract to Higher

Education. A tiered system operates in that 'the increase in so-called non-standard students has been mainly within the former polytechnics and other "new" universities' (Jones, 2006: 487–488), leading to the assumption that 'because the more elite universities recruit . . . fewer mature students one might conclude that they [are] not a highly sought-after commodity' (Woodley and Wilson, 2002: 331). It is further suggested that from a continuing lack of part-time courses or changes to existing teaching and support systems, as well as anecdotal evidence from staff, it would seem that 'mature students are useful when needed by the HE system but have no great intrinsic merit', and 'are tolerated rather than prized', despite faring at least as well, if not better, on courses than their younger counterparts (2002: 331). It is suggested that mature students deserve to be valued more by the HE sector given that they bring a range of transferable skills worthy of being recognised and celebrated (Wisker, 1996: 13).

Student financing

In their 2005 manifesto the ruling Labour Party announced the goal of 'breaking down the barriers that stop people fulfilling their talent' (2005: 5), adding that they had 'made difficult decisions – about . . . student finance' (2005: 6). Critics perceive a fundamental clash of interests between the governmental drive to widen participation and changes to student finances (Taylor, 2007: 35; Callender, 2002: 83; Edwards, 1993: 6). Lone parents have been particularly affected by developments such as the introduction of fees and loans, and declining student eligibility for means-tested unemployment benefits. While the Dearing Report conjectured that 'although lone parents currently form only a small minority of the student population . . . their numbers are likely to grow in future' (Department for Education and Employment, 1997), within a few years, changes to financing had had the effect of decreasing numbers of lone parents studying full time in Higher Education (Millar and Rowlingson, 2001, 239; Jackson, 2004: 5). The financial hardship that HE participation can increasingly entail for lone parents impacts negatively upon student retention, as well as acting as a deterrent against initial enrolment. The NUS goes as far as to suggest that the cumulative effect of government policies has effectively penalised lone parents for their circumstances (2009: 51), as they attempt to improve their opportunities through educational participation.

Research on the experience of student parent poverty by the Scottish Child Poverty Action Group argued that government initiatives to assist disadvantaged students in the context of the changed funding structure have failed to match the needs of students with caring responsibilities, compromising their ability to move into and through Higher Education. This has hence compromised the Government's widening participation agenda (Scott, Frondigoun, Gillespie and White, 2003: 6). Particular financial problems are perceived for students who are lone parents (Scott *et al.*, 2003: 13), with financial difficulties incurred through childcare costs and inability to work contributing to lone parents leaving courses early (Millar and Rowlingson, 2001: 63). The relationship between the student finance support system and the Department for Work and Pensions (DWP), the prospect of debt, loss of potential earnings and familial responsibilities also act as deterrents for lone parents contemplating Higher Education (Horne and Hardie, 2002: 69; Scott *et al.*, 2003). There is evidence that the relatively high cost of tuition fees and low availability of grants has placed UK lone parents in a worse position than many of their European counterparts (Moreau and Leathwood, 2006: 23).

UK lone parents are seen to face difficulties because of inherent 'contradictions between the operation of the Benefits Agency and the student support system' (Christie, 2005: 12; also discussed by Scott *et al.*, 2003, and Horne and Hardie, 2002). Research suggests that for student parents the period of transition from means tested benefits to student funding can be particularly stressful, while managing a limited budget of grant and/or loan apportioned three times annually has also contributed to a cycle of constant debt for many lone-parent students used to receiving their limited financial support via weekly or at least monthly welfare payments (Scott *et al.*, 2003; Horne and Hardie, 2002: 63, 69).

Several successive rounds of student funding developments have aimed to increase financial support for part-time students. While this has been welcomed, the developments have had their own disadvantages, for example excluding part-time students studying below 50 per cent of a full-time student workload (Layer, 2006: 16–17) or, most recently, rendering part-time students liable for repayment of their student loans long before their courses are due to complete.

Lone parenthood in late modernity

The drive engendered by the development of knowledge economies to widen participation in Higher Education to include previously excluded groups is one major trend of late modernity informing the relevance of investigating lone parents' experiences as HE learners. The second important trend supporting the relevance of researching this area is the increasing pervasiveness of lone parenthood as a family form.

While lone parenthood has become a persistent demographic trend internationally, the UK has particularly high numbers, with lone parents caring for almost one in four children (Learning and Skills Council, 2007: 8). This trend runs counter to a continuing unrealistic agenda in US and UK politics to 'put the clock back' in terms of reducing public expenditure on lone parents (Klett-Davies, 2007: 279). Contrary to the understanding of lone parenthood as social threat that has been prevalent in the US and UK in contrast with other European countries (Klett-Davies, 2007: 11–12), commentators consistently find that lone parents do not want to survive on benefits, and would prefer to work (see Bradshaw and Millar, 1991). In 2007 the Freud Report found that eight out of ten lone parents wanted to work (Freud, 2007: 16). However, UK lone-parent employment rates remain well below the national average (Leitch Report, 2006: 360), as well as lagging behind much of the rest of Europe (Freud, 2007: 16). This leaves UK lone parents more welfare-dependent compared to other European countries.

Individuals with lower levels of education are more likely to become lone parents, and British lone parents have a lack of qualifications. Given that the majority of lone parents continue to be women, supporting educational access is central to addressing persistent gender inequalities in the labour market. The Government has acknowledged the need for more high-status jobs for women and more part-time jobs, recognising women's desire to both be in employment and be with their families. The link between job remuneration and level of education has been further acknowledged, and hence the need to support educational attainment and improve careers guidance, in order to improving working mothers' pay and employment conditions (Hencke, 2006).

There has, however, been ideological slippage over recent years between discourses of opportunity and compulsion in returning mothers, and in particular lone mothers, to employment. This has addressed the UK's former status amongst the few European and

Anglophone countries not compelling lone parents to seek work (Gingerbread, 2007b; Department for Work and Pensions, 2007a: 40; Wintour, 2007). The age of the youngest child at which lone parents must be available for work varies widely internationally from as young as three months in the US to as old as 22 years in Ireland if the child is in full-time education (Freud, 2007: 92). When the UK Government followed the Australian, German and French models in lowering the age of the youngest child at which lone parents are required to seek employment, the necessity of improved childcare provision to facilitate this was acknowledged (Wintour, 2007). UK lone-parent employment rates were already increasing substantially when compulsion was introduced (Freud, 2007: 10; Wintour, 2007; Leitch, 2006: 14). In 2005, Department for Trade and Industry (DTI) statistics had shown women to be slowly narrowing the income gap, with single mothers moving fastest of all, showing the largest leap in income (Ward, 2005a).

Paid work is consistently promoted as being a critical determinant of life chances (Social Mobility Strategy, 2011: 60), and 'the best way out of poverty' for lone parents (Child Poverty Strategy, 2011; Klett-Davies, 2007: 33), but lone parent welfare-to-work policy too often stops short of providing adequate educational support. While governments acknowledge that training and education are central to promoting lone parents' economic self-sufficiency, there has been resistance (particularly in the US and UK) to investing in supporting the higher levels of learning that provide more stable long-term financial independence for lone parents (Klett-Davies, 2007). This is particularly relevant in the UK context given the relatively low educational qualification level of UK lone parents compared to many other countries. Particularly high childcare costs in the UK mean that it is often only financially feasible for lone parents to be in employment if they are in well-paying, and hence well-qualified, jobs (Klett-Davies, 2007: 32; Shaw and Woolhead, 2006: 178; Horne and Hardie, 2002: 60; Millar and Rowlingson, 2001: 28). There is also a demonstrated relationship between level of qualification and long-term employment for lone parents, alongside intergenerational benefits for their children (Polakow, Butler, Stormer Deprez and Kahn; 2004: 9). Those with only low levels of qualifications are able to command only low wages (Shaw and Woolhead, 2006: 178), and hence are likely to remain economically inactive (Millar and Rowlingson, 2001: 257).

The UK benefit system is structured with the aim of preserving the financial incentive to work (Ford, 1996: xi). In 1998 the then Labour administration, introduced the 'New Deal' programme to encourage benefit claimants into work. The Government evaluated the New Deal for Lone Parents (NDLP) and Working Families Tax Credit (WFTC) as having been successful in reducing worklessness amongst lone parents through delivering financial incentives (LSC, 2007: 8), with the Leitch Report claiming that by 2006 the NDLP had helped over 420,000 lone parents into employment (HM Treasury, 2006: 124).

But it is observed that, compared to the approach of other countries, and in contrast to the New Deal for Young People, the NDLP (Millar and Rowlingson, 2001: 238), the UK's New Deal programme, has appeared most concerned with moving lone parents into paid employment with the least amount of support for education and training. This fits with observations that in the UK there does not seem to be strong willingness to invest heavily in supporting participation by disadvantaged groups (Walsh, 2007). NDLP participants have been entitled to apply for financial support for courses of up to one year, not, therefore, including HE courses. Critics have argued that HE participation is the only way in which lone parents lacking qualifications can secure sufficiently high paid work to make childcare costs viable (Horne and Hardie, 2002: 60), and that lone parents looking for higher-level jobs requiring specialist training tend to have been poorly served by the NDLP scheme (Klett-Davies, 2007: 47).

There is a particular identified lack of financial support for lone parents' educational participation at Level 3 (A-level equivalent), compared to more comprehensive support at Level 2 (GCSE equivalent) and in Higher Education through the student finance system (Gingerbread, 2007a). The NDLP has generally supported training only up to National Vocational Qualification (NVQ) Level 2, equivalent to standard school leaving qualification at age 16, with support only exceptionally provided to Level 3. Claimants have been able to study for a Level 3 qualification at FE college on benefits with the fee waived, but childcare support has been uneven, with the result that lone parents moving into Higher Education are often already in debt from funding their Level 3 studies (Millar and Rowlingson, 2001: 239).

This lack of funding has been attributed to UK policy uptake of the US model of lone parent provision (Gingerbread, 2007a), which itself was based on findings that education and training provision did not speed up the process of returning lone parents to employment. The US government argued that putting workless individuals through college did not help them toward employment and self-sufficiency (Polakow *et al.*, 2004: 1). However, the US model is accused of being flawed in that the training it found unbeneficial was poor quality, and critics argue that the policies it informed have actually led to increases in lone parents claiming benefits (Gingerbread, 2007a). Polakow *et al.* contrastingly found completing post-secondary education to have had huge benefits for women welfare recipients in the US in terms of securing steadier jobs, higher incomes and greater family well-being (2004: 9). They have documented the substantial decrease in the number of US lone mothers obtaining degrees since 1970 (2004: 115), accusing US fiscal policy of amounting to lone mothers being denied their educational rights and deliberately trapped permanently in low wage work (2004: 10). DeParle's *American dream* (2004) further illustrates the shortcomings of US welfare-to-work policy for many lone parents.

Lone parents frequently find it difficult to source accurate information about financial entitlements (NUS, 2009: 4; Horne and Hardie, 2002: 66, 69; Connor and Dewson, 2001: 73), with lack of information flow identified as correlating negatively with returning to employment for the group (Jenkins and Symons, 2001. 131). A 2007 LSC report described part of the remit of the NDLP as being 'improving awareness of benefits, providing "better-off" calculations and assisting with benefit claims' (2007: 8). Given the increased risk-aversiveness documented amongst non-traditional learners, including lone parents (Reay, 2003), it can be difficult for individuals to embrace the opportunities offered by engaging with education and work when this entails leaving the relative certainty of the welfare safety net. Risk aversion is shown to correlate negatively with income – those with the lowest incomes are the most risk-averse, and lone parents are characterised by poverty (Jenkins and Symons, 2001: 139). Reay's research with mature working-class women students confirmed that going to university was often considered a 'risky' process, and that successful university applicants often ultimately failed to make the transition they had planned after Access courses because they considered the risk too great (Reay, 2003: 303, 312). For many lone parents, engaging with education has entailed the somewhat unattractive prospect of launching into the precariousness of a low and often uncertain income made up of grant, loan, Housing Benefit, Child Benefit, child maintenance, Child Tax Credits, perhaps part-time earnings and also applications to charitable trusts (Jenkins and Symons, 2001: 126). One of the aims of the incoming universal credit in replacing individual benefits with one payment, is to address the acknowledged difficulties for those managing a patchwork of entitlements. The results of this, however, remain to be seen, and the system is projected to engender its own particular risks and problems for claimants; for example through the inevitable hardship caused when bureaucratic payment errors result in cessation of all household income instead of just one element as previously. In addition, many lone-parent students will remain reliant on a combination of student financing and lone-parent welfare entitlement, though the terms of both areas are in contemporary flux. If anything, simultaneous major changes to both areas of financing will leave vulnerable groups, including lone-parent learners, additionally exposed to errors, as both clients and staff attempt to negotiate the complexities of unfamiliar bureaucratic procedures.

CHAPTER THREE

Researching lone-parent students

Accessing lone-parent students

This chapter introduces the lone parents who participated in the research, locating them in terms of demographic characteristics, family background, and motivations for entering HE as lone parents. The chapter begins by explaining how the lone-parent mothers were contacted, which impacted on the characteristics of those who participated. Identified benefits and disadvantages of this procedure are also discussed.

Lone mothers studying at university were recruited via a research website, to which Gingerbread, the largest organisation representing lone parents in the UK, agreed to provide a link from their homepage. Participants then responded electronically each fortnight to email 'prompts' asking them about particular issues and how managing studies and family life was going generally. Pseudonyms are used throughout this book to protect the anonymity of participants and their children; names of children, towns, universities and employers have also been removed from quotes.

There has been a tendency amongst some to regard Internet-facilitated research as somehow inferior to the assumed ideal of face-to-face contact (Sudweeks and Simoff, 1999: 42), the former sometimes seen as compromising the increased closeness and personal involvement between interviewer and participants assumed to be a feature of qualitative as opposed to quantitative research (Mann and Stewart, 2000: 82). and evidence of this belief amongst researchers persists. The view that the Internet is incompatible with meaningful qualitative data collection because 'the physical presence of the researcher is too restricted', resulting in a mere 'disembodied exchange of textual material' (Mann and Stewart, 2000: 3), was not borne out by this research. The counter-argument has emerged as being more significant: that computer-mediated qualitative research has in fact provided opportunities to cross boundaries between the researcher and the researched (Mann and Stewart, 2000: 77). Indeed, the co-existing anonymity and intimacy offered by internet communication proved particularly beneficial to engaging with lone mothers; for example, facilitating discussion of sensitive issues, without the shyness or fear of judgment sometimes present in face-to-face contact. This is particularly relevant given the often stigmatised social status of which lone mothers indicate feel only too painfully aware. Email can offer the advantage of providing 'a secure, private and familiar environment where personal issues might be explored' (Mann and Stewart, 2000: 79). Without prompting, lone mothers volunteered their experiences around issues including substance misuse and mental health problems, topics that may not have been as easy to discuss without inhibition face to face.

Email communication further lends itself particularly well to researching lone parents in enabling participants to respond from home in their own time, bypassing the need to arrange childcare in order to attend interviews, or reschedule real-time phone or web-chat interviews when children suddenly demanded attention.

The additional key suspicion against Internet research amongst sceptics is concern around ensuring authenticity. They first key factor seen as mediating against this possibility was that the substantial and prolonged time investment asked of already overstretched participants without reward offered little attraction to individuals with fraudulent intentions compared to ample alternative opportunities. Offering additional protection, participation required considerable exclusive insider knowledge as to the experience of being both a lone parent and a university student, and the longitudinal research design provided further opportunity for cross-checking the insights and consistency of participant's responses.

Identifying characteristics of the sample

Although the self-selecting sample yielded too few responses from demographic groups including younger, BME (black and minority ethnic) and LGBTQ (lesbian, gay, bisexual, transgender and queer) students to allow systematic comparison, individuals from these groups were present in the research. The rich, longitudinal data collected goes some way toward compensating for low numbers by providing in-depth insight into individual experiences. This signposts pertinent particularised facets of experience for minority demographics within the group as a whole.

Participants are categorised by the accepted distinction between mature and traditional entry-age students of a cut-off point of age 21 at commencement of study (Woodley and Wilson, 2002: 330). However, the vast majority of lone mothers in the study were aged over 26. Only two participants were under 26 at the time of research and none were under 21; hence all were mature students.

It was decided not to pursue the route of asking participants what type of HE Institution they attended (for example, Russell Group, 1994 group, post-1992), in order to avoid confusion. This was because responses demonstrated that individuals often did not know what type of institution their university was. This may reflect a propensity of lone parents to choose their HEI primarily on the basis of locality rather than academic or other factors, given considerations like contact with absent parents and wider family ties, housing and children's schools and childcare providers. While the impact of HEI type was not investigated systematically, it was nevertheless apparent from responses that the research included contributions from lone parents from across the spectrum of the UK HE sector. Some lone mothers raised issues they interpreted as being symptomatic of the HEI type they attended, as is discussed in subsequent chapters.

Amongst the lone mothers who took part in this study, there was a high representation of Arts compared to Science students, and in particular, large numbers of participants were pursuing Social Science courses. This may represent an increased disciplinary interest in taking part in social research. Despite juggling multiple roles, participants frequently engaged with the research beyond what was asked of them. Many were familiar with issues being explored in the research, whether through their own Social Science HE studies, or through active involvement with support organisations for lone parents. Several coordinated local support groups for lone parents, and others, were aware of relevant issues through their employment, including as social workers, adult education teachers or disability rights coordinators. Those working as part-time teachers in Higher Education while they pursued their own studies were inevitably often particularly aware of relevant issues.

Defining lone parenthood

The pivotal consideration in characterising the individuals who participated in the research is defining lone-parent status. Defining lone
parenthood is acknowledged to be more problematic than is often
assumed (May, 2004: 2). A lone mother is typically understood to mean
'a female head of a family comprising only herself and her dependent
children' (Jenkins and Symons, 2001: 128). But experiences contributed
to this book highlight the complexity of family in late modern society.
This includes variations in both family groupings and roles, and the way
in which these relations are interpreted as representing experiences of
what family means. The high proportion of lone parents reporting to
have a partner at some point in the duration of this research validated
the decision not to restrict inquiry to unpartnered individuals. In light
of the complexity of contemporary experiences of lone parenthood,
lone-mother status was measured predominantly by self-definition.
This decision was representative of the belief that 'examining the social
construction of "family", researchers now listen to the stories people tell
of family life and focus on everyday actors' own definitions of "family"'
(May, 2004: 1)

Acceptance of individuals' self-definition as lone parents was however
applied within reason. If a parent cohabiting with the other biological
parent of all of their children claimed to be a lone parent this would
clearly not be accurate. The in-depth longitudinal nature of this research
furnished ample opportunity for cross-checking discrepancies between
participants' self-defined status and concrete situations. The baseline
understanding of lone parenthood was that lone mothers must be
parenting at least one dependent child.

Experiences and understandings of what family means have diversified
so much in late modernity that individuals defining themselves as lone
parents may in fact be totally alone, supported by family, in a non-
cohabiting relationship with their child's other parent, or in a cohabiting
or non-cohabiting relationship with someone who is not their child's
parent and has chosen not to take on a parenting role or responsibility.
Other individuals in the same circumstances may not define themselves
as lone parents. As emerges throughout the narratives contributing to
this book, the level of family support a lone-parent student can call
on intersects pivotally with other central factors including financial
resources, to inform the feasibility of remaining afloat in their HE

participation. Lone mothers contributing to the research frequently described how having a partner did not fundamentally alter their circumstances as lone parents, as the following indicates:

> *I do have a partner (but am still a single parent, as this does not mean that we share [my son's] care), and in this relationship and others there has always been a mismatch, as one person can go out and the other one can't.* (Bex, age 34, one child aged 12, MA Primary Education with QTS [Qualified Teacher Status])

That in contrast one lone parent chose not to contribute further to the research shortly after she had met a new partner because she no longer considered herself a lone parent, whilst others explained that they were still a lone parent despite having a partner, validated the decision to rely on self-definition of status. The large number of lone parents who continued to contribute to the research alongside the making and breaking of relationships, discussed this in their emails. There was a considerable amount of casual dating, beginning and ending of relationships, and relationships moving toward being more serious, with talk of cohabiting, although no participants took this step while the research was in progress. This observed trend toward remaining living alone while in relationships may in part symptomise the threat that moving into cohabiting can cause to established financial arrangements for student parents, as participants discussed. It also represents documented broader patterns in family formation in terms of the trend toward 'living alone together' in long-term, committed and exclusive, but non-cohabiting relationships (Haskey, 2005). Approximately a quarter of research participants described such arrangements at some point in the study, corresponding with Haskey's findings that a quarter of lone mothers have a regular partner who lives elsewhere (2005:1). Haskey's research further identified just under one-third of all women with a partner living elsewhere to be lone parents with dependent children (2005: 17). Such findings further contribute to the rationale for including the perspectives of lone mothers who are in non-cohabiting relationships. That individuals continue to define themselves as lone parents in the context of long-term relationships may also represent rejection of the constraints of traditional values. This resonates with the Klett-Davies model of 'pioneer' lone mothers, characterised by their independence and bucking of traditional perceptions of lone parenthood (2007: 72–73).

None of the participants in this study reported having made a conscious decision to become a lone parent. This contrasts sharply with negative social stereotypes of feckless women actively and irresponsibly choosing to parent alone. Although some individuals had been lone parents since the onset of pregnancy, whether they had embarked on parenthood accidentally or deliberately, all who discussed it had hoped to co-parent with their then partner.

Lone mothers' discussion of couple relationships offered valuable insight into what it means to be a lone parent in contemporary Britain. Experienced and imagined problems in being in a relationship as a lone-parent student revolved around conflicting time demands, intellectual mismatch and negotiating changing identities and expectations. Partners' reactions to participants' university student status ranged widely from proud and supportive to threatened and sabotaging.

For those without partners, an important motivation for finding a relationship was to share the financial and child-raising burden, including having someone to babysit so that they could socialise more easily. Such relationship expectations were contradicted by the reflections of newly single participants that not having a partner left them freer to concentrate on studies and socialise as they wished than previously. Relationships past, present and imagined were frequently perceived as a distraction from study and vice versa. Over half of lone mothers in the research expressed some level of perceived incompatibility between being in a relationship and being a student. The most frequent concern was around inadequate time to devote to a relationship alongside juggling studying with the responsibilities of being a lone parent. A partner may not understand the need to study and consequently may be unsympathetic and make unrealistic demands on time. Another perceived problem was that partners were or may be 'put off' by a proactive, intelligent woman taking active steps to educate herself, or that since embarking on study the kinds of men they knew and met would not be intellectually compatible. Many of those without partners considered a supportive and sympathetic approach to their studies to be a priority in any potential relationship. This was reinforced by the reflections of participants with partners who were currently or had previously been engaged with adult learning, in that the learning experience made these partners more able and willing to empathise with their experience and needs as mature students, as the following expresses:

27

> *I have recently entered into a relationship and it's a nightmare!!*
> *It's so hard to make time for everyone, myself, my son and my*
> *partner!!! But as my partner has already gained a degree he is quite*
> *understanding!'* (Charlotte, one child aged 4, Year 2 Psychology)

Not all lone parents, however, saw student status as a block to achieving relationships. Some felt that being a student made them more attractive partners, although the inevitable problem of slicing up tightly stretched time remained:

> *Being a student has actually helped me to attract men in a way I*
> *think. A lot of men I chat to online are impressed that I am trying to*
> *help myself and not just living on benefits. (I'm not sure I like their*
> *attitude but it is often present). They are the type that would have*
> *been completely unable to have a relationship with the stereotypical*
> *lone mum who they are sure exists. In other words being a student*
> *and bringing up kids helps my status in some people's eyes.*
> (Ruth, age 47, two children aged 9 and 12, Year 3 BA Social
> Policy and Criminology)

Many of those who had not developed new relationships since separating from ex-partners felt that their former relationship had damaged their confidence and trust. Becoming an adult learner could, however, develop individuals' confidence so that their expectations of relationships changed; as one described:

> *Because of increased confidence, I would be a lot less likely to settle*
> *for a relationship which does not give what I need, or what my*
> *children needed.* (Rosa, two children, MBA)

Effects of lone parenthood

Relationship breakdown and ex-partners' absence have not been automatically assumed to be problematic in this study unless this was explicitly expressed by participants. Relationship breakdown is, however, frequently cited as a root of hardship, with lone mothers often experiencing it as having triggered serious financial hardship or depression (the latter particularly where individuals are left pregnant or with young babies to care for alone). Relationships can break down when participants' studying provokes unsustainable friction with unsupportive partners. The most serious documented problems with ex-partners include debt accruement, mental illness, alcohol abuse, actual or threatened physical violence and verbal bullying against mothers and children, and threatened or actual child abduction. These problems appear with surprising frequency and often occur in conjunction with one another. The most widespread and less extreme problems with non-resident parents are failure to honour maintenance and contact arrangements.

Lone mothers' narratives document domestic violence and related control of freedom by partners, as also observed in mature women HE learners' trajectories (Edwards, 1993: 172–173). Domestic violence is overrepresented in the histories of women and children in lone parent households. The legacy of domestic violence has a further knock-on effect on families' subsequent ability to manage life in terms of juggling paid work with family responsibilities; for example, because mothers lack self-esteem and support, and feel guilty about leaving insecure children with childcarers (Cohen, 2007).

Demographic characteristics

Ethnicity

BME women are overrepresented in Further and Higher Education (Mirza, 2007), and this is partly understandable in terms of what black feminists have interpreted as black women's belief in education as a way out of poverty and exploitation, and necessary to achieve anything in the face of discrimination (Edwards, 1993: 2). Black lone and partnered mothers in Britain have significantly higher levels of education than white lone mothers (Duncan and Edwards, 1999: 158), although Edwards' work suggests that the reality of BME women's HE experiences may be less than positive (1993: 98, 148), and HE participation has been identified to be more likely to lead to positive employment outcomes for white compared to BME lone mothers (Duncan and Edwards, 1999: 161).

The documented high concentration of BME lone mothers as HE students is not reflected in this research. It was not possible to systematically explore the relevance of ethnicity, as the majority of participants either reported White British ethnicity or did not respond to the question. Several lone-parent students contributing to the research discussed having children of biracial ethnicity. Although BME women were underrepresented in the research, findings that black women frequently perceive others' low educational expectations of them to be informed by their ethnicity (Edwards, 1993: 148) are reinforced in this research, as indicated by the following:

> *I do think that some aspects of my life have been affected by my experiences in various ways. Being female, black and then becoming a single parent and homeless, I found myself shoved onto a depressing council estate, on the top floor, with no lift, leaking roofs, thin internal walls, and disruptive, noisy neighbours, along with all the other black single mums, and the white mums who the council classified as 'working class'.*

> *As I've grown older, I've noticed that being female, black and single, I appear to be somewhere near the bottom of the rung in society. At the top of the hierarchy are white, middle-class men. White women come below that, and black women even lower.* (Beatrice, age 31, one child aged 8, Year 3 BA Education – Primary)

Social class background

Previous research has found that HE students frequently feel a strong sense of class identity (Taylor, 2007: 37), and that mature women students often perceive factors around race, sex and class as being responsible for low expectations of them educationally during initial schooling (Edwards, 1993: 98). British BME students are predominantly working class (Taylor, 2007: 35), and black women report perceiving these low expectations mainly in terms of class, while white women perceive them in terms of sex and class (Edwards, 1993: 148).

In this research, participants were almost equally divided in terms of defining their background as working class or middle class respectively. The high representation of self-identifying working-class individuals in this research contrasts with the picture of mature HE participation in the UK, where 2012 HESA statistics indicate around two-thirds of both male and female undergraduates to come from SEC 1–3 (HESA, 2012).

This discrepancy is likely partially to reflect the mismatch between official measurement and self-definition, indicating a greater propensity amongst those studying in HE to self-identify as 'working class', when this may not in fact tell the same story as socioeconomic status. It is likely, however, to also be important as indicating the effect of lone-parent status upon socioeconomic status, skewing representation by social class compared to the broader group of mature women students as a whole.

Self-identified middle-class and working-class participants in this research were equally likely to report other mature returners to education in their family. This may denote that participants come from families of both social classes in which there exists a culture of pursuing adult learning, rather than these familial experiences of HE participation representing broader social class trends.

There are currently around 45,000 more mature women students studying in UK Higher Education compared to mature male students (HESA, 2012). This increased educational participation by mature women learners can be seen as representing recoupment of earlier restricted opportunities, in line with Egerton's suggestion that educationally excluded groups recoup earlier disadvantage through HE participation at mature ages (2000: 64). This is particularly relevant for mature women students, many of whom grew up with values and even policies containing strong ideological views of girls from different classes and families (also Edwards, 1993: 39); remaining true as when observed by Edwards nearly 20 years ago. Working-class girls have often been expected to exit education early, while education has been taken more seriously for boys and middle-class girls. For working-class women in this research, educational discouragement had often centred on assumptions about insufficient aptitude, alongside beliefs that their future was marriage, motherhood, and office or manual work, and that concentration on education would be wasted. Christie *et al.* criticise 'the presumption that a greatly expanded HE sector automatically enhances social justice' arguing that this has been 'challenged by the persistent social class gradient in participation' (2005: 4).

Both this research and existing studies have found working-class women to report initial schooling experience as leaving them with negative, alienated feelings of education. This includes receiving messages in school of the importance of not 'getting above yourself' (Edwards, 1993: 46), and that 'education was not for the likes of them' (Jackson, 2004: 44). Despite the potential 'second chance' offered by adult learning, both this research and existing findings have shown these negative messages frequently to be reiterated rather than challenged in Higher Education. For example, working-class women students have been found to feel intimidated by the sophisticated-seeming language used by university staff (Leonard, 1994: 169), with Taylor arguing that 'working-class women's confidence is potentially undermined within Higher Education as their voices are not legitimised in the same way that middle-class ones often are' (2007: 45). For learners who are working class, from minority ethnic backgrounds, and lone mothers; class, ethnicity, femininity and parenthood can compound one another, demonstrating the way in which inequalities feed into and reinforce one another (Reay, 2003: 313).

As has been indicated, while utilising self-definition of social class was deemed desirable, it was not unproblematic. Lone mothers' responses to being asked to define their own social class reveal the thorniness of the issue for many. One in six of those who responded said that they were not prepared to define themselves in this way, or disagreed outright with social class as a category. For still others, social class proved a slippery and hard to grasp concept, with sometimes confused and unsure responses, as the following demonstrate:

> *I'm not sure how to describe the social class position of my upbringing, we have always been pretty well off and as my dad has always worked in small towns as the only doctor he has always been pretty important in the community. I suppose we are middle class? Who knows.* (Daisy, one child, Year 4 undergraduate)

> *Social class is somewhat harder, I'm unsure as to where I would place myself, certainly not lower or higher classes so somewhere in between!!!* (Sadie, age 27, four-year-old twins, Year 3 LLB)

Lone-parent students also discussed mixed social class backgrounds in terms of their own parents each coming from different classes, family histories documenting upward and downward social mobility through the generations, or because of a mismatch between family values and material resources. The longitudinal nature of the data further indicated changes over time in individuals' own social class identification and willingness to be categorised in this way:

I guess I would have to say that regards to social class we were lower-middle, the occupations weren't particularly held in high esteem, but boy did my parents earn decent wages which meant they could afford the sorts of things that the typical white/blue collar worker could afford. I'm not sure what my social class is at the moment! I've no money, I don't work (officially still a student) and am a single parent – that used to be equal to 'scum-bag' type, but I don't think I fall into any particular category at the moment – I don't really do the class system. I know too many 'posh' people that are complete gits and pigs! (Gloria, age 39, three children aged 12–17, PG Diploma HE, February)

I'm living in council rented property, own a car, working class, heterosexual, single, English (and always have been). (Gloria, October)

These reflections from the same lone mother further document the trend identified in the research of lone-parent student status informing perceived upward or downward social mobility from childhood upbringing, as the following also illustrates:

My family class has changed because I am a single mother without any consistent work. I would estimate my social class to be low in comparison to my parents. (Connie, age 23, one child, Year 1 Business Behaviour)

The extent of contradiction and confusion in terms of social class led to it being considered a problematic analytical category, approached with caution. That research participants emphasised the salience of lone-parent status upon previous social class position and broader life experience, suggests that lone-parent status is frequently experienced as an overarching demographic variable informing identity formation. It is deemed particularly significant that, even for those participants clearly defining a social class position, there is no discernible relationship between social class and documented experience and attitude along a range of themes that are highlighted in the existing literature as reflecting potential class differences amongst students. The themes upon which social class identity surprisingly does not appear to impact range from

33

financial hardship to parental academic encouragement in childhood.

Lone-parent learners' narratives illuminate the pervasive impact of lone-parent status upon wide facets of life experience, showing that it frequently has overriding significance compared to other key aspects of identity, including social class. While class identification is demonstrated to impact considerably in some respects, in other areas, lone-parent students' experiences also contrast with findings in existing commentaries on mature women HE students that have unearthed class effects not present here. This point of difference between lone-mother HE students and the partnered mature women learners with whom they share so many facets of identity and experience, underlines the salience of lone parenthood as a variable. There are, however, key respects in which self-defined social class does relate to experience, including attitudes to and experience of debt, support from extended family, and themes around fitting into university. These areas are discussed in detail in Chapters 5, 6 and 7 respectively.

Parental employment during childhood emerged as a prominent influence on participants. Occupations varied widely; and there were many narratives of occupational change and career development in the work lives of participants' parents, with a substantial body of tales of upward social mobility through the generations, sometimes strikingly so. Public sector occupations were heavily represented amongst participants' parents across the social class spectrum, and work and education both featured strongly as themes in lone mothers' upbringings.

Early educational experience and encouragement

Lone mothers' trajectories indicate social class background, gender and parental encouragement to intersect pivotally to inform individuals' formative educational experiences. Lack of encouragement at home and school emerge as key factors in informing negative outcomes from initial schooling. Lone parent learners also indicate the relevance of the educational experience of other family members, including other adult returners to education.

One-third of research participants reported being encouraged academically as children by their parents or teachers, representing a spectrum from positive encouragement to do their best and realise personal goals, through to overbearing pressure to go to university. Lone mothers contributing to the research described privileged educational experiences, including: passing Eleven Plus and Twelve Plus exams; attending single-sex, convent, grammar, independent and boarding schools; being placed in the top set; home tuition and education abroad. Participants also frequently reported leaving school with high numbers of GCSE, O-level and A-level passes, with several being encouraged by parents and teachers to apply for Oxbridge, and some pursuing this successfully.

One in eight participants described being discouraged educationally, mainly by parents and wider family, but also by teachers or school careers advisors. These trajectories of educational discouragement included being kept away from school to contribute to the domestic running of the household. Such experiences frequently contributed to leaving school early with few or no qualifications. Evidence of non-traditional learners generally demonstrates their early education often not to have been compatible with 'learning', with individuals frequently perceiving themselves as having been labelled as 'troublemakers', 'underachievers', or 'not very clever' in initial education (Weil, 1986: 224). Existing research on mature women students and lone parents chimes with this study in identifying a trend toward lack of career encouragement in childhood from family, peers and teachers (for example, Jones, 2006: 494). Expectations or pressure to leave school early and marry young, can culminate later in lone parenthood for individuals who may feel they have not chosen the paths laid out for them by others (May, 2004: 393; Edwards, 1993: 46). For those who become mothers in their teens, evidence suggests that pressure often occurs from schools to leave early without completing education (Zachry, 2005: 2571). Research has found the early adulthood trajectories of mature women learners frequently to include having left school with no qualifications and no great career ambitions or direction, to go into 'stop-gap' jobs in traditional female occupations with little status or prospects, and after a short time fulfilling their own and their parents' expectations by finding a man and having children (Edwards, 1993). It emerged as significant in this research that both extremes of overbearing and uninterested parents appear paradoxically to have contributed to similar trajectories of early school-leaving, low self-esteem and relationship breakdown, in turn leading to lone parenthood. While the research included participants from working-class backgrounds who had exited school early and those who had proceeded with post-compulsory education immediately after schooling, girls encouraged to exit initial education early for unskilled jobs reported this influence as pivotal to their early entrance to the labour market, as others have also found (see Edwards, 1993: 41). Both concrete circumstances and family values are cited as having kept lone parents from focusing on initial education. Nevertheless, while family financial need does impact upon early school-leaving, it is significant that the level of educational encouragement does not appear contingent upon social class.

A perceived gender bias in both subject choice availability and teachers responding to the needs of boys, alongside the competing demands of schools' ethos of concentration versus peer pressures, have been blamed for culminating in educational disadvantage during the childhoods of many subsequent mature women learners (Wisker, 1996: 3). A prevalent corollary of personal responsibility results in both individuals and institutions perceiving educational failure as personal failure, obscuring the impact of class experience. Mature working-class women students therefore frequently internalise their own failure at initial educational success, as borne out by both this research and existing studies (Reay, 2003: 306). Lone mothers in this research discussed the ways in which these negative past school experiences contributed to their feeling 'daunted' or 'intimidated' at the prospect of learning and writing essays (also Jones, 2006: 491). It is suggested that coming from family backgrounds without experience of Higher Education can leave non-traditional learners vulnerably ill-equipped for independent learning and with unrealistic expectations of Higher Education (Laing *et al.*, 2005: 169–170).

Insights from this research have further located lone-parent students' experiences in the wider context of family educational background; for example, through illuminating siblings' educational trajectories. This wider context contributes to understanding of whether participation in learning takes place against the backdrop of an unsupportive, supportive, or sometimes competitive family culture of educational engagement. Just over one-third of lone parents in the research discussed their siblings' education. Some described siblings who had not achieved academically, and this could either make it more difficult to be academic, or result in great pride at bucking the tradition. Some had witnessed siblings failing to realise academic potential because of lack of effort, or being forced into paid employment, marriage and motherhood. However, the most significant two recurring themes were of siblings who had or were also currently participating in adult learning, and of individuals who felt that siblings had been more academically able and/or encouraged in childhood.

Just over one-third of lone parents discussed other family members returning to education as adults, including siblings, parents, aunts, uncles, cousins, adult children and even grandparents. Some were studying at the same time as their mother, sisters or daughter.

Lone parents from middle-class and working-class backgrounds are equally likely to report other family members returning to education as adults. Those with other returners in the family indicate being more likely to receive support for their studies, although families where the research participant was the only returner could also be supportive.

This documented trend of siblings who had been deemed more academically able in childhood represents a pattern of reported damage to educational self-esteem caused by feeling cast as a comparative failure. This impacts significantly alongside parental expectation upon initial educational attainment. The following quote illustrates the development of such feelings of perceived inadequacy:

> As for school experience I remember enjoying primary school and having some good friends, but then not feeling very confident at all at secondary school. I think part of this stemmed from the fact that my older sister had passed the Eleven plus and had gone to grammar school and I didn't. In other words, I felt like a failure even though I was put in for an exam to a private grammar school by my school and was placed on the reserve list for a place. The fact that I hadn't passed knocked me in many ways for many years. I never felt that I was good enough and my sister was always better than me. (Jennifer, age 44, four children aged 10–20, Year 3 BA Education Studies and History)

The theme of being happy at primary school but losing confidence at secondary school ran through participants' memories, being discussed by one in eight, despite not being explicitly asked about. Research participants variously discussed reasons for this change emanating from both home and school. The broad theme was of feeling lost and insignificant in the impersonal largeness of secondary school. Older participants were more likely to report negative secondary school experiences, with one-quarter of over-40s, compared to one-fifth of under-40s, reporting this to be the case:

My teachers on the Access course often made the comment that they simply didn't understand how I had 'failed' at school. Looking back I can see only too easily how the whole system in a way was designed to fail people as much as to not fail others. All the discussion these days re lower standards etc. frustrates me as it is simply the case (as far as I'm concerned) that in years gone by only the select few were able to get through to HE. Now that more and more people can do it to my mind it exposes the fallacy that it was ever that difficult. All those people I used to look up to and think were so very clever were just lucky. (Ruth, age 47, two children aged 9 and 12, Year 3 BA Social Policy and Criminology)

While a range of competing features of family background, many of them lodged in structural inequality, may contribute to steering an individual's prospects; the unifying factor in lone-parent students' narratives in this research is the potential of interpersonal support from family and wider informal networks to mediate disadvantage and inform success or 'failure' in Higher Education.

Family life and values

Lone mothers' reflections on their childhood backgrounds illuminate family attitudes to lone parenthood, as well as how participants' childhoods had compared to others around them. Relatively few had themselves been raised by a lone parent. Several described not having known any lone-parent families as children, that it would have been unthinkable in their family, or that they had been brought up to look down upon, and not to associate with those from lone parent families. Some of those who had experienced lone parenthood first-hand as both children and adults reflected on improvements to the opportunities available for lone parents, as the following indicates:

My own mum who was a single parent in the 1970s turned to me recently and said 'I envy you, the choices you've made and been allowed to make. When I left an unhappy marriage I lost everything, the expectation was to simply find another husband to "take me on".' In the year 2004 being a single parent in HE is not a walk in the park but it is a lot easier than it was in 1974, for people in my mother's position it was in fact impossible. (Kristin, age 26, one child aged 8, PGCE [Postgraduate Certificate in Higher Education] History)

Research participants often described feeling as a child that their family was in some way different to those of others around them. This could be because of different family values, financial means, or lifestyle factors. Alongside those from lone-parent families, for others, perceived difference lay in being adopted, having a parent who largely lived away from home for work, or perceiving a distinct identity from surrounding others in terms of social class, nationality or accent. A feeling of difference in childhood from other surrounding families was mentioned equally frequently by participants identifying as middle class and working class, and difference of any kind was frequently reported to result in bullying by other children.

One area suggesting social class difference was in terms of expected gender roles. Several lone mothers identifying as working class discussed perceptions around the inevitability of distinct gender roles. In contrast, the only self-identified middle-class participant who comparably overtly discussed such gender roles had an opposing perspective:

> *I strongly believe that both men and women should attempt things that do not always seem compatible with their gender role. I have developed reasonable practical skills (decorating, drilling, etc.) that I guess I may not have bothered with if I had had someone else to do it for me. (Bex, age 34, one child aged 12, MA Primary Education with QTS)*

Such observed difference may indicate the potential of key demographic variables, including gender, social class and ethnicity, to mediate one another, impacting upon the ease or restraint individuals feel affect their ability to self-author their life trajectories, as previously highlighted. The research does not however indicate a straightforward relationship between social class and gender expectations. Despite the discussed presence observed here and by others of working-class girls assumed to be destined for lives of unskilled work and domesticity, as a whole, lone mothers in this research were equally likely to report being encouraged or discouraged educationally by their parents during childhood, regardless of social class background. The following quote is one of many describing participants' experiences of educational encouragement from parents:

I would regard my family as working class, though these things don't really seem static. My parents were very interested in my education and I think they would have liked my sister and I to enter higher/ further education. (It would have been a lot more sensible to do it then – but I probably wouldn't have had the motivation.) They always attended parents evenings and meeting with the school. I have never felt that anything I was aiming for was 'above my station'. There was certainly never a feeling of 'people in our class only do xyz' . . .
(Karina, two children, PG cert. Managing Health and Social Care)

Many participants discussed their experiences of being raised by parents who wanted something better for their children than they themselves had experienced. It was often working-class mothers who encouraged their daughters to strive high in order to avoid the factory or farm work that they themselves had been restricted to, while working-class fathers were more likely to discourage daughters from remaining in education, although there were exceptions to this.

Some lone mothers identifying as working class did berate parental aspirations for them that had been restricted to typing or nursing. Individuals discussed how their own ambitions had exceeded those prescribed for them, even as teenagers; but in the absence of parental support such dreams had often taken decades to begin to realise as mature adult learners. For many, success in initial schooling had been compromised by home life. This was constituted either by assumed care responsibilities for younger siblings, or ill parents or extended family members; or by parental unavailability and neglect through long work hours, abandonment, mental illness or bereavement. Participants' narratives documented understanding that such lack of parental support stemmed from material conditions challenging the optimal nurturing of children, rather than a lack of value on education per se:

We were solidly sub-working class, living on the breadline. However, my mother worked hard at home before we started school to ensure we could all read and write, add up, etc. She was extremely supportive till she had the fifth child when I was around high-school age, and she seemed to no longer have the time to assist. My father was unwilling and unable to help with homework. I think after this point, I lost interest in school work, despite staying on to do A-levels, and

failing miserably. (Marie–Therese, two children aged 9 and 12,
Year 2 BA Social Sciences and Politics)

Work, study and deferred gratification

Lone mothers' narratives documented the importance of, and value
attached to, work in their childhoods. Many talked of how hard their
parents had worked, the work ethic that they had instilled in their children, and although some had grown up in periods of significant worklessness nationally, there were no reports of workless families, despite the
in-depth nature of the research. The strong theme of the importance
of work, echoed consistently across childhood social class backgrounds,
applied to research participants' mothers as well as fathers, even in
contexts in which individuals described many other mothers not having
been in paid employment. The majority of participants had grown up
in households where their mothers had been in at least part-time, if not
full-time employment, contributing to the development of their own
expectations of being a working mother. Contrary to findings from
other studies of lone parents (see Klett-Davies, 2007), no participants
saw being a lone parent as justifying not being in paid work, education
or training. Lone mothers' reflections suggest that a strong work ethic
may have contributed to engagement with education as productive time
use to develop employment prospects while raising children alone. In
addition, presence of such a family work ethic can be seen as supporting
lone mothers' motivation to persist in their university studies in the
face of substantial obstacles. This illustrates the strong agency frequently
required for lone mothers to manage the challenges of HE participation.

Such persistence in the face of obstacles indicates the value on
deferred gratification necessary for lone parents' success in HE. This
value is indicated regardless of participants' social class background,
standing in contrast to the tradition of commentaries associating a
middle-class background with increased focus on deferred gratification
and educational achievement (see Willis, 1977). Furthermore, given
this evidence that both lone-mother HE students and their families
place strong value on the deferred gratification of education and
employment opportunities, this raises the question of what past events
have interrupted participants' learning, and sometimes employment,
biographies. As well as the early education experiences discussed above,

lone mothers' trajectories testify to the disruptive effect of becoming a parent, and subsequently a lone parent through relationship breakdown, on participation in education and employment. Paradoxically, these life-change events not only inhibit personal and professional development, but can also act as a trigger for it, as discussed later in this chapter.

The importance of deferred gratification runs throughout participants' narratives. For example, many described feeling aware that other students were out socialising while they stayed at home studying, but comforted themselves with the reflection that sacrificing social activity to prioritise their studies in the short term would ultimately repay them with a more comfortable life, the rewards of which would include increased social opportunities. For some, such individual focus on deferred gratification stood in stark contrast to childhood parental pressure to leave school early and take up paid employment. The trajectories of some lone parents, particularly from working-class backgrounds, illustrated radical transformation as individuals developed learner identities, placing increasing value upon deferred gratification for themselves and their children.

The relationship between lone parents' HE engagement and gratification resulting from this is complex. Financial gratification must be deferred, projected by lone mothers' instrumental motivations to use university participation as a means to achieving greater economic security as sole providers for their families. In contrast, the intrinsic gratification of HE participation contributing to nurturing of the self and perceived quality of parenting is frequently immediate. For many, educational participation chisels a pocket of 'me time', or care of the self beyond the role of parent serving others, albeit within the context of competing demands and overstretched resources. That individuals sometimes see their HE participation positively as constituting 'me time', and at other times negatively as a stress upon emotional and physical well-being, illustrates the ebb and flow of experience illuminated by the longitudinal approach.

Why Higher Education?

Intrinsic and instrumental motivation

Approximately half of the lone mothers described their motivations for entering Higher Education. They often felt that it was something they should have done a long time ago, sometimes directly attributing this delay to the lack of support received from parents, teachers or partners in the past. Individuals discussed the interwoven significance of a range of instrumental and intrinsic motivations for their HE engagement, as discussed throughout the remainder of this chapter.

Research with mature students has acknowledged the extent to which motivations for educational engagement vary between vocational reasons and personal development (Woodley and Wilson, 2002; Leonard, 1994; Edwards, 1993). Such diversity of motivation is inevitable given the heterogeneity of mature HE students as a group, ranging from those with no formal qualifications at all who needed much confidence building, to highly qualified individuals managing a career break and wishing to update or retrain, as found by Wisker (1996: 3). Male and ethnic minority students have been documented to enter Higher Education for predominantly career-related reasons compared to women, white and older students (Brennan et al., 1999; Edwards, 1993). The significance of career-related motives for study have been found to decline with age; with vocational reasons prevailing for students under 30, after which they become of equal value to personal motivations. For students over 35, personal reasons have been found to dominate. These include subject interest, career change, self-fulfilment, and achieving self-respect after perceived failure in initial education (Gallagher et al., 1993). The well documented prevalence of personal satisfaction motives for HE participation amongst mature students as a whole (Murphy and Roopchand, 2003; Reay, 2003; Woodley and Wilson, 2002), translate into successful learning outcomes, with intrinsically motivated students demonstrated to perform better in Higher Education (Byrne and Flood, 2005: 11).

Despite the high representation of mature, white women who participated in this study, this was not matched by a corresponding prevalence of intrinsic motivations for HE engagement, observed extensively amongst this group by other commentators (Murphy and Roopchand, 2003: 256; Reay, 2003: 304; Brennan et al., 1999: 7–11; Leonard, 1994: 167; Edwards, 1993: 56, 83; Gallagher et al., 1993: 5). Existing research on lone parents has identified the significance of instrumental motivations for educational participation amongst this group (Polakow et al., 2004: 116; Wisker, 1996: 5). This study identified a complex interweaving of intrinsic and instrumental motivation for lone parents' educational engagement. The unique position of sole responsibility for meeting both the material and emotional needs of children disrupts the breadwinner model of women as secondary wage earners and primarily responsible for children's practical and emotional care, that remains deeply entrenched in both social policy and cultural values. Lone mothers' responsibilities as sole breadwinners stand them apart from other mature students for whom intrinsic educational motivations dominate, as one explained:

> *Having to be mother and father . . . and fulfil two roles (multi-tasking to the extreme).* (May, four children aged up to 18, Year 2 Social Sciences and Human Biology)

Instead, lone mothers frequently feel forced to think instrumentally about providing for their families' present and future material needs, acting as what Crompton and Harris have termed 'careerists by necessity' (1999: 138). The narratives of lone mothers in this book indicate hoped-for future career development, financial stability and enhanced material opportunities as a result of HE participation to be primary educational motivators, even if these goals accompany desires for intrinsic satisfactions.

Such difference in experience from mature students as a whole indicates the strong impact of motherhood, and particularly lone motherhood, upon individuals' motives for HE engagement, altering the balance of intrinsic and instrumental goals. Comparing lone parents' motivations and experiences to literature on mature students as a whole, illustrates how parenting alone heightens the intensity of priorities that are relevant to all parents. Hence, both instrumental and intrinsic motivations for HE engagement appear to be felt particularly acutely by lone parents. Such differences between the specific case of lone-mother HE students, and the much more extensively documented experience of mature women students with family responsibilities as a whole, demonstrate the need for research differentiating between the two groups. This impact of breadwinning pressure upon the prevalence of intrinsic or instrumental motivations for HE engagement fits with documented social class differences in motivational orientation amongst mature male and female students with caring responsibilities. Working-class learners report increased instrumental motivation, compared to prioritisation of intrinsic motivation amongst middle-class learners (Cappleman-Morgan, 2005: 5).

Lone-parent status informs both the particular instrumental and intrinsic goals individuals hope to achieve through HE participation. Individuals' motivations for educational engagement frequently map on to one or more of the three key areas dominating the group's experiences of HE participation, as explored in Chapters 4–6: time, finances, and childcare. Key motivations have been documented by existing commentators to include job prospects, earning potential, improved personal circumstances, providing for dependants, setting a positive example for children, doing something for themselves, escaping the house, meeting new people, and getting off state benefits (Horne and Hardie, 2002). These goals are all strongly represented amongst lone mothers in this study, and illustrate the extent to which intrinsic and instrumental goals are complexly interwoven for lone parent HE learners.

Lone parent experience further impacts upon the HE courses individuals choose to study. Instrumental goals lead many lone mothers to opt for teacher training courses, perceiving a particular compatibility between teaching as a career and their responsibilities as sole parent. Many lone mothers attribute their enrolment in social science courses to interest in issues around social justice, stemming from their own experiences as lone parents. This resonates with findings around mature women students' interest in social sciences frequently being informed by their own life experience (Edwards, 1993: 83). The prevalence of social science courses amongst lone parents further fits with identified patterns in instrumental versus intrinsic orientation, with social science students documented to be most influenced by career goals, followed by science students, and humanities students the least instrumentally orientated (Gallagher et al., 1993).

Lone-mother HE students describe hoping that HE participation will ultimately facilitate a future with more time and financial security, and less reliance on childcare than in their lives as lone parents to date. This includes those indicating their engagement with study to have been informed by feeling unable to continue fulfilling the requirements of formerly held demanding jobs in their current circumstances as lone parents. Those participating in teacher training described their hopes of a future career that would both offer a stable salary and maximise time with their children after school each day and during school holidays, representing the combination of instrumental and intrinsic motivations.

However, such belief in the future rewards of HE participation frequently demands a strong commitment to deferred gratification, particularly for those without family experiences or support to draw on in validating long-term benefits of educational participation. In the immediate term, the very problems in terms of finances, time and childcare that lone mothers seek to alleviate though HE completion, are frequently magnified for the duration of their studies. For example, while those training to be teachers are often motivated by hopes of enjoying hours of work and holidays that fit better with children's schooling than other occupations, participating in teacher training courses frequently engenders particular problems for lone parents in terms of travelling long distances to training placements, early start times and long working days.

In addition to family-oriented instrumental and intrinsic goals, lone parents frequently report a further important motivation for HE participation to be securing employment which is more interesting, challenging, or useful to society. This is particularly the case for those training in nursing, teaching and social work; and chimes with research on mature working-class women students who indicate the desire to 'give something back' to society (Reay, 2003: 301). For mothers in this research, the change in values and perspective entailed in the experience of becoming a parent were often indicated to catalyse development of an interest in environmental and political concerns, as observed by Edwards with regard to mature women students (1993: 51, 53).

Educational triggers

Researchers of adult learners have frequently identified the significance of pivotal moments in individuals' life trajectories in triggering (re) engagement with education. Such moments have been variously con-ceptualised as 'critical incidents', 'fateful', 'trigger' or 'epiphany' moments (Hyde, 2007; Jones, 2006: 494; Brine and Waller, 2004: 101; Crossan *et al.*, 2003; Komulainen, 2000; Merrill, 2000; Parr, 2000; Leonard, 1994: 167; Gallagher *et al.*, 1993: 6). Crompton and Harris' further identification of such epiphanic moments as informing women's engagement with paid employment is similarly relevant to understanding the motivations of lone-parent learners (1999: 139). The occurrence of such critical trigger moments emerged as central to the trajectories of many of the lone mothers in this study, corresponding with findings of participation in adult learning as either responding to life change or seeking it (Jones, 2006: 496).

Specific educational triggers described by lone mothers in this study include: availability of funding; fear of, or actual redundancy; reduction in childcare commitments; marital breakdown; geographical move (also Gallagher *et al.*, 1993: 6); illness or bereavement; or the 'jolt' parenthood provides in terms of having 'someone to provide for' and needing to have a 'solid job' (also Leonard, 1994: 167). Exemplifying the way in which such concrete circumstances inform engagement with Higher Education, one lone mother in this research explained:

> *I could not study on my course if I was at work full time, no way! Neither could I do this if [my daughter] was under school age.* (Marcia, age 43, one child aged 7, Year 3 BSc Clinical Nursing).

A particularly salient area of pivotal moments in informing educational re-engagement are traumatic experiences, or 'mega trauma', including psychological trauma or physical abuse experienced either in childhood or adulthood (also Parr, 2000: 38, 100). Such events can be central to informing individuals' desire to change their identity through engaging with education (2000: 46), and are often relevant in the narratives of lone-mother HE learners. Much of the language around the significance of such critical moments in learning trajectories has strong resonance with circumstances frequently defining lone parenthood. Critical incidents, or 'status passages', are therefore seen as marking entry to a certain status or role involving changes in a person's identity (Crossan *et al.*, 2003: 56, 60), or even a 'metamorphosis' of the self (Komulainen, 2000: 453). Frequent triggers including shifts in caring roles and responsibilities (Crossan *et al.*, 2003: 59), experience of discrimination (Woodfield, 2007: 71), and the shedding of constricting traditionally stereotyped gender roles (for example through divorce) (Komulainen, 2000: 457) as preconditions for individual self-realisation through education, are particularly relevant to lone mothers, and were frequently indicated by individuals in this study. This contributes to understanding why the change in circumstances of becoming a lone parent is so frequently documented as being the overall motivator for HE participation. Research on mature women students has found that they are substantially more likely to be divorced compared to contemporary trends, with further trends toward separation during the course of HE study, and documented on-going relationship problems (Edwards, 1993). Relationship breakdown can hence be either catalyst or consequence of returning to education (Jones, 2006: 495; Edwards, 1993: 49).

Existing research has identified a strong impact of parent status upon overall educational motivation for both young students (Zachry, 2005) and mature learners (Edwards, 1993). Indeed, in this research, becoming a parent or lone parent was indicated to be by far the dominant motivator for educational engagement, with more than half of those who described events leading to their entry into Higher Education, citing one of these as the key factor.

Becoming a parent or lone parent can act as the catalyst for the return to learning that individuals have long put off embarking on, representing an example of the acknowledged way in which major change can lead to an individual's reassessment of life and priorities, providing the opportunity to fulfil a long-held desire to return to learning (Parr, 2000: 47; Brine and Waller, 2004: 101). In fact a significant body of those in this research reflected that they would probably not have enrolled in Higher Education at all had they not become lone parents, as explained by Rosa:

> *My being a single parent has meant that in some ways I can be more selfish when it comes to study, as I don't have a partner to consider or set aside time for. If I hadn't become a single parent I would still have had the desire to return to study, but would have been less likely to act on it, as would have been more stuck in the rut of work, financial success, promotional and career ladders, etc. So I am very happy that I decided to go back to study and think that every cloud definitely has a silver lining; becoming a single parent forced me to go back to a simpler way of life and to do some of the things that make me more secure and happy.* (Rosa, two children, MBA)

The negative impact on individuals' learning trajectories of lack of educational support and encouragement from teachers, parents and partners has been highlighted earlier. Similarly demonstrating the strong impact of absence or presence of networks of support, lone mothers stress the significance of encouragement from supportive individuals in childhood or adulthood as being pivotal in informing educational engagement (Hinton-Smith, 2007a; Hyde, 2007). For example, one lone mother described how her motivation for HE participation had been the role model provided by a good friend:

*College was never mentioned at home or school. I come from a rough
area where most girls get pregnant and most men get jobs in factories
or get into crime. In fact me and my sister are the only people in my
entire family to have gone to uni; we have a huge extended family so
it's quite strange that no one else has. Although no one in my family
has returned to education, my oldest friend of 22 years has returned
to uni. She has been my best mate for so long she is like family and
she is the reason I came to uni as she inspired me and made me
believe I could do it.* (Charlie, age 29, two children and 8 and 9,
Year 2 BA Developmental Psychology)

Illustrating the two primary educational motivators of lone-parenting
status and networks of support, another reflected that:

*I was very encouraged by the positive feedback from the tutors on my
access course and to be honest I'm not at all sure what I would have
done in my life had I not become a parent when I was 21.* (Bex,
age 34, one child aged 12, MA Primary Education
With QTS)

It has been observed elsewhere that discovery of learning can involve
the influence of a key person who is helpful in building up a learner's
damaged self-esteem (Weil, 1986: 224). Factors including the kind of
relationship a participant has with a partner, and direction of family
support can intersect to impact critically upon the determining effect
that events like becoming pregnant or a lucky break in getting a job
have upon an individual's life (Procter and Padfield, 1998: 246).

Filling a void

The potential of mature HE engagement to remediate the dissatisfactions
and inequalities of individuals consigned to domestic, childcare roles, the
majority of whom have been women, has been theorised in political
terms by commentators. In 1965 Betty Friedan advocated Higher
Education as the key to what she called 'the problem that has no name' –
the isolation and dissatisfaction of 'wifing' and mothering roles. Edwards
has drawn on this legacy to suggest that adult educational engagement
can be a political instrument for, and of, power, offering a way out of
inequality and oppression for groups who are powerless. For women

especially, it is claimed that education can be an escape route from domestic life and second-class citizenship into the public sphere (Edwards, 1993: 1). Such dissatisfaction is not necessarily exclusively feminine, but may relate primarily to the undervalued primary parenting role. This can be a motivating factor for educational engagement (Hinton-Smith, 2007a), and increased educational provision and support is advocated as a solution (Greif, 1992: 267). The opportunity to be alone, an individual, independent, and to take a break from the responsibilities of parenthood, represents aspects of the rewards adult learners experience from participation in university learning. At the extreme end, lone mothers in this research and elsewhere describe enjoying the feeling that people at university do not know they have children (also Edwards, 1993: 89).

Trajectories documenting the role of HE participation in fostering a sense of freedom and time for oneself can be seen as representing what we contemporarily perceive as 'personal development', with lone-mother HE students frequently discussing the role of university participation in terms of 'broadening horizons'. One described her motivation for HE participation as being a way to prevent her from 'becoming brain dead', while another had commenced her adult education as a response to the boredom of being a jobless teenage mother.

Lone mothers frequently explained that their HE engagement was motivated by the desire to fill a void, making explicit a tacit theme in existing work (see Jones, 2006). The sentiment of one reflection that study served to 'fill a hole created by my last long-term partner' (Josephine, one child, BSc Social Policy), was iterated by many others. Lone mothers frequently speak explicitly of their studies filling time left empty by the absence of employment opportunities, intimate relationships, social activity, or the full health to participate actively in society (see also Duncan and Edwards, 1999: 137). Several indicated hoping that their university participation would address absences in their lives beyond the academic remit of studentship. Many hoped that HE engagement would additionally create opportunities to make friends or meet a new partner.

The longitudinal dimension, and inclusion of individuals at varied stages of their HE learner journeys, charted reflective development in lone mothers' subjective interpretations of the meanings attached to their HE engagement. This included individuals' changing perceptions of the true triggers behind their decisions to re-engage with education, as the following identifies:

It's pretty clear to me now that university provided the perfect 'way out' of the bad relationship without needing to go down the route of finding a great job (with a good salary) and the struggle of childcare. At the time, that wasn't necessarily how I viewed it! It was more that I felt with [my son] being at school, the time for postgrad study was right. (Beth, age 33, one child aged 8, Year 2 PhD Archaeology)

That HE engagement can coincide with exiting an unsatisfactory relationship is a recurring theme. Lone mothers' reflections suggest that the leaving of a partner, who may have dominated family life and decision-making in various ways, can lead to an increased sense of autonomy, free time, self-confidence and closeness with friends, which can underpin and catalyse the feeling that there is space in life for something else alongside parenting.

Child-oriented intrinsic and instrumental motivations for HE engagement

The needs and futures of children are ever-present in lone mothers' narratives of educational motivation. Motivational factors for HE engagement, including new opportunities, career advancement, providing a better future, and improved quality of life, are all discussed in terms of projected benefits to children. The key motivation for HE engagement of the desire to achieve financial stability and career advancement is frequently linked to the importance of earning enough to support a family as a lone parent:

I remember growing up and being bullied for not having a mum at home and for never having the new, trendy clothes, etc. There are bigger motivations than money, but I guess as a parent it is a natural feeling to want to be able to look after your children. I know it must have been very difficult for my dad as a single parent bringing up two girls, and I will always love and respect him for doing the best he could. In a way I want to learn from him and do things differently. Things like being able to take my son abroad, to broaden his understanding of the world, which I never had the opportunity to do as a child. I would also like to be able to save some money for when he is an adult, for either university, or a deposit for a house, or to travel – for whatever he needs. (Stacey, one child, BA Sociology, Business and Management)

51

For many, an important aspect of this desire to earn more money is the hope that an HE qualification will contribute to achieving more satisfactory housing for their families. Lone parents frequently talk of achieving the means to 'escape' the area where they presently live.

Family-oriented instrumental and intrinsic motivations are tightly interwoven in lone-parent HE learners' motivational trajectories, with individuals hoping that HE participation will help them to meet their children's needs financially, practically and in terms of becoming 'better' parents. For example, one mother's motivation for HE engagement had been a desire to become better informed about her son's Special Educational Needs (SEN), since she felt that he was being failed by professionals. Lone-mother HE students often perceive their educational participation as enhancing the quality of their parenting skills, as other commentators have observed of parents generally (Shaw and Wool-head, 2006; Duckworth, 2005; Eccles and Daris-Kean, 2005). A strong intrinsic motivation to provide a positive role model to children is further significant for lone-parent HE learners (Jackson, 2004: 57; Reay, 2003: 309; Horne and Hardie, 2002: 64; Scott *et al.*, 1996: 234; Edwards, 1993: 59,119–121). The following quote encapsulates the complex interweaving of a combination of intrinsic and instrumental HE motivations for many lone parent learners:

> *The single mum status did influence my decision to train as a lawyer*
> *– no one else to help me to pay the bills! I want my children to be*
> *able to stand up in class at school and say my mummy is a lawyer –*
> *and be proud of me rather than saying my mum just stays at home.*
> (Sadie, age 27, 4-year-old twins, Year 3 LLB)

Research has found women with children to see their engagement with learning in terms of helping their children achieve educationally, positioning themselves within a framework that articulates responsibility as 'good parents', and seeing themselves as passing on their education to their children in a variety of ways. The desire to act as positive role models for children is seen to represent a particularly strong aspect of this motivation (Zachry, 2005: 2566; Reay, 2003: 309). The providing of such a positive role model in terms of the potential of achieving a Higher Education and professional employment has been documented to be particularly significant for individuals from working-class backgrounds (see Cappleman–Morgan, 2005: 5). However, no discernible difference emerged in this research in what lone parents hoped to achieve from their HE studies according to social class identity, with both self-identified middle-class and working-class participants equally emphasising plans for graduate employment and continued postgraduate study, and hopes for their children's futures.

The complex range of motives for lone mothers' engagement with HE learning sit uncomfortably alongside their ongoing perception of others' opinions of them as scroungers, and it is significant that the hope that engagement with learning will help to free them of the stigma of dole-scrounging lone parent is a cited motivation for HE participation (NUS, 2009: 20, 22). This continuing perception of social stigma attached to lone motherhood is iterated in other commentaries (Freud, 2007: 53; Klett-Davies, 2007; Cappleman-Morgan, 2005: 5; Polakow, *et al.*, 2004: 237). To rid oneself of the stigma of lone parenthood, from teenage parenthood to welfare dependency, is an important recurring motivational factor for HE engagement. Lone parents describe the need to prove to themselves and others that they can succeed. Among others citing the desire for freedom from welfare dependency, two described their motivations:

> *To not be on benefits anymore. I would say my self-esteem is much higher being a 'psychology undergraduate' rather than a single mum on the social.* (Anne-Marie, one child, Year 1 Psychology)

and

> *To lose the stigma attached to lone parent that will still never truly disappear. But really, and more importantly, I did it for the security for the future for me and my daughter.* (Kristin, age 26, one child aged 8, PGCE History)

The following three chapters explore in detail key areas defining individuals' experiences as they negotiate the challenges of HE learning, in pursuit of freedom from the financial constraints and unwelcome stereotypes they encounter in their lives as lone mothers.

CHAPTER FOUR

Juggling time

'I love being a working mum,' says Nancy, 'but I'm constantly juggling time. And the one person there's never any time left for is me!' (Asda magazine, Sept. 2006: 90)

Academic and popular texts alike are littered with metaphors of 'juggling' and 'balancing' parenthood, home and work in the lives of women. The following three chapters explore in detail the key areas of barriers experienced by lone mothers in their HE participation, how the interrelated nature of these concerns play out in daily lives of themselves and their families, and how these are negotiated. Lone mothers' trajectories document the complex balancing or juggling acts they manage in terms of time, finances and childcare, being the three major areas of significance impacting upon HE participation. Problems around these areas have been identified as providing key reasons for mature working-class women students leaving HE courses prematurely (Reay, 2003: 312). Moreover, these three broad categories are frequently inseparable as lone-parent students' lack of time largely stems from the financial necessity to juggle paid employment with studies, and lack of funds to buy adequate childcare needed to provide time for study. Nevertheless, these key areas of challenge are not entirely collapsible. Even the most financially comfortable lone parents, able to afford full-time childcare and meet the costs of living without the need for paid employment, nevertheless experience the stretching of time inherent in being a sole provider and carer of children in the context of cultural expectations of 'intensive parenting', as explored by commentators (Wall, 2010; Cha, 2009; Dew, 2009; Jacobs and Gerson, 2004).

This represents the way in which, to a considerable extent, lone mothers' experiences can be seen as constituting a difference in degree, rather than one of kind, from the contemporary experiences of parents generally. Lone mothers' in-depth reflections on their daily lives balancing complex loads of responsibility, including study, paid work, childcare and care of elderly parents, alongside some attempt at space for care of the self, reflect broader trends of life in late modernity. The challenges described by participants in this study indicate that their concerns in many ways merely represent the particularly intensive end of those experienced by parents, and society generally.

Lone-parent students' accounts of juggling time relay the relationship of their home and university lives, addressing conflicting priorities and telling stories of guilt, sacrifice and self-actualisation, as explored throughout this chapter. Two-parent families are seen as responding to the demands of the modern family and employment by operating 'shift work' parenting. Although this may be considered far from an ideal solution in terms of family quality of life, it nonetheless provides a strategy not available to many lone parents. Land's suggestion that lone parenthood can be likened to running a small business with a permanent labour shortage (2007) certainly resonates with the time deficits described by lone mothers in this research, as reflected by Shelby:

> *I often think my situation is magnified by being a single-parent,*
> *as being a parent is in itself difficult, but trying to be both is near*
> *impossible! I also feel that the added burden of being the sole*
> *breadwinner is often overwhelming – how do you balance the*
> *commitment of a good career, with being a good mum?* (Shelby, age
> 32, one child aged 6, PGCE FE)

Many lone mothers described the competing pressures on their time as leaving their heads so overburdened that they became forgetful, with clear negative implications for ability to study effectively, as well as on wider life. Others describe negative effects along the lines of feeling like 'I've aged five years' (Heather, age 30, one baby, Year 2 BA Urban Studies and Planning).

Unsurprisingly, time emerges as a major issue for lone-parent students, discussed by almost two-thirds. The overwhelming majority of those discussing their use of time lament not having enough of it. There being insufficient hours in the day is a frequent complaint:

> *I think the only thing that would really help, would be an extra five hours or so in every day'* (Stacey, one child, BA Sociology with Business and Management)

Accounts of 'juggling' or 'balancing' commitments are also prevalent in commentaries documenting mature women students' educational participation and the dual or multiple roles combining study and care-giving responsibilities more broadly (Jones, 2006: 496; Murphy and Roopchand, 2003: 255; Merrill, 1999: 154, 159; Edwards, 1993: 33). Mature learners are documented as juggling various combinations of care for elderly parents, labour market commitments, childcare, domestic responsibilities, studying, and voluntary work; and wanting to meet the demands of all (Reay, 2003: 301, 307). In this research, the loads juggled by individuals were made up of various patterns of study, childcare, paid work, partner relationships, care for ageing parents, ill ex-partners, friends or other family members, volunteering, and religious participation – although the most commonly discussed roles being juggled were those of student and parent, being discussed by half. Findings elaborate upon how increased longevity and delayed childbearing can leave individuals simultaneously caring for ageing parents and dependent children, and the impact of these care responsibilities, as highlighted more briefly elsewhere (Scott *et al.*, 1996: 235). Lone mothers further describe how the demands of HE study can force them to cut back on such additional care responsibilities beyond those for their own children, and the ensuing guilt experienced. In addition to the physical demands of parenting alone, lone mothers describe the impact of sole responsibility for their families' emotional care and for what I have termed 'mental domestic labour', including myriad responsibilities from scheduling dental appointments and remembering birthdays through to listening to the problems of children's days at school. This means that, even if individuals manage to delegate particular tasks and responsibilities, it nevertheless remains they who must organise and worry about it. Women in The European Union, a collective of feminist academics representing European Women's Studies Institutes, also acknowledge the burden of responsibilities implicit in what they have termed the 'mental burden of domestic labour' or 'domestic management' (2011).

Time is thus not merely a concern of the physical dimension, and the assumption that leisure is something one does when not occupied by paid work or unpaid housework therefore is false (Edwards, 1993: 64, 70). This burden of mental alongside physical domestic responsibility is experienced by many students with family responsibilities as the shouldering of an enormous burden of commitments which, not surprisingly, interferes with studies.

Research has indicated women students to report more stress and negative health impact resulting from juggling the different pressures of work, study and family than men (Moreau and Leatherwood; 2006: 34, Gilbert and Holahan, 1982: 643). One lone mother participating in this research perceived the juggling demands on her as being a gendered issue, reflecting, 'am I more prepared as a single parent? Probably, more prepared as a woman! I think women just "do" juggle, and "plan", quite honestly'. She reiterated this gendered perspective in a later email:

> *Women have a desire to succeed . . . Women multi-task naturally, whilst juggling the emotional pull of leaving children with someone else* (Veronica, age 41, one child aged 10, Year 2 PG Diploma Management Studies)

Existing research indeed indicates that those part-time students who manage to combine study with wider life least problematically tend not to have responsibility for children (Moreau and Leatherwood, 2006: 17). The challenges mature students face in juggling the various elements of their lives have been acknowledged at policy level, with the then Secretary of State for Universities advising Vice-chancellors in 2006 of the need for evening and weekend courses to 'meet the needs of older students who need to study in new ways and balance work and family' (Shepherd, 2006).

The impact of individual circumstances

A range of factors affect the type and extent of problems and worries experienced by lone-mother university students. Those studying by distance learning report fewer problems than those studying on tradi-tionally taught university courses. The obstacles that distance learners do describe are frequently more generalised life problems that often do not relate specifically to Higher Education. Similarly, part-time students describe fewer problems managing their combined commitments compared to those studying full time. These variations both indicate that, unsurprisingly, the presence of fewer competing demands upon resources renders participating in learning less problematic. Existing findings that part-time students are affected more by extra-institutional matters than full-time students (Yorke and Longden, 2004: 104) have not explored why this is the case, although the implicit assumption is that part-time students frequently have family responsibilities. Narratives in this research contribute to understanding by documenting learner journeys for both part-time and full-time students with family responsibilities. That part-time students are more positive about their daily routines as student parents and their support needs being met by their HE Institution, and less likely to report problems, suggests that the balancing of the dual roles of student and parent alone is not the key issue to address. Rather, shouldering the burden of a full-time study load may be pivotal to managing HE study alongside lone parenthood, with part-time study potentially being more manageable. This bolsters calls for increased open learning opportunities to embrace those not able to manage full-time study (Wisker, 1996: 10).

Perhaps surprisingly, lone-parent students with one child more frequently describe obstacles to study compared to those with two or more children, despite the increased childcare and domestic labour burden associated with additional children. This contrasts with existing findings that mothers with more children are less likely to complete their studies (Zachry, 2005: 2571). This may hide the experiences of lone parents struggling to manage learning with more than one young child who have already exited their studies early because of the unmanageable pressure. Children's ages can also be potentially more significant than number of children. This is indicated by lone mothers of preschool children in this research being far more likely to report feeling 'tired' by their attempts to manage HE participation with lone parenthood, resonating with evidence that parents of younger children are more likely to leave courses early because of the increased domestic responsibilities associated with younger children (Scott *et al.*, 1998: 233). Most lone parent HE students in this research with preschool children had only one child, potentially reflecting decreased willingness amongst parents of several preschool children to engage with education or, once again, an increased propensity for parents with more young children to exit courses early. Surprisingly, no significant variation emerged in how likely those with and without preschool children are to report obstacles to their studies, although perhaps inevitably the majority of problems described by those with preschool children focus on childcare. Lone parents report the same general obstacles to study regardless of the number and ages of their children, although there are trends in the particular form these problems take, according to the ages of children. Such specific obstacles are discussed further later in this chapter.

Also relevant to considering the problems faced by lone mothers in their HE engagement are their worries, or projections as to what factors they expect to cause them problems in the future. Once again, those in part-time employment are more than twice as likely to discuss worries compared to the unemployed or those in full-time employment, pointing further to the stresses of their multiple roles. There was no significant difference in how frequently distance versus traditional contact, and part-time versus full-time students discussed worries. Part-time students indicate more frequently than full-time students the conjecture that their worries do not differ significantly from those of childless students or non-student dual-parent couples. This may be informed by part-time students' participation in learning environments in which it is assumed that everyone is engaged in juggling multiple commitments, regardless of parent and partner status. In contrast, the breadwinning and childcare responsibilities of lone parents may feel particularly at odds with the circumstances of the majority of full-time university students, pointing to the continuing implicit relevance of the 'Bachelor Boy' ideal of university participation (Edwards, 1993: 63).

Lone-parent students aged over 40 describe worrying more compared to the under-40 age group. Perhaps unsurprisingly in terms of the burden of responsibilities, lone mothers with more than one child also describe more worries compared to those with only one child; although, as discussed earlier, this contrasts with the increased prevalence of actual problems experienced by lone parents with one child. Perhaps surprisingly, those with preschool children are significantly less likely to discuss worries than those with older children. This can in part be attributed to preschool childcare providing more comprehensive cover, better suited to meeting the study needs of lone parents. This is compared to the shorter days and term dates of formal school provision, particularly during the initial reception year of schooling, when many children attend school only until lunchtime each day.

The remainder of this chapter discusses in detail the key areas of time stress salient for lone-parent students, effects of negotiating these stressors, and strategies employed by individuals in managing them.

Time for study

Clearing time to study amongst the competing time demands of parenthood is revealed by lone mothers' narratives to require meticulous time planning and rigid self-discipline not traditionally associated with the university student experience, as indicated by Helena:

> *Regarding transitions, [my son] was born halfway through my PhD so I had to adjust my hours of work from being very flexible and long to a strict day of 9–18 hours.* (Helena, age 31, one child aged 2, Year 3 PhD Medicine)

University teaching and assessment requirements in traditional Higher Education have been documented to be incompatible with the responsibilities of mature students with family commitments (Wisker, 1996: 11). Lone parents indicate the availability of time to devote to study in busy lives to be inadequate, and trying to manage study with children or non-cohabiting partners present is frequently described as unsatisfactory. The distraction caused by children is a key theme around trying to study. Amongst the frequent and varied discussion of studying time, the unanimous underlying sentiment is that 'I wish I had more time to study'. The large number of lone parents who rely on time children spend visiting non-custodial parents as a key opportunity to study means that times when most people traditionally take a break from work, like weekends and public holidays, for lone-parent students frequently represent periods of intensive studying, free from the usual interruptions of children.

The development of increased open learning opportunities has been advocated for meeting the needs of mature students with family responsibilities who are not able to fit full-time study into their lives (Wisker, 1996: 10). Distance-learning students frequently describe having been attracted by the flexibility of being able to complete their studies at home in their own time. However, this apparent solution also often entails its own particular problems when lack of childcare means that study cannot be completed at a library with necessary resources to hand, and that studying at home as a lone parent invariably means being subject to distraction by children. Parents of older children describe studying while children entertain themselves, do their own homework (although this often causes tensions over demand for the one home PC), 'play out' with friends, or at times, are kept entertained by games consoles or DVDs. One lone mother described regularly taking her young children to indoor adventure playgrounds in order to be able to write essays. A recurring theme is the difficulty of settling down and 'zoning in' to study when the freedom to do so comes only in short bursts between periodic interruptions of either children's demands for attention or routine responsibilities like ferrying children between school, daycare and activities. The often inevitability of interruptions also impacts on the kind of study that can be undertaken at given times:

> I just study when I get the chance and/or the inclination! I have to say that being a single parent I think it must be harder than for someone without children as, speaking for myself, I cannot study as such when madam is around. However, I do 'tidy' assignments up etc., little bits that don't require great concentration and you can dip in and out of. However, for really concentrated effort, e.g., critical analysis (what's that!) I have to be alone here and just study, no housework, no phone calls, nothing. (Marcia, age 43, one child aged 7, Year 3 BSc Clinical Nursing)

As in existing studies (Edwards, 1993:6), lone parents often express reluctance to be unavailable to children by studying while the family are at home together. Those who do study when children are at home and awake frequently experience tensions about whether they should be more available for their children:

> I also work one day a week, and luckily I have flexible hours and my boss is very understanding. However, the amount of time I have for studying is negligible. [University] have timetabled the course under the assumption that all the students will have the weekends free to 'catch up on the reading', but when I try to, my son accuses me of never spending any time with him. His resentment is growing in direct proportion to my exhaustion. (Michelle, age 35, one child aged 12, MSc History of Science)

Another described resorting to allowing her six-year-old son to share her bed at night during times of intensive study because she felt that university commitments prevented her from giving him sufficient contact during waking hours.

Parents of children too young to entertain themselves, or whose working day does not permit time for study, are often left with no choice but to study after children have gone to bed at night, as also observed elsewhere (NUS, 2009: 67; Edwards, 1993: 74, 76). Significantly, all of those describing relying on studying at night report it to be a difficult time to concentrate. Lone parents are inevitably tired at the end of a busy day in paid work and/or caring for preschool children, and several described routinely falling asleep at their studies at night. Assessment deadlines can demand staying up all night to study, and lone-parent students tell regular stories of early starts and late nights to complete assignments. Some regularly pursue the traditional student strategy of 'burning the midnight oil' into the small hours when assignments are due for completion. Many others, however, say that they are too tired to study by the end of the day, or feel that the impossibility of catching up on lost sleep during daytime hours because of having to care for children prevents late night studying from being an option.

Unsurprisingly, the pressure of attempting to revise for exams with children around demanding attention is described as particularly stressful (also Hyatt and Parry, 1990: 19). However, while continuous assessment has frequently been seen as preferable for adult learners compared to exams, this can also pose particular problems for lone-parent students, leaving university assignment requirements in almost constant conflict with domestic responsibilities (Wisker, 1996: 10).

In addition to the challenges children pose to finding time to study, lone parents with non-cohabiting partners often experience this as a further drain on precious studying time. Partners invariably visit in the evenings, after work and once children are going to bed – just the time when time-strapped lone-parent students need to commence their day's study. This conflict of demands results in either forfeiting study time, or continuing while partners are present. Either scenario results inevitably in feelings of guilt and inadequacy at failing to manage time and commitments satisfactorily, a major issue for lone-parent students that is discussed later in this chapter.

Study and school holidays

Study requirements in traditional Higher Education such as assessments to be completed over the Christmas holidays, are identified as particularly problematic for mature students with care responsibilities (Wisker, 1996: 10). Half of the lone mothers in this research describe problems fitting time to study around children's school holidays. Academic timetables requiring students to attend classes, do large volumes of reading, complete assignments or revise for exams over school holidays are problematic. Perhaps unsurprisingly, distance learners are far less likely than traditional students to find fulfilling university commitments during children's holidays difficult. Nevertheless, distance learning can create its own specific problems in terms of studying during the holidays:

> *My only problem with the OU is that their 'year' runs from end Jan to Oct and this of course covers all the major school holidays which makes study very difficult : 0 (. I think this is being reviewed though and some courses now run at different times.)* (Ruth, age 47, two children aged 9 and 12, Year 3 BA Social Policy and Criminology)

Parents with preschool children are significantly less likely to find studying in the holidays a problem compared to those with only school-age children, often reflecting the generally shorter holiday closures of preschool childcare. However, these parents' problems in keeping up with their studies can be particularly acute during periods of childcare closure, because the level of supervision required by preschool children precludes the possibility of completing any studying at all during children's waking hours. For these lone mothers, holiday study can usually only be attacked when preschool children are being cared for elsewhere or have gone to sleep at night, as explained by Danielle, who had little support:

> *[My son's] nursery was closed for nearly two weeks so I was really stuck for assistance . . . consequently got no study done as every night I fell asleep putting him to bed and woke up later . . . it was a bizarre Christmas . . . and I was glad when it was over.* (Danielle, age 33, one child aged 3, BA History and American Studies)

For lone parents with only school-age children, it is often the school holidays that create the only major problem area in terms of finding time to study, as indicated by Bex among others:

> *Holidays are actually the times when I have found it hardest to get work done as [my son] is not at school.* (Bex, age 34, one child aged 12, MA Primary Ed. with QTS)

Similarly, Lara explained that:

> *The main problem is that there is no childcare for the period over Christmas when you have to revise, so you have to try to revise round your child, which is difficult.* (Lara, age 28, one child aged 5, Year 3 BSc Zoology)

Studying during the school holidays is particularly problematic for lone parents of younger school-age children, for whom there is often no childcare infrastructure in place, yet whom nevertheless are young enough to require supervision.

The net result for lone parents is that remaining abreast of academic work during children's school holidays usually means either managing around a houseful of children or shouldering additional childcare costs, and that study has to compete with other demands from entertaining children at home to days out. Whichever strategy is followed frequently results in feelings of guilt and is often rather unsatisfactory, as Ruth lamented:

> *So far the holidays are the usual nightmare! Me in the kitchen desperately trying to study with two bored boys fighting round the house.* (Ruth, age 47, two children aged 9 and 12, Year 3 BA Social Policy and Criminology)

Some lone parents refuse to study in the school holidays because they feel that this is time for spending with children, but the majority feel that it cannot be avoided, as May explained:

> *Unfortunately my first TMA [tutor marked assignment] is due soon after the New Year so it still means 'nose to the grindstone'.* (May, four children aged up to 18, Year 2 Foundation Social Sciences and Human Biology)

Having to focus on study often means compromising time spent on more traditional holiday activities like summer day trips or Christmas gift shopping, and there are frequent tensions in terms of which activities to compromise:

> *Christmas is stressful when you are at uni, mostly because the exams have been booked just after the new year, meaning Christmas is meant to be the time to revise. Though with family commitments and wanting to make Christmas great for your kids something has to give, usually revision time.* (Lara, age 28, one child aged 5, Year 3 BSc Zoology)

Academic study time during school holidays has to compete further with the many commitments that there is insufficient time for during term time, including household jobs, catching up with friends and family, and allowing children to have friends home to play. Lone mothers describe becoming highly skilled at salvaging moments for study during the school holidays:

> *It's quite simple really – I'm a bad mother! As soon as my son heads out (or even upstairs) I grab the chance to work – should he resurface when I am mid-thought I growl loudly – then feel really rotten afterwards! He is actually an absolute treasure about all of this and well used to occupying himself.* (Samantha, age 47, one child aged 11, BA Humanities)

Assignment extensions

Despite frequently highly developed time management skills necessitated by lives as lone-parent HE students, inevitably there are often times when unexpected additional challenges, including illness, childcare problems or work pressure, tip the balance and render it temporarily impossible for individuals to meet the expectations placed by HE Institutions. In such cases lone mothers are dependent on the willingness of tutors to sanction absence or extensions. This willingness varies considerably between HE Institutions, and impacts pivotally on the lives of individuals and their families at the most difficult of times in terms of family health and well-being.

The willingness of universities to grant assignment extensions in times of crisis is central to lone parents' perceptions of their institution's supportiveness of their circumstances. Just over a quarter of lone mothers in the research described experiencing staff at their universities who were prepared to grant extensions on assignments. Distance-learning and traditional-contact students are equally likely to be granted extensions, and just three lone parents reported having been refused extensions, representing both distance and traditional contact students. One in ten lone parents reported that their university permitted no concessions for lone parents in terms of extensions, which were either refused to everyone, or were granted but resulted in loss of marks:

> *My previous experience of HE was a BSc in Social Psychology with the University of [. . .]. That was a full time formal contact course. No concessions were made for single parents, though I only asked for an extension once, and that was when a relative died. Even so, it was difficult to get that extension. That course was a real slog and there were certainly no allowances made for personal circumstances.* (Karina, two children, Year 1 PG certificate Managing Health and Social Care)

> *Re out of hours services, I can see my personal tutor before lectures, during lunchtimes, after lectures, and we have email contact. She is very good at replying to communications, even out of hours. I do not find her as sympathetic as the course tutor in terms of me being stressed, etc. When I initially approached her about not coping with it all and asking to hand my assignment in later than other students she thought this would be unfair to the others!* (Sheila, age 43, one child aged 7, Year 3 BSc Clinical Nursing)

Lone-parent students describe having marks deducted for late assignment submissions when they have had to care of sick children, and have had no one else to do so, although they would not have been penalised in this way had they been sick themselves. Those studying part-time report requesting and being granted more assignment extensions compared to full-time students. While common sense assumptions may decree that a part-time workload should be more manageable alongside other commitments, this apparently decreased ability for part-time students to manage to meet institutional deadlines can be interpreted in several ways. It may indicate the more fractured lives experienced by part-time students, in which a greater conflict between competing roles and responsibilities compromises attention to studies. However, it may also suggest that HE Institutions with greater concentrations of part-time students are more orientated to addressing the needs of students with external responsibilities. It may further be the case that the learner identity of part-time students is less integral to overall identity. Studentship can hence be more easily balanced with other core elements of identity. This means that at times of multiple demands, part-time learners are quicker to drop study commitments in order to focus on competing demands, rather than subjugate other responsibilities to learning, as participant feedback later in this chapter shows full-time students more often to do, indicating more pervasive learner identities in which student status represents a more central facet of core identity.

University timetables

Teaching timetables feature significantly in lone-parent students' discussion of their efforts to juggle home and university life. Nearly half of lone mothers in this research discussed their university timetables, the majority of these describing how their university's organisation of timetabling impacts negatively upon their lives. Over a hundred separate discussions of timetabling over twelve months included only three positive comments. The degree to which lone parents' experiences of managing academic timetables are positive depends to a great extent upon the thoughtfulness and attitude of HE Institution staff and policy toward the competing responsibilities of mature students with care responsibilities.

Some distance-learning students perceive this status to render academic timetabling issues irrelevant to them, while other distance learners do describe timetabling problems. By far the most significant recurring context in which academic timetabling is discussed is with regard to problems created by timetables not being available sufficiently in advance. A related frequently cited problem is academic teaching timetables that change each term. While highlighted in this research to be highly significant to lone-parent students, the importance of such timetabling issues has been absent from most existing studies, although it has been acknowledged more recently by the NUS (2009: 29).

The problematic nature of these staples of university life came from lone parents' reliance on often-inflexible formal childcare structures. Academic timetabling was discussed in relation to childcare by almost one-third of lone parents in this research. Timetables changing each term and made available at short notice leave lone parents unable to secure childcare to cover their university commitments. Already financially struggling, lone parents are left frustrated at what they see as the unnecessary additional cost of having to overbook childcare to ensure adequate cover. The following quote encapsulates many of the inter-relating issues for lone parents around timetabling:

> *As a student mum of a young child I really feel uni life does not cater well enough for us; for example I didn't find out my timetable till the last day of the week I started (I had to book my daughter in nursery for the whole week). This wasn't just the cost, I just felt I wanted to be more organised and be able to plan for the time away from my daughter. Even once the timetable was sorted, during the first four weeks the lecture/seminar times were revised on several occasions. Which is a real pain as I have to give four weeks' notice if I want to change the times of nursery.* (Julie, one child, Year 1 Bachelor Degree)

The following example expresses the popular sentiment that academic timetables should be provided further in advance, to help meet the needs of lone parents:

> *Personally, I would like to see university cater more comprehensibly for single parents. That includes providing an annual timetable in advance of at least three months.* (Shelby, age 32, one child aged 6, PGCE FE)

Apart from short-notice and changing timetables leading to financial and attendance problems, they also result in problems regarding the all-important issue of children's happiness in childcare. Several lone parents described how childcare arrangements that keep changing at short notice to accommodate timetable requirements result in unsettled, unhappy children.

Timetabling issues impact further on lone parents' university participation, highlighted by those reporting choosing course modules to fit between seminar times and childcare availability, rather than academic interest:

> *Basically I had to choose my options according to which lectures*
> *I could go to rather than those I wanted to do.* (Andrea, age 23,
> one child aged 1, BA Development Studies)

Classes and exams timetabled for early mornings, evenings, and Saturdays all create problems, essentially because of clashing with school and nursery hours (also Gallagher *et al.*, 1993: 22). Sometimes lone parents resort to leaving lectures early because of finishing times not corresponding with school hours (also Jackson, 2004, 52). Other complaints include lectures being cancelled at short notice, after childcare has been arranged and individuals have travelled into university, and exams being rescheduled. What may be minor gripes and inconveniences to students who are not balancing such a precarious load of responsibilities, often have a profound effect in terms of disturbing the equilibrium for lone-parent students, preventing them from fulfilling their universities' expectations.

Managing study and family with employment

In addition to attempting to balance the competing demands of family and university, many lone parents are economically compelled to participate in paid employment, adding significantly to their juggling load. Bradshaw and Millar's research found lone mothers to be:

> *Acutely aware of the dilemma of trying to be both a 'good' mother,*
> *who cares for her children, and a 'breadwinner', who provides for*
> *them financially. This dilemma was felt to be especially acute because*
> *they were the only parent.* (1991: 33)

The dilemma is inevitably increased for those lone parents also attempting to manage HE study. Many mature students take part-time courses while remaining in employment (Woodley and Wilson, 2002: 332), and it has been suggested that being in paid employment can make individuals feel less guilty about attending university because they are also providing financially for their families (Wisker, 1996: 5). In a study of 6,000 part-time students at six major UK HE Institutions in the late 1990s, 83 per cent of students were found to be in paid employment, with some movement from full-time to part-time employment over the duration of studies (Brennan *et al.* 1999: 5–6). This suggests the impact of studies on ability to manage employment, and vice versa. It is stressed that 'undertaking part-time study is not an easy option for students, especially for the vast majority who are combining study with full-time or part-time work (1999: 7). Paid work in term time has increased in recent years generally amongst undergraduates in England, partly reflecting changes in HE funding (Moreau and Leathwood, 2006: 23), and this imperative is likely to increase given the most recent hike in course fees, trebling the current annual cost to up to £9,000. It is often fear of leaving university with heavy debts that results in students taking on paid employment (Yorke, 2004, 116), and mature students with dependants frequently discuss the financial necessity for part-time, and even full-time employment while studying. Aside from the increased number of students working, those students who are in paid employment now work significantly more hours than their counterparts did in the late 1990s. Students from lower socioeconomic groups are most likely to be in paid work and also work the most number of hours in term time. However, there is little difference in overall earnings between students of different socioeconomic groups because of lower hourly rates earned by the poorest students (Moreau and Leathwood, 2006: 24). It has been suggested that working-class women students in particular are 'doing it all, undertaking education and employment in order to exist, if only just' (Taylor, 2007: 41).

Low-income lone parents struggling to continue HE study alongside paid work are indicated to face strained family relationships, exhaustion, stress and guilt (Polakow *et al.*, 2004; Scott *et al.*, 2003: 26). Research shows that employer support is vital for success in managing paid work with HE studies, and that there are inequalities in the receiving of such support (Brennan *et al.*, 1999). Unsurprisingly, there is evidence that academic achievements are adversely affected by part-time employment (2004: 117; Scott *et al.*, 2003: 27; Naidoo and Callender, 2000: 243), causing students to miss lectures and tutorials, and submit assessments late. Providing an alternative perspective on how HE Institutions may perceive contemporary students' multiple priorities, it has been asserted that 'an emerging concern for HE Institutions is the low priority which students attribute to their studies. Increasingly, students now expect their university to fit around their lives rather than vice versa.' (Byrne and Flood, 2005: 114).

This research indicated lone-mother HE students to be working a wide range of hours from two hours a week up to an intensive full-time week plus overtime. They were also employed in a wide range of employment sectors, with many in well-established professional careers, some completing their degrees as part of these. Lone mothers undertaking postgraduate study often described finding part-time work as university researchers or sessional tutors whilst completing their studies. Perhaps unsurprisingly, those in full-time employment emerged most likely to conceptualise managing their various time commitments in terms of 'balancing' or 'juggling', with approximately two-thirds doing so, compared to half of those in part-time work or unemployed. While two-thirds of those working part time or unemployed described issues fitting their studies and parenting together, this was true for only just over half of full-time employees, indicating that adding paid work to the equation decreases the significance of the perceived burden of the task of managing children and study together. Lone mothers in part-time employment more frequently reported problems and obstacles to successful HE participation than both those in full-time employment and the unemployed. Wider discussion around these problems indicates that while unemployed lone-parent students undoubtedly suffer particular financial hardship, they may also benefit in terms of increased time to devote to their studies. At the other end of the spectrum, those in full-time employment are more likely to have reliable childcare mechanisms in place. It is frequently those in the squeezed middle, balancing part-time work with full-time or part-time study, who appear to particularly acutely experience the stress of managing a cobbled together pastiche of informal and often unreliable childcare provision.

Lone-mother HE students in employment frequently describe the challenge of managing work, and how it impinges on their ability to meet the needs of children and study:

> *I am shattered lately; I only commenced full-time work in March and now I am back at uni I feel that with my son . . . and work, I cannot manage it all. I am contemplating leaving work. I mentioned going part time before and they said no way. But unless they agree to a four day week, I shall leave.* (Beth, age 33, one child aged 8, Year 2 PhD Archaeology)

Structural occupational demands, including opportunities for flexibility and part-time work, are identified as pivotal in determining how women live their working lives in terms of their domestic relationships and gender identities (Woodfield, 2007: 62). Increasing occupational demands co-exist alongside a parallel gendered expansion in what is expected of parents at home, meaning that individuals may be finding it difficult to juggle the demands of work and family life, not only because they increasingly participate in both simultaneously, but because of the increasing demands of both spheres. It is argued for instance that (particularly middle-class) parents are expected more and more to take responsibility, not only for their children's physical care and sustenance, but also for every aspect of their emotional and intellectual development, with for example, ferrying children around after-school activities cutting into both work and home time for parents (Jacobs and Gerson, 2004).

Prioritising competing roles and responsibilities

In the hierarchy of competing commitments, the demands of paid employment often come first by necessity, because of employers' inflexibility and work being essential in terms of providing financially for the family. University course requirements, with their assignment deadlines, often come next, with lone mothers' own and children's well-being lagging behind:

> *The most difficult part is really doing the assignments. I have to fit them in around the work day (I work full time) and the children. It's quite hard to fit it all in or get a good long stretch to sit down and do an assignment. By the time I've had a full day at work and done the tea, etc. I could just flop in a chair and relax. But I feel guilty if there's studying to be done.* (Kiera, two children, PG certificate Managing Health and Social Care)

Discussion indicates the extent to which, as one of the three major inter-related areas of issues for lone-parent students, (lack of) time necessitates careful planning, but nevertheless frequently results in some needs and responsibilities being compromised through inability to fit everything in. While some manage to balance study and domestic responsibilities, for others it can become a debilitating drain on emotional and physical energy (Wisker, 1996: 7). Circumstances can deteriorate to the extent that lone parents resort to taking time off study and paid work to concentrate on their own and their family's health and well-being, regardless of the consequences:

> *I am off work sick (sick of work) and I really feel as though I am*
> *suffering from exhaustion. I just want to sleep all of the time and*
> *so have not got a lot of studying done. I may not get paid for these*
> *days off, but feel that I need to seriously de-stress and try to make a*
> *decision regarding this next course.* (Beth, age 33, one child aged
> 8, Year 2 PhD Archaeology)

For the majority of lone mothers in this research, time overstretched between competing demands often made it difficult to manage effectively. Lone-parent students frequently describe how the burden of clashing responsibilities leaves them feeling that every task is inevitably rushed, with several explaining feeling that because of not being able to give one hundred per cent of their attention to any one thing, they never do quite a good enough job at anything, be it university assignments, housework or parenting:

> *Nothing ever done well enough, rushing, I'm just taking one day at*
> *a time: I got through this one — let's hope I get time to make enough*
> *progress tomorrow to get the 'credit earning' jobs done! Don't like it*
> *that way, because I don't feel that I'm learning as much as I should*
> *be — nor am I happy with the quality, because it's all so rushed.*
> (Gillian, age 48, two children aged 13 and 15, Year 3 BA
> Primary Education and Teaching)

There is often a collapsing of different tasks and roles into each other in lone-parent students' lives, and with the insufficient time formally allocated to study previously discussed, individuals often try to incorporate snatches of study time in amongst family and domestic responsibilities, with varying success: 'I've tried studying whilst waiting for the taties to boil, but there's just not enough time to get "into" something before you have to pull your mind away again' (Gillian). The open-ended stretching of lone-parent students' time that contributes toward such unmanageable loads for some, results to a large extent from the shared characteristics of both family and university in being greedy institutions, each grappling to demand primary allegiance of their members. The 'poverty of time' (Reay, 2003: 301) experienced by lone-parent students emanates from the task-defined nature of responsibilities to both family and academia, juxtaposed with the time-defined nature of paid work. The shared task-defined demands of study and family render them potentially more challenging for lone mothers to juggle compared to family and paid work (Edwards, 1993: 64).

The volume of lone parents clearly conceptualising their time in terms of 'juggling' or 'balancing', despite there being no question explicitly focusing on this, as well as the even greater proportion describing scenarios interpreted to constitute juggling, reveal such managing of dual or multiple roles frequently to be fraught with tension (also see Jarvis, 2003: 3; Murphy and Roopchand, 2003: 255). Three quarters of lone mothers in this research described managing the various responsibilities in their lives in ways constituting juggling, without necessarily explicitly defining it as such, while nearly half directly mentioned 'balancing' or 'juggling'. Lone mothers' reflections in this area are largely couched in negative terms of having insufficient time to balance or juggle all of life's demands, and hence feeling that they are 'failing' at the balancing act, frequently left feeling:

> . . . *frustrated and very stressed having to juggle between home and work.* (Helena, age 31, one child aged 2, Year 3 PhD Medicine)

Parents with preschool children are significantly less likely to discuss their lives in these terms compared to those with older children, perhaps once again linking to contrasting childcare cover for these age groups. Perhaps surprisingly, those with only one child are also significantly more likely to describe their lives in terms of juggling compared to those with two or more children. For some lone-parent students whose one child is still young, this heightened sense of juggling can be seen as representing the stress of adjusting to the changing circumstances of becoming a parent for the first time. For part-time students, with their decreased academic workload, managing the combination of responsibilities is the salient issue, rather than this being dominated by intense study loads as for many of their full-time counterparts:

> *I'm feeling fairly apprehensive as I have to work 30 hours per week and have two children, aged 9 and 10, and so it is not the difficulty of the subject that worries me the most, but my ability to keep on top*

of everything. (Sophie, two children aged 9 and 10, Year 1 PG Human Resource Management)

Mature learners are acknowledged to organise their role identities in complex hierarchical fashions (Merrill, 1999: 177–178). Juggling inadequate resources between competing demands, lone-mother HE students' trajectories show them to be acutely aware of the need to prioritise. Nearly two-thirds identified their priorities despite there being no specific question focusing on this. Despite overwhelming commitment to participating successfully in Higher Education in the face of considerable obstacles, their position as sole carers necessitates that family responsibilities must ultimately override study commitments:

> *A little voice in my head still feels that nothing is as emotionally, mentally, or physically engaging or tiring as bringing up a little person.* (Beatrice, age 31, one child aged 8, Year 3 BA Primary Education)

Research on mature women students has found that while some do attempt to prioritise their studies, the majority reflect the assumption that responsibility for others, particularly children, must take priority, leading them to organise study around family life rather than vice versa (Pascall and Cox, 1993: 143). Academic commitments must therefore frequently be unavoidably relegated to low on a long list of competing priorities. Beyond care for dependent children, this duty of care is located in the broader context of individuals' fulfilment of care responsibilities toward adult children, ageing parents, and wider networks of family and friends:

> *My mum is in hospital after suffering a series of strokes, so at the moment I am balancing hospital visits on a daily basis, looking after my dad, keeping other relatives informed, working evenings, running a home, assisting my 18-year-old [son] with his life and what was the other thing? Oh yes! I'm doing a full-time MA!!* (Kate, two children aged 18 and 24, MA)

Amongst immovable obligations and parameters, including paid employment, the school day, ill children, lectures, and various appointments, personal study is often the time demand that can be most easily shifted out of the way, when necessary, which means that it frequently is. The following extreme example exemplifies how personal priorities inevitably push study out of the way:

> *A week ago my daughter was told she probably has lymphoma. She is 24, in her first year at [university], and to all intents and purposes otherwise healthy. My mother being ill was awful, but nothing compared to what I feel now. The impact on work has been to bring it to a halt, albeit temporarily. It has ceased to be a priority.* (Kate)

This inevitable feature of study time to be sidelined in times of stress provides a distinct perspective on the identified need for universities to make their study requirements more flexible in recognition of the needs of widening participation students. This represents a site of tension given that the very flexibility of study, compared to family and paid employment commitments, often ensures that it is readily relegated at the first sign of clashing responsibilities. Lone mothers understandably see their overriding priority to be family, and in particular children, although the necessities of financial demands and university requirements frequently challenge this. Half describe their children as being their priority over study, paid work, or other commitments, despite indicating that sometimes the water can become muddied in terms of what to prioritise. Nevertheless, when children or parents suffer acute illness it becomes clear that family is the first concern.

Christie *et al.* divide day students' juggling strategies into three categories: those who feel they are missing out on the full pleasures of study; pragmatists who recognise that study cannot take priority over other life responsibilities; and finally those who distance themselves from the ideal of the normative student, seeking to maintain separate worlds of home and university (2005: 14). While these strands of experience are all observable amongst lone mothers, the longitudinal dimension of this research reveals the picture as more complex than representing clearly distinguishable types of learners. Rather, the different situations encountered by HE learners juggling family responsibilities as they travel through the course of their studies, necessitate constant renegotiation of priorities, causing individuals to slide between categories of attitudes to learning.

Often having no choice but to put children first, and fit studies around their needs and childcare arrangements, clearly represents a deviation from the expected hierarchy of prioritisation held by many academic staff, and thus automatically places lone parents in a difficult position. Lone parents iterate the importance that studies must fit around children's needs, although universities are criticised for having other ideas as to what should take priority. When paid work or study demand to be treated as the priority, this is often resented:

> *Oh, I nearly forgot to mention a recent incident that should fall well within the spec of your study . . . I'd been working extra hard to have completed the writing up by Feb . . . because my son (who will be 18 months) will be starting nursery. As it will be a big change for him (from childminder to full-time nursery), I really wanted to be 'there for him' and more relaxed. It will also be a change in my working patterns as the nursery shuts early, so it is important that I can lighten my workload. However, following a meeting with my supervisors, it appeared that I will have to include extra data in the thesis, which means that there is no way I will be finished on time for Feb. I was very upset about this, particularly as it should have cropped up months ago, but my supervisors being busy people, the meeting kept being put off and they did not read the chapters I was sending them. Although I understand that to them I am just another PhD student, and that they are very busy professionals, I found that the gap between their lack of commitment and the impact this has on my personal life was glaring.* (Helena, age 31, one child aged 2, Year 3 PhD Medicine)

Similar resentment can ensue at the perceived attitude amongst others that paid work should be prioritised over being there for children:

> *I get the impression that many people feel I should be working full time as soon as possible. Why? – So that I may pay my dues to society? Well I'm not so sure. I don't want my son to be a latchkey kid.* (Shelby, age 32, one child aged 6, PGCE FE)

Prioritising children's needs is rendered particularly important because of lone mothers' status as sole carers, and because children have experienced relationship breakdown and frequently the loss of their other parent. Sometimes a mismatch is perceived between children's interests and parents' needs:

> *I started my degree at a very bad time – not long after my ex and I split up. It was quite a bad relationship and my children and I were left with quite a few issues that I really should have sorted out first. Doing this degree was the right thing for me to do for me, but I'm not left with any time to try and sort my children out, so I don't think that it was the right thing to do for them.* (Leanne, three children aged up to 9, Social Sciences)

This expresses a theme also indicated by others – that as well as meeting family's needs, it is important to reassert oneself as an important individual with needs:

> *I think partly this is down to the fact that I had my son when I was 19 and so for almost all my adult life have had to put someone else first and think about what was best for him and I've always come second (if at all), so now doing the course I am doing something I want to do and something for me, so then if I don't end up with a better career to others it may seem like I've wasted my time.* (Eva, age 28, one child aged 9, Year 2 Primary Education with History)

While beyond the academic remit of HE participation, it may also partially represent an expression of what has been termed 'care of the self' (Reay, 2003: 301) in terms of personal development, as indicated by the above quote, the competing juggling demands on lone-parent students simultaneously often pose a threat to such care of the self. Lone mothers' time is largely constructed around others' demands, and as the last item on a long list of priorities, it is a poverty of time for this care of the self that is invariably the net result of the competing commitments of lone motherhood, HE study and paid work, alongside additional individualised life demands. With insufficient time for everything, prioritising means cutting corners. As paid work and care responsibilities invariably have to take precedence, followed closely by academic work, it is usually sleep, health and housework that fall by the wayside for lone-parent students in times of stress. Relaxation, reading for pleasure, watching television, exercise, leisure, friends, socialising, and giving time to children, including reading with them, all feature prominently in lone-mother HE students' accounts of what gets skimped on when necessity demands it:

Time is divided mostly into work, domestic responsibilities, study, sleep and then leisure. Work being 35 hours with five a week travelling. Leisure gets sidelined as I cannot NOT sleep or clean or look after my son and heir! (Josephine, one child, BSc Social Policy)

Many lone mothers describe prioritising precious time by deciding to remain single until children are older, in order to devote attention to studies, rather than adding a relationship to the melting pot of demands. Some conjecture that having a partner would simply add more to the juggling act, perceiving prioritising family and studies to leave no time for a relationship:

Unfortunately choices sometimes have to be made and for me my children and my study come first and second with men trailing a poor third I'm afraid. (Kate, two children aged 18 and 24, MA)

Some of those who do have non-cohabiting partners, explain the terms of their relationship as including an understanding that children and university take priority. Balancing a relationship with studies and children can also be made easier by having a partner living some distance away, minimising disruption of routines.

For mature returners to learning, HE participation can include a desire to engage with the university experience in its perceived entirety, including the social element alongside academic attainment (Edwards, 1993: 59). These hopes of becoming involved in social experiences and other activities apart from learning are scuppered for lone parents by time constraints limiting their ability to join in the social life of university (also Gallagher *et al.*, 1993: 33). This difference in experience can leave mature learners with outside responsibilities feeling irritated at younger students (also Woodfield, 2002), and as one lone parent explained:

I think the thing that affects me most is that people don't realise that your time is severely restricted and that you just don't have a social life. In fact uni is my social life & I'm too busy trying to complete all the assignments to go for 'coffee' every day. (Heather, age 30, one baby, Year 2 BA Urban Studies and Planning)

While time constraints hamper ability to engage with university social life, lone mothers frequently feel that their heavy loads and stretched resources limit the time they have to devote to existing friendships. Less attention is paid to friends than prior to studies, leaving previously enjoyed social lives severely curtailed or almost non-existent, as Edwards has also found with regard to mature women students generally (1993). Lone mothers frequently express the feeling of not being able to justify devoting valuable time to socialising: 'I feel that if I'm not up to date with uni work then I can't justify going out and having a good time' (Heather).

While it is wholly understandable for 'non-essential' time commitments to be cut back in order to streamline finite resources to prioritise children and studies, it is also significant that many of the activities trimmed back represent facets of what we contemporarily understand as 'me time'. Far from being a self-indulgent luxury, making time for care of the self may be vital to safeguarding well-being and protecting the individual from stress overload. For example, while socialising may not seem a priority, lone mothers in this research identified it as representing an important part of rebuilding self-confidence after relationship breakdown.

Representing this frequent relegation of care for their own well-being, more than half of lone mothers in this research described feeling tired or lacking sleep, with many left feeling exhausted by the amounts crammed into their days:

> *The routine this year is gruelling and I do wonder when I'm*
> *supposed to have the time to study. My day is from 5.45 a.m till*
> *10 p.m. every day with the responsibilities and the study – nothing*
> *else. I do find that this is exhausting and inhibits focused thought.*
> (Denise, age 35, one child aged 9, Year 2 BA English)

Adjusting to a new regime of study, paid work and domestic responsibilities can be particularly exhausting. Unsurprisingly, lone parents with preschool children are significantly more likely than those with older children to discuss their tiredness, with three-quarters doing so. Tiredness is frequently mentioned alongside the meeting (or not) of housework responsibilities. While for some the responsibilities they are juggling leave too little time for sleep, others say that when the hectic day finally ends and they have time to think, their worries keep them awake. There are significant recurring themes in terms of the worries that lone-mother HE students describe; this being particularly the case for those studying full time. Managing university workload is not just a practical problem, but also a source of intense worry. For some of those studying full time, university commitments expand to eclipse other priorities to an unsustainable extent:

> *I began to get horrific flashbacks to last April, when I had been working through the night on a regular basis to meet assignment deadlines, trying to keep the housework up, as well as relate meaningfully with my daughters. It all fell apart because, in order to do all that, I had drained myself completely and there was nothing left and it was VERY scary.* (Gillian, age 48, two children aged 13 and 15, Year 3 BA Primary Education and Teaching)

The following reflection indicates further the stress lone mothers can experience from the ways they feel forced to prioritise time:

> *So my experience of HE as a lone parent: shit, tough, tiring, lonely, poor, physically/mentally exhausting, not having your own children as your top priority in the attention stakes, never ending, guilt, tears, debt, shall I not continue?!* (Kristin, age 26, one child aged 8, PGCE History)

The following section explores in detail the internalising of responsibility and guilt that is so salient in lone-mother HE students' trajectories of trying to successfully balance their heavy loads of competing time demands.

Individualising responsibility, role conflict and guilt

> *Guilty mums – why are women plagued with guilt? It could be over friends, family, partners, jobs and diets, but mostly it's about children. For mums, the fear of not measuring up to some unrealistic ideal is overwhelming.* (Closer magazine, September 2006: 3)

Narratives of 'maternal guilt' are as ubiquitous in popular and academic texts (see Sutherland, 2010; Waldman, 2009) as those around the challenges inherent in managing, caring and providing for children. This is perhaps inevitable given the near-impossibility of managing all of the prescribed tasks to ideal standards. Lone mothers' reflections often reveal them to assume juggling and guilt to be the sole domain of women:

> *Whereas most women have a guilt complex if they feel that they are taking up too much time for themselves with study, etc. I don't believe men have even heard of the word!!* (Jennifer, age 44, four children aged 10–20, Year 3 BA Education Studies and History)

Similarly, existing research has suggested that mature women students experience increased role conflict compared to male returners to education because studentship is more compatible with men's expected work roles than women's expected family roles (Gilbert and Holahan, 1982: 637). These assumptions pivot on the condition of men being exempt from primary domestic responsibilities within the family. In fact, the assumed gender dimension can be seen to stem fundamentally from women's structural position as forming the vast majority of primary care givers. When men take sole or primary responsibility for children's daily care and long-term upbringing, they too can be plagued by guilt about their competence and success. In addition, as expectations alter generally in terms of the extent of fathers' participation in the qualitative experience of family life alongside providing as breadwinners, narratives describing guilt at not spending more time with children amongst fathers become generally more observable (see Rentoul, 2007). In terms of reported guilt around giving insufficient time to children and perceiving oneself as a 'bad' parent, lone mothers' experiences can be seen as representing the extreme end of the intensive parenting expectations of all parents in late modernity (see Jacobs and Gerson, 2004: 80–82). The deeply culturally ingrained idea of 'maternal guilt' is perhaps accurately, if less tersely, conceptualised along the lines of 'key carer guilt'.

The dominant sources of guilt are documented to be the juxtaposed and irreconcilable pulls of feeling a failure at not studying hard enough, and yet also taking too much time away from family to study (also Cappleman-Morgan, 2005: 8; Wisker, 1996: 7). Guilt about not studying hard enough can remain even when students are away from their studies, for example while on maternity leave (Edwards, 1993: 68). Lone mothers reveal their guilt to be largely centred on the perception amongst both themselves and their families of studying taking time for the *self* away from what are perceived as the legitimate claims of the family, and a mother's perceived responsibility for domestic and childcare tasks (also Jarvis, 2003: 271; Reay, 2003: 309). When asked to reflect on specific sources of guilt, lone mothers frequently focus on the guilt they experience over taking time to study while children are at home after school, at weekends and during the school holidays. Devoting time to study is often seen as making the family suffer, despite the primary goal of HE participation often being to improve the family's standard of living and prospects (also Merrill, 1999: 156). In this research, as elsewhere, individuals describe experiencing guilt for feeling angry about their burdens, seeing it as irrational and unfair to afflict their families with their tiredness and inability to cope (Edwards, 1993: 71).

It is significant that individuals with their feet in the two worlds of parenting and HE learning are unlikely to be able to comply fully with the demands and ideals of full-time self-sacrificing motherhood and domesticity, yet frequently nevertheless idealise family life in these terms. Similarly unable to meet the full demands of studentship in terms of total immersion in the university academic and social experience, they therefore measure their own experience as deficient. Organised routines can be fragile, having to be dropped whenever unexpected family crises arise. Mature learners frequently drop and rearrange everything, allowing everyone else's lives but their own to proceed as usual. In doing so, they can pre-empt any sense that their studies are negatively affecting family responsibilities (Edwards, 1993).

Both domestic and study responsibilities appear to have large amounts of flexibility and autonomy, but in concert can be restrictive. This contributes to falsely individualising time-management problems, with never-ending individual combinations of commitments presented as the product of individual choice. This has been documented elsewhere to leave many seeing the answer to their problems managing home and university as being more organised (Edwards, 1993). While extensively indicating the guilt they experience at pursuing their own studies, in contrast to existing findings, lone-mother HE students in this research did not attribute their problems to their own time management, instead perceiving themselves to be operating at the maximum of their capacitates. Of all those describing what would improve their experiences as lone parents and students, only one named changes that she was responsible for making herself, and these were presented alongside external factors:

> *Overall I think had I been more organized and planned things better, it would have been a lot easier – had I had more support in terms of help with [my son] within the home – studying would not have been so tough – more support in general, from friends, tutors, financially would have meant I could have divided my time up more effectively and allowed me to have more of a social life, without feeling that I was neglecting my son or my studies.* (Lucille, age 25, one child aged 4, PG Diploma Law)

While not faulting their current coping strategies, others conjecture that their HE participation would have been easier had they made different retrospective choices, including going to university straight from school or completing their studies before having children, allowing them more freedom to devote their full attention to studying. Mature students' internalisation of assumptions of such a 'proper' time to go to university validates the legitimacy of the 'Bachelor Boy' model of the ideal student, with its inherent assumption that full participation in the experience of being a university student requires an individual not to have conflicting responsibilities.

Such individualised rationalisation of the challenges inherent in juggling HE participation with lone parenthood obscure the responsibility of institutions to ensure family-friendly responsibilities, even if individual learners also acknowledge that they are doing the best they can under their current circumstances. Existing research iterates that mature students, juggling challenging loads of study and family responsibilities, largely view themselves as having to deal with the consequences of their decision to be in Higher Education, and internalise blame for their inability to manage, or direct anger and frustration at their families, deflecting 'down' negative feelings into relative power vacuums – the 'kick the cat' syndrome. Thus the cultural forces and institutional values working against individuals' ability to manage both sets of task remain hidden from view. The underlying assumption is that individuals can avoid conflict and 'bad' feelings if only they are 'good enough', with them attempting to meet standards ostensibly set by themselves, but which are actually socially constructed (Edwards, 1993).

It has been asked whether we should focus on the difficulties Higher Education presents for women or those that women present for Higher Education, and further suggested that it is the HE sector's inability to deal with difference that is problematic for mature students, with problems experienced by mature HE learners combining family and education therefore conceptualised with the onus on individuals dealing with them themselves (Edwards, 1993). These observations are equally true of the experience of lone mothers. Jackson suggests that HE Institutions blaming mature students with children for 'inadequate time-management skills' as being the problem, at the expense of acknowledging the highly skilled multi-tasking many undertake and problems in the structural organisation of Higher Education (2004: 52). Rather, educationalists have often focused on how family responsibilities 'interfere' with ability to study (Edwards, 1993: 9). For example, Gilbert and Holahan investigated the 'effectiveness' of mature students' coping mechanisms at balancing the often conflicting demands of the student and parent roles (1982: 63). Such causal assumptions obscure the responsibility of HE Institutions in informing the realistic potential for such students to succeed in their juggling, and the often failure of HE Institutions to develop sufficiently family-friendly practices and policies. As one lone parent observed of her HE Institution:

> *Staff openly admit that they take no account of people with children when planning this timetable.* (Michelle, age 35, one child aged 12, MSc History of Science)

The common thread of the inequity of expectations on individuals to simultaneously fulfil irreconcilable demands of care, breadwinning and investing in the future through HE participation is obscured to the individuals balancing the demands, and also in the eyes of others. It is suggested that HE Institutions do acknowledge the juggling that students with primary care responsibilities must carry out, but that most traditional full-time HE Institutions see families as baggage that must be dealt with by individuals rather than by the institution. Achievement for this group is thus perceived to constitute 'success' at balancing university alongside family sufficiently successfully to complete one's HE studies. Hence, it has been observed that HE courses targeting mature returners often include advice on 'balancing home and studies' (Edwards, 1993: 33).

Far from being an accidental by-product of the process, guilt can be seen as serving a central function as one of the ways in which greedy institutions such as the family and the university ensure voluntary compliance and commitment from their members (Edwards, 1993: 70). In terms of the family applying guilt to ensure compliance, the suggestion that guilt deliberately generated by partners of mature HE learners to ensure continued allegiance to serving the family amounts to 'domestic sabotage' (Leonard, 1994: 171), resonates strongly with lone-parent mothers' reflections on the demands on time made by non-cohabiting partners.

Lone mothers juggling university participation with family responsibilities largely perceive their various commitments as quite legitimately laying claim to their time, and see themselves as having responsibility for managing them. Nevertheless, their narratives indicate that awareness and anger that the demands being juggled can be unreasonable and incompatible does sometimes surface. Lone mothers indicate acute awareness of socially defined standards and discomfort about not meeting them, hence they strive to meet such expectations as soon as possible. The way in which time-strapped lone-parent students prioritise devoting weekend time to children, housework and partners can be seen as the giving of time as an end in itself, a symbol of care-giving rather than just a means to an end in terms of completing necessary tasks. Giving attention and emotional support to family members, and showing interest in their lives, whatever the demands on one's own time, is regarded as a crucial part of being a parent or partner. Lone-parent students often express the desire to compensate their children for their absence by devoting their full attention to them when they are at home (see Edwards, 1993).

Solutions and strategies

Having reviewed the key competing demands on time encountered by lone-mother HE students, the following section discusses in greater detail the strategies they employ in managing to juggle these roles and responsibilities. For some, the load is inevitably ultimately too great to manage, resulting in course withdrawal, with the ensuing associated financial loss to both individuals who may have accumulated debt without benefiting from obtaining a qualification, and subsequent loss of future earnings, and also to HE Institutions, who lose revenue per capita for every student who fails to complete their course. When lone mothers are unsuccessful in improving their future prospects through HE participation there is a further loss to their families, and to society generally, in terms of wasted human capital. In this research, over the course of an academic year, only two lone mothers formally withdrew from the study because they had withdrawn from their HE courses. Of these, one exited the course because of financial problems, and the other because of the competing time demands:

> *I had quite a few problems again towards the end of last semester and didn't finish my degree. In fact I had a bit of a breakdown, finally admitted to my parents how hard I found it coping alone, working, studying and bringing up my daughters.* (Gillian, age 48, two children aged 13 and 15, Year 3 BA Primary Education)

Two more lone mothers described having previously exited HE courses without completing, before subsequently returning to university for a second attempt. These individuals both indicated the primacy of being unable to manage time demands in informing their previous course withdrawal, as Ruth explained:

> *I was constantly running from one place to the other, looking at my watch, and fearing I wouldn't get there on time. I had one child at school to be dropped off and collected and the other (three years old) at a nursery. When my timetable was received for the first semester in Year 2 I had (I think) three late lectures (i.e. late afternoon) and two early ones (i.e. 9am). As I have very little help from family with childcare this was simply not do-able and I was exhausted as it was from the stress of the first year. I saw my tutor who was very sympathetic. We thought that if I could miss the late lectures and maybe one of the early ones and receive notes from the lecturers then I could get through. He needed to consult with the head of dept. She gave a very definite no. I could have continued anyway and missed the lectures and then done battle with the uni to stay, but I didn't have the fight in me. Bear in mind that at the same time as this I was 'fighting' (and still am) with the education authorities re my son (now 11) and his education.* (Ruth, age 47, two children aged 9 and 12, Year 3 BA Social Policy and Criminology)

Existing research on part-time students exiting HE courses early found employment demands to influence withdrawal for just over half, while around a quarter cited the needs of dependants, the weight of the workload and financial difficulty (Yorke, 2004: 118). For mature women students with children, key reasons for leaving Higher Education prematurely have been indicated to be reversed, these being family responsibilities (73 per cent), work responsibilities (53 per cent), financial difficulties (36 per cent), and lack of family support (35 per cent) (Scott *et al.*, 1996: 240), alongside overload, stress, health problems, and lack of suitable childcare (1996: 236). Despite the documented significance of responsibilities defining lone parents' lives in informing non-completion, the learning trajectories of those who had previously exited courses early but subsequently returned for a second attempt at HE completion, represent the resilience of many lone-parent learners, offering optimism that some of those who fail to complete their initial attempt may return in the context of more favourable personal circumstances and learning conditions.

While some do not ultimately continue their learning journeys in the immediate term, those who do manage to do so identify a range of coping mechanisms assisting them in dealing with the considerable constraints they face. The effects of an acute poverty of time are central to the strategies that lone-mother HE students are forced to employ in negotiating daily life, determining decisions around study and employment. When lone mothers exit paid work or HE courses, or limit time spent on HE assignments to a level below what is expected by academic staff, they risk compromising their academic confidence, success, future employment and financial prospects. In making apparently irrational decisions, they may appear not to be acting as rational decision-makers. Their narratives, however, suggest that in many such cases, whether consciously or unconsciously, they continuously make sophisticated cost–benefit evaluations of the projected trade-off between the resources of time and money that they are able to safeguard for their families. Such evaluation takes place within the context of both resources being stretched, often to their limits, and frequently in direct competition with one another. The negotiation of juggling finances is discussed in detail in the following chapter.

The positive response to the heavy demands shouldered by lone-mother HE students is rigid time-planning, and routines allowing no margin for error are frequently relayed. One lone mother explained how she got her baby daughter up at 4 a.m. one morning every week in order to travel to university. The following extended example illustrates the extent to which every minute is often accounted for:

It can be difficult but I make sure that I get up about 6.40 a.m., have a shower, make packed lunches and breakfasts, get the washing done and hung up to dry, wash and wipe the pots, help [my son] to get ready, dry my hair and have a quick tidy round before I take the children to school so that when I come back, for about 9.00am, I can get down to studying right away as the important bits are out of the way and the kitchen is clean and tidy. Other things like hoovering and ironing I tend to do in the evening, usually when [my son] is out at his sports. I am out every evening as on Monday I teach at [. . .] college, Tuesdays I take [my son] to his sports (so if I need any bits from ASDA I don't waste time and go in the day, I call in the evening while I am out taking [my son]), Wednesdays [my daughter] does Karate, Thursday [my son] does football after school and again at 6 p.m. to 7.30 p.m., Friday [my daughter] does Karate again. I do my big shop for the week at 7.30 a.m. every Saturday when ASDA is not busy, so that again I'm not wasting the time that I have on my own during the week by going shopping. (Jennifer, age 44, four children aged 10–20, Year 3 BA Education Studies and History)

Through careful micro-management of everyday responsibilities, cutting corners where possible to create little pockets of extra time, the precarious load of responsibilities remains (just about) balanced, and the emergency pressure valves of non-submission of assignments, or exiting work or study are for the most part kept at bay. A major area of such corner-cutting is housework, with sentiments along the lines of the following frequently expressed:

I do find that when there is an assessment due in that the housework goes out the window and the kids often moan at having no clean clothes!! (Charlie, age 29, two children aged 8 and 9, Year 2 BA Developmental Psychology)

During term time when I have deadlines to adhere to, I do tend to lapse on housework and listening to the children read; the other daily tasks are normally still done. (Francesca, age 34, four children aged 6–18, Year 1 BA History)

Time-strapped lone-parent students achieve this minimising of domestic responsibilities by redefining what is essential (also Edwards, 1993: 76), but such skimping on domestic tasks inevitably results in the reappearance of the monster of guilt.

There is, however, an alternative aspect to common-sense assumptions that being sole carer must increase the burden of family responsibility and thus decrease opportunity for other commitments. Commentaries on mature women students often do not differentiate between students with and without partners, and existing studies consistently document having a partner to be a drain on time in terms of domestic labour and emotional demands (Wisker, 1996: 67). Being, to a greater extent, masters of their own time, lone mothers frequently perceive themselves as benefiting from being able to make autonomous decisions to skimp on housework, cooking or attention to children in order to devote time to academic study, without encountering a partner's disapproval:

> *When you're single there are no distractions and no excuses (once the children are asleep), to get on and do whatever makes you happy.* (Stacey, one child, BA Sociology with Business and Management)

While some lone parents conjecture that it would be easier to manage being a parent and university student in terms of financial and practical support if they had a new partner, this contrasts with the reflections of many of those who had juggled study with a relationship, also resonating with commentaries on mature women students (Jackson, 2004: 68; Wisker, 1996; Leonard, 1994; Edwards, 1993). Relayed experiences of the frequently experienced incompatibility of new relationships with lone parents' learning offer evidence of the potentially facilitating relationship between single status and increased freedom to study.

Often, primarily partners rather than children are perceived as preventing individuals' engagement with studies, with some partnered students consequently describing envying lone parents the freedom to do what they want when they want (Edwards, 1993). The independence of thought and future symbolised by learning is seen as a threat by some partners (Jackson, 2004: 68; Leonard, 1994: 164), with animosity sometimes extending to physical violence (Wisker, 1996: 5; Edwards, 1993: 172–173). One lone mother in this research felt one benefit of single parenthood was that it was easier to manage her responsibilities now that her ex-partner's aggression was no longer a factor in the household. Unsupportive attitudes from marital partners are seen as posing one of the greatest threats to mature students' educational participation (Leonard, 1994: 176). From this perspective, lone parenthood may be seen as an advantage, and lone parenthood has indeed been theorised by commentators as often representing independence (Klett-Davies, 2007; May, 2004: 394). Existing research has similarly indicated that some lone mothers perceive their single status as facilitating increased attention to career development more broadly (Crompton and Harris, 1999: 140). As with other themes in this research, feedback from lone mothers frequently conceptualised such domestic autonomy, or lack of it, in heteronormative terms as representing the deeply entrenched gendered expectations implicit in heterosexual relationship roles:

> *The amount of guilt and stress that they [partnered student mothers]*
> *felt about 'neglecting' the family, especially their children, I believe,*
> *was down to pressure from their husbands. I don't feel guilty, I*
> *have enjoyed what I have done and I have got on with my work*
> *during the day, knowing that when they come home from school*
> *and at weekends that I can't expect to get the peace that I need to*
> *concentrate; therefore I use my time when they are at school to get*
> *as much done as possible and weekends and evenings are for taking*
> *them to their activities and getting household chores done.* (Jennifer,
> age 44, four children aged 10–20, Year 3 BA Education
> Studies and History)

It is also significant, however, that experiences of relationships as compromising rather than facilitating freedom to study amongst participants in this research were unified in the relationship having ended, because it was perceived as terminally unsatisfactory in some way. It is frequently the case therefore that former partners had been seen as being particularly unsupportive. It is very possible that more supportive partners would conversely be facilitative of studies, and this is indeed indicated by some of the more positive accounts of new relationships that had not presently developed into cohabitation.

That lone mothers are able to make room for study by downsizing definitions of their domestic role and responsibilities in a way that partnered parents often cannot, suggests that other forces in the relations of the nuclear family may be more significant to hindering individuals' creative potential than the physical responsibilities of child rearing. This problematises suggestions that mature students experience difficulty relinquishing parenting obligations in order to make room for study (Gilbert and Holahan, 1982: 637). Although individuals do find it difficult to justify cutting down on domestic responsibilities to partners, and experience guilt when they do so, the different experiences of partnered and unpartnered parents demonstrate the willingness and ability to shift non-essential domestic responsibilities in order to prioritise study. While there is inevitably a solid core of child-rearing responsibility that lone parents cannot shift away from themselves, there is, nevertheless, room for manoeuvre when immediate learning requirements necessitate temporary reordering of priorities.

In addition to redefining domestic responsibilities as non-essential, when this is not possible, another strategy employed by lone mothers in facilitating the time to engage with studies, is to build and rely upon vital informal networks of mutual support. It is suggested that such 'survival networks and pooling of resources' are essential to managing lives constructed of planning, organising and creating orderly patterns from a patchwork of demands of others' individual needs and wants (Edwards, 1993: 73).

Benefits of juggling time

Despite the extensive challenges in managing intensively stretched time experienced by lone-parent HE students, their narratives further illustrate the potentially positive effects of combining parenthood with study. For some this stems from substituting participation in paid work for university, and finding the latter easier to manage with their role as sole parent:

> *I have more time than ever being a student because I've always worked in the past. I do things as and when they arise and find that I have plenty of time. To begin with I found the lack of routine a bit daunting because my life was pretty regimented before I became a student.* (Eva, age 28, one child aged 9, Year 2 Primary Education with History)

The very tightness of time inherent in juggling lone parenthood and university can itself be experienced as beneficial in further ways:

I think being a single parent can affect your health positively. You have little time for self-pity and are subsequently, rarely ill. You don't have time! (Shelby, age 32, one child aged 6, PGCE FE)

Relatedly, it is rare for lone parents to describe experiencing boredom in their circumstances as HE students, except occasionally during gaps between academic courses.

Having discovered to their own cost the high price of participating in Higher Education as lone-parent learners in terms of the stretching of demands on time, individuals often describe envisaging, or at least hoping that, completion of their HE studies, and hence the cessation of this priority on their time, will free up resources for other temporarily sidelined activities. This imagined future is ambivalent for some, however, given that it entails the loss of identities developed as HE learners. This is encapsulated in the following reflection on the benefits of university participation and the imagined life after completion:

> *. . . learning something new. Opening my eyes to things I've never known or experienced or heard about before. Above all, what will I do with myself? How will I fill those evenings and weekends – perhaps . . . a social life?* (Samantha, age 47, one child aged 11, BA Humanities)

The following chapter explores in detail the financial impact for lone mothers of participating in the rich but challenging world of university beyond the home and family.

CHAPTER FIVE

Juggling finances

Alongside the juggling of time discussed in the previous chapter, lone-parent students must also juggle their finances. Despite lone parents qualifying for more student support than any other group (Callender and Kemp, 2000: 16), and thus having the highest average student income, they remain the poorest of all students in England and Wales (NUS, 2009: 4). Their vulnerability is frequently compounded by a lack of family financial support and savings (Callender and Kemp, 2000: 12). Three-quarters of lone parents studying full time have reported financial difficulties, compared to fewer than half of all students (Callender and Kemp, 2000: 13). For lone parents in this research, financial problems, unsurprisingly, emerged as a central concern, dominating individuals' everyday lives, and constituting a major source of stress. Almost all of the lone mothers in this research discussed their financial concerns, contributing rich insight into qualitative understanding of the constraints faced by this group of HE students. Many discussed financial concerns frequently and extensively, with several raising money issues separately up to eight or ten times over the course of the year. The nature and extent of strain on limited financial resources varies considerably for lone-parent students, depending on a number of factors explored throughout this chapter. These include housing status, participation in paid employment, and availability of reliable financial support from non-resident parents and extended family.

Additional biographical factors also impact on the prevalence of financial worries. For example, older lone parents frequently perceive their age to be a problem, specifically within the context of a labour market that places an increasing premium on youth. They indicate worrying about the employment implications of their advancing age in terms of securing satisfactory graduate work in what they perceive as an ageist job market. Commentators have similarly identified both the perceived and actual detrimental impact of age upon graduate employment (Woodley and Wilson, 2002: 335; Brennan *et al.*, 1999: 11; Merrill, 1999: 190). The influence of social class in informing the occupational level and income bracket at which mature students re-enter the employment market after graduation has also been documented (Taylor, 2007: 47; Burns and Scott, 1993: 40). Lone mothers' narratives indicate that they frequently perceive age as impacting more significantly than social class upon the opportunities available to them.

Children feature repeatedly in lone-parent students' discussion of finances, particularly in relation to income and housing problems. Meeting children's material needs is the priority, even at the expense of substantially 'going without' oneself. In addition to the time-related guilt discussed in Chapter 4, lone mothers describe the guilt ensuing from trying to juggle overstretched finances, including taking the cost of course fees from the family budget, and children having to go without material possessions while their parent completes HE study. Lone mothers' discussion of the effects of their HE participation upon their children resonate with observations as to the perceived contradictory effects of the HE participation of parents as a whole upon their children's lives, sometimes causing suffering in the short term, despite the goal of ultimately improving the family's long-term standard of living and prospects (Edwards, 1993: 66), as well as altering family values. The evidence that, although lone mothers are often motivated to engage with Higher Education in order to improve finances, it can temporarily exacerbate material hardship, attests to the extent to which they must be willing to defer gratification. That lone parents must frequently defer gratification and undergo interim financial hardship, insecurity and debt in order to succeed in Higher Education undermines widening participation amongst disadvantaged groups, given identification that for students from working-class backgrounds, Higher Education frequently represents too 'risky' a business (Reay, 2003: 303, 312).

The number and ages of lone-mother HE students' children does not impact significantly on their discussion of financial issues. Neither is there significant variation in how frequently full-time and part-time students discuss financial issues, although full-time students' discussion of finances is generally more positive. This is notable given that their studies leave less time for paid employment, and may indicate their increased entitlement to student finances. Following sections address in detail lone-mother HE students' access to income through paid work and entitlement to financial assistance.

Lone-parent HE students, employment and welfare entitlement: incentives and disincentives for paid work

Government assistance is central to financially supporting lone-parent students, although individuals report widespread problems in terms of income assessment. HE participation is frequently explicitly located by lone mothers within the context of their entitlement to means-tested benefits. The intricacies of this entitlement fundamentally inform employment decisions, childcare access, and life balance between study and paid work.

NUS research has found that 94 per cent of student parent respondents receive some form of benefits (2009: 49). The sources of welfare provision on which lone-parent students rely include Child Benefit as currently payable to all parents regardless of income, and means-tested benefits and associated entitlements, including Income Support with free school meals and milk tokens, Working Families Tax Credit (WFTC) and childcare subsidy, Child Tax Credit, Council Tax Benefit, Housing Benefit, assistance with mortgage interest and NHS charges, Incapacity Benefit, Disability Living Allowance (DLA) and Carer's Allowance. The introduction of the Universal Credit replacing all of these benefits as part of the 2011 Welfare Reform Bill is likely to impact strongly on lone parents. By 2014–15, cuts to welfare entitlement are estimated to be equivalent to an 18.5 per cent drop in income for lone parents (Taylor-Gooby and Stoker, 2011: 8). Financial implications of contemporary policy developments for lone-parent students are discussed in more detail in Chapter 8.

Lone mothers in the research indicated widely divergent incomes. Of those in full-time employment, six disclosed their annual incomes, which ranged from £18,000 to £41,000 per annum, while part-time employees divulged incomes between £9,000 and £18,000. Significantly, those who were unemployed and studying who discussed their incomes, reported total annual household incomes of between £10,000 and £14,000, thus not substantially below many of those who worked part time, or even full time. This can be seen as representing the significance of the benefit trap for lone parents, potentially negating the value of paid work after factoring in additional expenses and stresses, and decreased eligibility for means-tested benefits. Given the acknowledged tendency of the UK Tax Credit system frequently to provide a disincentive for lone parents' participation in employment beyond a certain level of income and hours (Jenkins and Symons, 2001: 121), the instrumental rewards of juggling study and employment alongside family responsibilities may be intangible for lone parents, given that the cost of increased stress brings little financial recompense in the immediate term.

One in eight lone-mother HE students researched explicitly discussed the hours they worked in terms of ensuring benefit entitlement, with two key employment patterns represented. The first of these patterns was limiting hours of employment to earn under £20 per week in order to maintain Income Support eligibility, given deduction from benefits of any earnings beyond this threshold. A more frequent pattern was represented by those working a minimum of 16 hours per week in order to qualify for Working Families Tax Credit, including help with childcare costs. Some lone-parent students reported working 16 hours per week in order to qualify for childcare support, which was then used to pay childcare costs which covered study time. This example of one of the ways in which lone-parent students frequently resort to 'robbing Peter to pay Paul' in terms of managing their stretched resources of both time and money, exemplifies the complex juggling act often necessitated in order to negotiate HE study and employment alongside lone motherhood.

The majority of those in receipt of Working Families Tax Credit reported being in part-time employment, although others were working full time. Lone mothers' reflections on the support they receive from the Tax Credits system indicate that not only is it effective in pursuing the Government's goal of moving lone parents into employment, but also that many lone parents themselves perceive this process and its efficacy:

> As I've already mentioned, I think the Tax Credits system is a
> Godsend and I know I'm not alone in thinking this. It encourages
> you to work and does not make unrealistic expectations of father's
> contributions. This year my total income will be about £18,000.
> (Samantha, age 47, one child aged 11, BA Humanities)

However, this is not the experience of all: others indicate that in the context of their own personal circumstances and eligibility, the benefit system failed to provide an incentive for employment:

> *[Out of work] I have also received free school meals for my son,*
> *a £1,000 parent allowance and £85 towards childcare costs. In*
> *addition, I am exempt from Council Tax and get free dentist care – it*
> *all adds up and I'm beginning to think I may be worse off working!*
> *I also qualify for Child Tax Credit of £42.40 a week and the usual*
> *Child Benefit.* (Shelby, age 32, one child aged 6, PGCE FE)

This financial disincentive for employment is further reinforced by expert advice received by some lone parents:

> *I have been told by the CAB [Citizens Advice Bureau] that I would*
> *be financially better off not working and I know in terms of studying*
> *I would have finished the course by now if not working BUT as I*
> *said to the CAB adviser 'I am a nurse, I can't give up my job'. If*
> *I did give up work then when I wished to return I would have to*
> *relearn or start again near the bottom, depending on the position I*
> *managed to obtain.* (Marcia, age 43, one child aged 7, Year 3
> BSc Clinical Nursing)

Child maintenance represents a further key financial issue for lone mothers, with many expressing misgivings that maintenance from non-resident parents is not received more generously and regularly, if at all (see Jenkins and Symons 2001: 130). It is one of the primary elements of income for lone parents and an important financial resource, and as such can impact upon willingness to participate in paid work. Child maintenance has been disproportionately disregarded from Working Families Tax Credit compared to Income Support, meaning that lone parents who receive maintenance have had a substantially increased incentive to work rather than remain unemployed, and whether maintenance is received reliably has hence been identified as an important factor in lone parents' willingness to engage with employment (Jenkins and Symons, 2001). Lone mothers describe dissatisfaction at the apparently inconsistent way in which child maintenance is included as income in the assessment of various benefit and student funding entitlements. The introduction of the 2011 Welfare Reform Bill is likely to impact considerably on lone parents' receipt of maintenance, given changes including the introduction of payment by the resident parent for using the services of the Child Maintenance Enforcement Commission (CMEC) replacing the Child Support Agency (CSA).

A third of lone parents not in employment suffer from disability or long-term illness, and a similar proportion have a child with a disability (Gingerbread, 2012), representing considerably increased prevalence compared to the general population. Research has found lone parents indicate health problems to pose a substantial barrier to getting or keeping paid work (Ford, 1996: xv). Such considerations around exacerbating family disruption, uncertainty about income, and health problems are likely to be similarly relevant to lone parents' decisions over whether to engage with educational opportunities as well as paid work. The following quote illustrates the intersection of long-term limiting illness and financial assistance entitlement in the life of one lone mother juggling HE participation with caring for her children and managing her health problems:

> I am classed as a disabled lone parent, because I suffer from Fibromyalgia (severe muscle pain, constant, very nasty!) and Chronic Fatigue (feel generally ill to the point of passing out if I over-exert myself!) so that makes me too mouldy to work full time (over 15 hours & 59 mins per week). I do not get Tax Credits unless I do 17 hrs a week. I cannot physically cope with 17 hours of running around at work every week. Therefore, I can only do around 10 hours. This means that everything over £20 I earn is knocked off my Income Support, pound for pound. (Nicky, age 37, two children aged 8 and 10, BA Health and Social Care)

Alongside material hardship, lone parents describe the additional stresses of difficulties sourcing accurate information about financial entitlements, and Benefit Agency incompetence, resonating with existing findings (Working Links, 2007; Connor and Dewson, 2001: 73; Horne and Hardie, 2001: 66). It is significant given the sample size that despite not being asked about it, five out of 77 lone parents described the hardship caused by overpayment errors by various benefits agencies, often over many months, and the consequent demands for repayment from lone parents' already limited resources. The range of elements which lone mothers report as comprising their household incomes illustrates the way in which income is frequently cobbled together from a number of often unreliable sources, including grants, loans, Housing Benefit, Child Benefit, child maintenance, Tax Credits, earnings from employment, and sometimes also applications to charitable trusts (see Jenkins and Symons, 2001: 126). It is significant that up until the 1980s, family benefit entitlement was assessed according to net income after taking into account childcare and travel to work costs (Land, 2007). This acknowledgement of the significance of these costs to those who are on low incomes and responsible for children has been lost under the current system. Lone parents' narratives of managing their families' finances on benefit entitlement in this research draw out similarities with the US context, in which, it is suggested, there is often a necessity for poor lone parents to patch together various sources of income in order to survive because of the inadequacy of official Government provision alone to support a family (DeParle, 2004: 92).

Existing qualitative research has suggested that lone parents can find it difficult to predict their likely income from such a patchwork of means-tested benefits (Ford, 1996: xv) and that uncertainty about income is a disincentive to making the transition to work for the group (Jenkins and Symons, 2001: 126). Such uncertainty may similarly provide a disincentive for educational engagement. Indeed, lone mothers frequently indicate perceiving the Government to be at fault for failing to adequately support lone parents into learning opportunities:

> *Throughout the whole process of going back to college and then on to uni, the government have made it the most difficult. My personal experience with members of staff and tutors has always been positive, whereas the government hasn't been of any encouragement at all. There seems to be a real lack of funding for colleges and universities to help and support lone parents. If the uni was supported better by government funding and policies, perhaps they would be in a better position to support us.* (Stacey, one child, BA Sociology with Business and Management)

Lone-mother HE students' experiences highlight that confusion and misinformation from Benefits Agency staff can leave individuals resorting to researching and proving entitlement themselves:

> *P.S. I finally sorted out my housing benefit. I looked up the actual*

official regulations and quoted them all. So they finally had to agree I was right. But the best bit is that all the senior benefits staff had a meeting about it and they also realised that they been assessing all the other student parents' income wrong for the past two years. So now they are going to re-assess them all and will pay all those people the extra money they should have been getting since then. I think they hate me at the council now! (Andrea, age 23, one child aged 1, Year 2 BA Development Studies)

In taking matters into their own hands, lone-parent students can be seen as capitalising on research skills, literacy levels and advice and Internet resources that not all lone parents may have access to. This is one example demonstrating the extent to which the success of lone parents in negotiating structural constraints, including the obstacle course of HE funding, can depend very much upon determination and resources not shared equally by all.

The experiences of financial problems described by lone-mother HE students further illustrate the identified 'contradictions between the operation of the Benefits Agency and the student support system' (Christie *et al.*, 2005: 12; also Scott *et al.*, 2003; Horne and Hardie, 2002). In addition, lone mothers describe their experiences of changing financial support entitlement. Alongside negative experiences of such changes reducing entitlement, one lone mother described the alleviation of a particularly stressful, impoverished period.

Luckily the law changed right at that point and entitled lone-parent students to claim Income Support through the summer hols. (Ruth, age 47, two children aged 9 and 12, Year 3 BA Social Policy and Criminology)

Attesting to the fluctuating nature of relevant policy, this entitlement has since once again been reversed, as discussed in Chapter 8, with ensuing repercussions for lone-parent students. The contradictions and unpredictability of financial support entitlement frequently experienced by lone-parent students means that although, as one explained, they can be experienced as a 'Godsend' enabling otherwise financially impossible HE participation, reliance on such support also places individuals in a position of vulnerability. The same lone parent who heralded the Tax Credit system as a Godsend also reflected that:

> *I long to be tax credit free, so no government can suddenly take them away.* (Samantha, age 47, one child aged 11, BA Humanities)

The following expresses the frustration felt by many at the way in which sources of income and entitlement are assessed for lone parents attempting to improve their families' circumstances through HE participation:

> *When you are entering education as a means to put your life back together in your mid 30s as a single mother it appears that we are penalized at every point in the process. A portion of our benefits are taken away and replaced by loans. We are unable to benefit from maintenance payment from the fathers because it is taken pound for pound from the benefits portion. Our potential higher income is then eaten into via the loan repayment which then in turn inhibits us from achieving the financial ground necessary to be able to keep pace with our contemporaries. Does this picture stimulate anyone to put in the effort of this process? It seems like the government is trying to make us self sustaining before time in a vain attempt to cut cost, but this is very short sighted and puts too much pressure on for many of us.* (Denise, age 35, one child aged 9, Year 2 BA English)

The following section addresses the impact of the assessment of student loan as income in determining lone-parent student's entitlement to means-tested benefits.

Lone parents and student financing

In addition to means-tested benefits, lone-parent students rely on student financial support, including student grants, incorporating course fee waivers, and paid directly through individual HE Institutions including the Open University, or through LEAs. This can include additional elements including Parent's Learning Allowance, Dependant's Allowance and a childcare subsidy grant covering up to 85 per cent of costs, as well as help with the cost of purchasing a home computer. Access to these elements of support is dependent upon individual circumstances and when lone parents commenced their HE studies. Other sources of student financial support include PGCE Bursaries, NHS Bursaries for nursing training, including travel expenses, and competitive postgraduate

Research Council funding from bodies including the Economic and Social Research Council (ESRC). In all of these areas, lone parents, as other student groups, are likely to be affected by decreased access to funding opportunities resulting from 2010–2011 spending cuts.

Like benefit entitlement, negotiating student funding can often entail a similarly complex balancing act, as the following illustrates:

> *I have applied for a student loan, which the max I can get is £500 per year being a part-time student. Once you have received this, you can then apply for a grant from your college which is £250. If you have applied for this you can apply for a fee waiver for your fees, which I have received both years. However, because I received the grant of £250, the college have to work out how much I have paid towards childcare, travel costs, and books, and if this is lower than the £250 grant then I will not receive anything from the Access to Learning/Hardship fund. I am still awaiting a decision on this.*
> (Maria, two children, Year 2 BA History and Archaeology)

Immersion in the student financing system necessitates that lone mothers simultaneously straddle two worlds of financial assistance entitlement. This exacerbates the complexity of the patchwork of entitlements they must negotiate, and is frequently a great source of stress. The transition between student financing in the form of grants and loans during term time, and means–tested support including Income Support and Housing Benefit, available to some lone parents during university vacations but not term time, is a key area of financial problems.

By far the dominant themes; however; in terms of lone-mother HE learners' discussion of student financing, are the problem of loss of entitlement to benefits for which they were previously eligible, leaving them dependent on student loans which must be repaid (also Horne and Hardie, 2002: 61; Connor and Dewson, 2001: 77). A Gingerbread factsheet, *Money For Higher Education Students: A Guide for Lone Parents*, explains the situation facing the group:

> *You cannot choose to claim benefits instead of applying for all the Student Support your family is entitled to and you must tell the office(s) that pay your benefits and/or tax credits that you are now a student and about changes to your income. (2006: 3)*

This is seen as a great source of injustice for lone mothers, who indicate their resentment at perceiving the benefits system as effectively forcing them to accumulate debt. Many indicate their refusal to see their student loan as the 'income' it is considered as for assessment of benefit entitlement:

> *My annual income is around £10,000. This is about the most
> I have ever received in a year. But of course it's not really income
> because I have to pay £4,000 a year back.*

> *I thought it would be better once I had gone to uni because I would
> have the student loan on top of my benefits. I then discovered that
> my Income Support would stop, because they count the student loan
> as an income! I was furious, even the incompetent government must
> be able to know the difference between a loan and an income? I am
> now living on borrowed money. I started uni debt free, I will leave
> in £12,000 of debt.* (Stacey, one child, BA Sociology with
> Business and Management)

This assessment of student loan as income can have far-reaching financial consequences for lone-parent students' entitlement to support:

> *I have had to contact a solicitor over my ex stalking my eldest daughter
> (age 12). Last year when this happened, I qualified for legal aid as
> student loan was classed as a loan. This year, it is classed as income,
> meaning I am not eligible for legal aid and have to pay my solicitor up
> to £2,500 to drag this back into court again.* (Marie-Therese, two
> children aged 9 and 12, Year 2 BA Social Sciences and Politics)

The perceived injustice of lone-parent students' income assessment is compounded by discrepancies between various benefits as to whether student loans are included as income. For those receiving Child Tax Credit, the system can be seen as advantageous:

> *My annual income in total is around £23,500 give or take a bit.
> Luckily none of my incomes are affected by any of the other incomes,
> i.e., child tax credit don't take maintenance or student loans as
> income.* (Charlie, age 29, two children aged 8 and 9, Year 2 BA
> Developmental Psychology)

This contrasts with the situation of those further down the financial ladder in receipt of Income Support, for whom a student loan is included as income. It represents a facet of the drive to 'make work pay' by ensuring financial incentive for participation in paid employment, but not automatically validating the steps towards this represented by HE participation.

Inclusion of a student loan as income is seen as discriminating against lone parents because, compared to other students, parental responsibilities can exclude paid employment as an alternative to accumulating debt (Horne and Hardie, 2001: 65; Callender, 2000: 12). Despite this inequity and the additional barriers lone parents confront in participating in paid employment, in this research nearly half of participants reported being in employment whilst studying for their degree, while only nine said that they were unemployed (that the two groups do not cumulatively reflect the whole sample indicates that not all disclosed their employment status). Full-time, part-time and unemployed employment statuses were all reported by those with both school-age and preschool children.

The longitudinal perspective enabled insight from those who graduated during the research, revealing the negative impacts of the shift from grants to loans for lone parents to extend beyond immediate financial hardship, into graduate life. Lone-parent graduates describe how student loan debts leave them unable to afford to take up graduate jobs after their degrees. The continuing absence of a higher student loan repayment threshold for lone parents, despite their sole responsibility for financing childcare, and higher accommodation and living costs from a single income, places them at a substantial disadvantage. Lone-parent graduates consequently describe feeling bitter that having completed a degree, believing it to be the key to a better future, they can find themselves once again reliant on benefits. Lone parents indicate being prepared to work for the deferred gratification of the promise of increased economic self-sufficiency, self-esteem, job satisfaction and prospects, although there may be no immediate financial recompense. They can seldom afford, however, to work at a job that leaves them worse off financially than being unemployed, even if this is in pursuit of the deferred gratification of career goals for the future.

Becoming an HE student can often exacerbate existing financial hardship for lone parents, as studying demands that they decrease employment hours and/or incur additional childcare costs in order to study. However, while lone parents extensively document the financial challenges of negotiating HE study, a concurrent strand of evidence indicates some to experience their various learner-related entitlements to loans, overdrafts, credit cards, Tax Credits, childcare assistance, Council Tax exemption, and teaching and nursing training funding incentives, as actually leaving them financially better off than before. This is particularly the case for those previously reliant on Income Support. Significantly, all of those claiming that studentship had improved their finances were studying full time. Lone parents are, however, acutely aware that the majority of additional funds at their disposal as students are in fact debts:

> *Being a student has given me access to more money, even though most of it is now a debt, but this has meant that we have been far better off than when on benefits.* (Bex, age 34, one child aged 12, MA Primary Education with QTS)

Availability of larger sums of money in the form of student grants and loans, overdrafts and credit cards, can make it easier to afford one-off expenses like accommodation rental deposits, compared to managing on Income Support. It can also be used to finance otherwise unaffordable luxuries for the family:

> *My first year's bursary paid for us all to go to Disneyland Paris for three days. A pure luxury, but one that was desperately needed at the time to keep us all sane, and give us something to look forward to short term, and a glimpse into the future of what my salary may end up providing long term. My circumstances would have been dire long term if I hadn't taken the journey to university and beyond. I would have become very frustrated with the way we lived, and would have had no long-term hopes for any better improvement for us all.* (Naomi, age 44, three children aged 13–16, Year 2 MSc Interprofessional Health and Social Care)

Increased access to lump sums of money, albeit frequently from debt, can impact in much more profound ways for lone parents and their children than Disney holidays. While some relay frustration that sources of student financing are not included as income for mortgage assessment purposes, as discussed later in this chapter, this appears a grey area in which lender policy is not uniform, as indicated by others:

The upside of the PGCE grant and loan being treated as income is that HSBC agreed to give me a mortgage! I cried in their office and managed a Halle Berry speech thanking them for believing in me and taking a long-term view! Through my local Housing Association I have been able to part purchase a three bedroom house, in the same town as my family (this is extremely rare as it is a relatively affluent area with only private housing). I am thrilled as my son will remain in the same catchment area for schools and we are now 'safe' and in permanent residence. (Shelby, age 32, one child aged 6, PGCE FE)

Hardship assistance: Access to Learning Funds

In times of severe and unexpected financial hardship lone-parent students frequently resort to accessing grants or loans through their university's Access to Learning Fund (ALF). These awards are widely discussed by lone-parent students, and are both invaluable, and problematic in terms of eligibility. The NUS have found 42 per cent of lone parent students to have applied to their university's Access to Learning Fund (2009: 47), while almost a third of those in this research claimed to have done so. Almost all indicated having been successful in their applications, and the awards received were all reported to have been grants rather than the loans also available. It is significant that of 25 lone parents who had received Access to Learning grants in this research, eleven described how negative their experiences of the application process had been, despite not being asked about this. Nearly all of these criticised the depth of written evidence and verbal justification of personal circumstances required to secure an award. In comparison, only one research participant reported having found the ALF application procedure easy and satisfactory.

Those who complained about the application process described feeling uncomfortable having to ask for 'handouts', and one 45-year-old FE tutor relayed her embarrassment that her ALF application involved being expected to discuss her personal finances at a public desk, although her subsequent request for a private room had been met. Others described experiencing the ALF application procedure as 'demoralising', 'degrading', 'humiliating', 'like begging', and resenting the burden of having to 'prove' their need. The following is just one example of many similar reflections:

Having filled in a form with all my ingoings and outgoings I also had to justify everything on my bank statement for the past three months. Many of these things were also questioned, for example, whether I need a car. I was told instead I should use the bus to take my daughter to nursery even though this would involve a 20 minute walk to get to the bus stop, over an hour on the bus and then another 15 minute walk to the nursery before I did it all in reverse to get back to uni! They have since asked for lots more information including receipts for everything I brought for my house back in October! There are also the usual government restrictions on how much I need to spend and how much support I should receive from a partner or my parents! (Andrea, age 23, one child aged 1, BA Development Studies)

Lone parent applicants' experiences of the intrusiveness of the formal application procedure are frequently exacerbated by perceived attitudes of university staff:

The woman responsible quizzed me about any money that had gone into my account and it was most unpleasant. When I told her that I wasn't sure about one payment she said 'Well I think if someone paid money into my account I would know where it came from.' (Bex, age 34, one child aged 12, MA Primary Education with QTS)

The recurrence of descriptions of the ALF application process as (sometimes prohibitively) intrusive amongst lone parents contributes to understanding why many universities report large amounts of unclaimed ALF allocated funds. The most worrying insight explained how a lone-parent ALF applicant had been required to provide a letter from her ex-husband in order to qualify for an ALF payment:

I apply for a financial award and apart from digging around for info, most embarrassingly had to ask for a letter from my ex husband to confirm his maintenance. I objected to that but felt unless I did conform would not have received help I really needed. (Josephine, one child, BSc Social Policy)

While the need for stringency is understandable, requiring lone parents to make contact with former partners in order to qualify for vital emergency financial assistance is troubling, particularly in light of higher recorded incidences of domestic violence amongst the group compared to the general population. Gingerbread highlight that 'in many cases, lone parents are fleeing violent relationships', and lone mothers are over three times more likely to have experienced domestic violence than women in other types of household (2007d: 7). Lone mothers in this research relayed experiences of violence from ex-partners and even abduction of children by non-resident parents.

Beyond their university's ALF, lone mothers describe their experiences of accessing further emergency financial support from non-governmental sources, including assistance with fees, childcare and travel expenses from sources such as the European Social Fund (ESF) and Gingerbread, providing assistance with, for example, subsidised holidays and day trips. Applying to various sources of financial aid can represent an additional time-consuming diversion from other commitments:

> . . . the main problems being with funding. I am still waiting for confirmation of childcare grant, which means at present I have no money to pay for my son's nursery fees!!! I have to apply to about 34 different agencies for money and it's really time-consuming, especially when I have a son to care for and a degree to be doing!!
> (Charlotte, one child aged 4, Year 2 Psychology)

Debt

Previous sections of this chapter have discussed lone-mother HE students simultaneously inhabiting the worlds of student and lone-parent financial support, and the stresses caused by moving between the two systems. While increased access to larger bulk-sums of money through student financing has been indicated as advantageous in some cases in affording larger costs like accommodation rental deposits and kitchen appliances, this nuance of student funding compared to means-tested benefits also poses particular problems. Lone mothers' narratives indicate the difficulties faced in making the transition from weekly paid benefits to managing to budget with a still-low income, but paid in bulk termly. Managing a tight budget with large infrequent payments, particularly when individuals are used to low weekly payments, can frequently foster developing debt problems. Lone mothers describe the impact of personal debt in their families' lives, documenting the stress and anxiety it causes alongside other financial strains.

Lone parents as a whole are one of the social groups most susceptible to debt problems (Fawcett Society, 2007: 1), and research indicates that up to 61 per cent of lone-parent students have taken on debts, excluding student loans (NUS, 2009: 44). In this research, debt emerged as a significant issue for lone-mother HE students, supplementing findings that this group is the poorest of all students in England and Wales, and the group with the largest debts. Lone parents have been indicated to be the student group with the highest loan uptake, at 94 per cent, compared to three-quarters of other students, and have also been shown to have double average levels of student debt (Callender, 2002: 89–90). Students who accumulate the largest debts in Higher Education are those who were poor before going to university and those who come from the most disadvantaged backgrounds, with the most financially vulnerable groups being lone parents and students from social classes IV and V (Callender, 2002: 89–90). This is despite evidence suggesting that individuals from working-class backgrounds are more debt-averse than their middle-class counterparts (Taylor, 2007: 40; Naidoo and Callender, 2000: 241). Evidence highlights that lone parents often enter Higher Education already in debt because of inconsistent governmental assistance with NVQ Level 3 (university entry level) courses (Millar and Rowlingson, 2001: 239).

Forty-eight lone parents in the research discussed debts and loans, rendering this a key theme. Perceptions of what constitutes debt vary; when asked about debts, some lone parents cite mortgages on their homes, whereas many more of those with a mortgage do not include this when cataloguing their debts. One lone mother relayed on three occasions how steadfast she is about not accruing loans of any kind, before recounting subsequently her reliance on Department for Social Security (DSS) budgeting loans to replace household appliances, paying the balance back directly from her Social Security benefits.

HE participation by working-class students is seen to be compromised by a perceived increased debt-aversion (Taylor, 2007: 40). Accumulating large amounts of debt in pursuit of a Higher Education can inevitably feel like a greater risk in the context of lower wages, decreased capital in the form of savings and home ownership, and family histories dominated by non-professional employment. Such documented working-class debt-aversion does not, however, tally with evidence from lone mothers in this research. Discussion of debts and loans is one of the few areas in which social class emerged as significant. While equal numbers of self-identified working-class and middle-class lone mothers report having taken out student loans, working-class lone parents are significantly more likely to describe using other types of credit, loans and debts. This may indicate that greater financial need, through less lucrative employment, and extended family and ex-partners less able to provide financial assistance, can force some working-class lone-parent students to overcome any debt-aversion in pursuit of their educational goals. Reay's work, in which HE participation is suggested to be perceived too risky a business for many mature working-class students, focuses on Access students (2003). It may be that working-class lone-parent students who do persist to Higher Education, represent the least aversive to taking on risk, including debt.

Although the student loan is the obvious and most frequently cited source of lone-parent student debt, the group also incur debts from a range of other sources. The next most frequently cited source of debt is credit cards, with one in eight lone-parent students discussing using credit cards to provide either daily necessities or 'extras' like holidays. This points to the continuing relevance of existing evidence of the group's reliance on commercial debt (Callender and Kemp, 2000: 23). Lone mothers' narratives in this research contribute further insight to understanding the group's experiences of debt through documenting the substantial problem of stress and hardship caused by being left liable for debts incurred by current or ex-partners, often without the lone parent's knowledge. This is suggested to be a significant problem facing lone parents generally (BBC, 2007). In addition, lone parents acknowledge their reliance on bank overdrafts, bank loans, and Career Development Loans.

Just under half of the lone-parent students researched reported having taken out student loans. Perhaps expectedly, distance learners are significantly less likely to report taking out student loans. Lone parents aged under 40 are significantly more likely to report having taken out student loans than those over 40, with just under two-thirds of those under 40 and just under half over 40 having done so. While the age limit cap on student loan eligibility at age 54 was removed as discriminatory in 2005, subsequent to pressure from organisations including NIACE, and it is additionally anticipated that the bulk of students with dependent children would fall under this age anyway, older students may be either more financially secure in terms of resources like home ownership, or additionally reluctant to take on debt given their age. Lone-parent students in part-time employment emerged as more likely to have taken out student loans, with nearly two-thirds doing so, compared to nearly half of unemployed students and just over one-third of full-time employees. This may represent the increased financial stability of those in full-time employment, and the fact that many lone-parent students not in employment may be studying part time, and hence not eligible for student loans prior to 2011. Lone-parent students with two or more children are significantly more likely to report having taken out student loans compared to those with only one child, pointing to the increased financial demands of additional children. Those with preschool and school-age children are equally likely to have student loans, with approximately half of each group doing so.

In terms of student loans, some lone-parent students don't see their situation as differing significantly to that of students without dependants, while others see lone parents as being particularly vulnerable in negotiating the student loan system. One lone parent explained how the Student Loans Company had unexpectedly refused to provide a loan for her course fees because she already had outstanding debts to them from a previous period of study — although she was paying the earlier debt back as agreed:

> *I think the Student Loan Co. (SLC) should be looked into during your research and how they affect single parents (and others) from studying without financial burdens. It turns out that they are not going to pay my final year tuition fees as I owe loan monies from 1996 (I have been repaying these since 2002). Whilst you have an outstanding loan they will not pay any new 'loans or fees'. I renegotiated my monthly repayments, I offered £30 and they said £100 — I agreed because I thought they would pay my fees . . . as soon as the Direct Debit is set up they write to confirm that the fees will not be paid and to inform me a CCJ was entered against me in 2001 (the first I heard of this). Previously, the university waived my fees but this year a new scheme was introduced where you get funding via your LEA who refer everyone to the SLC.*

> *I now have to find my final year fees. The form I filled in for the LEA stated I would get 80% of my fees paid + £250 for books*

(non-repayable loan) as I was a single parent on a low income.
(Lucy, age 34, one child aged 5, Final year LLB)

Those who disclosed the extent of their student loan borrowing reported anticipated final debts of between £12,000 and £17,000. The changes to HE funding announced in the Browne report (2010) will determine that many future HE students, including lone parents, will leave university with very much greater debts, and the ensuing implications of financial hardship as they embark on their graduate working lives. This will be a key area for future researchers to document.

Informal financial support

Alongside formal income from paid work, benefit entitlement, student financing, and emergency grants and loans, lone mothers describe their reliance on informal financial support from networks of family, friends and current or former partners. Many describe the frustrations caused by non-resident parents who do not contribute adequately to children's financial support, and the difference made to their lives when significant others, usually their own parents, but also partners and friends, offer financial assistance. The small handful of favourable financial developments documented by lone mothers in this research invariably centred on receiving help from loved ones – usually parents with the will and means to help – but also unexpected windfalls from extended family, including inheritances, as well as satisfactory maintenance settlements from non-residential parents and financial help from current partners. Alongside the childcare, practical and emotional support often provided informally through these networks of care, financial assistance can be vital to sustaining lone-parent students' households, and, in doing so, facilitating their ongoing participation in Higher Education. Such assistance can take the form of regular contributions or emergency hand-outs in times of financial crisis, and includes help meeting the cost of flat rental deposits, household bills, clothing, food, gifts, holidays, day trips and school activities. For many this informal financial support acts as a much-needed buffer between lone parents and the formal provision that is often experienced as inadequate to cover needs, as has been documented in the US context by DeParle (2004: 92).

Comparison of lone-parent students' narratives shows that those without such informal support mechanisms to call on are left at a serious disadvantage. Existing research has indicated that financial assistance from grandparents for lone-parent families is relatively limited in the UK compared to some other countries, including, for example, France, where it is more expected (Millar and Rowlingson, 2001: 239). Lone mothers' narratives indicate significant variation in experiences of accessing financial support from networks of family and loved ones, also indicating the range of reasons why such support may not be forthcoming. Such mechanisms may be lacking because of the absence of a support network, financial inability within the network, a family background placing a low value on supporting education, or loved ones' own illness or problems leaving them unable to assist the lone-parent student. Those lone mothers without such resources to draw on are often acutely aware of the disadvantaged position this places them in:

> *I had always thought that being on benefit and undertaking a PhD would be straightforward (in the sense of not having to worry too much about money if you accept your living expenses have to remain low), but I had underestimated the stress I would be under. It's become more clear to me that the majority of single parents who I have come into contact with who successfully move forward with research have other levels of support. For example, they may have parents who support them financially or a reasonable arrangement with their ex.*
> (Beth, age 33, one child aged 8, Year 2 PhD Archaeology)

Effects of financial hardship

Of lone-mother HE students' extensive discussion of financial issues, the overwhelming majority of this focuses on lack of money. This ranges from the most severe scenarios, including financial stress culminating in nervous breakdown, through to more positive accounts of learning to be adept at managing limited funds resourcefully. Financial problems are an equally prevalent aspect of lone-parent student experience regardless of social class identification.

Despite extensive discussion of finances, including the emotional stress and material impact of financial constraint, only half of lone-parent students described experiencing financial lack to the extent that they felt it constituted the genuine hardship and real threat to continued HE participation, as illustrated by the following response:

Money is definitely the biggest threat to me completing my degree and definitely the thing that worries me most. It is often a case of not knowing how on earth you are going to pay for the things that crop up. (Andrea, age 23, one child aged 1, Year 2 BA Development Studies)

Perhaps surprisingly, those in full-time employment are significantly more likely to describe financial hardship, with approximately two-thirds doing so, compared to nearly half of those in part-time employment and one-third of those not in employment. Distance learners are significantly less likely to experience financial problems as centrally informing their daily lives.

Both this research and existing commentaries raise a number of key areas of financial constraint affecting lone parents' engagement with learning opportunities. It is important to address these issues, both individually and in terms of their cumulative effects, in order to facilitate lone parents' engagement with Higher Education on as equal footing as possible with other students. Financial necessity is shown often to inform important educational decisions for lone parents, including opting to study at less prestigious institutions with lower course fees, choosing courses including nursing or teaching because of the additional government subsidies they attract, or unwillingly dropping out of studies altogether due to lack of funds. Such choices in turn impact pivotally on opportunities after HE participation, given evidence that choice of institution and subject influence how valuable a degree is perceived to be by employers (Ramsey, 2008).

Being careful with money, budgeting, 'going without' particular luxuries or necessities, and deferring financial and material gratification in the medium term, are central themes around finances for lone-mother HE students. The detail provided by those who contributed to this research addresses a continuing gap in understanding poverty amongst the group, in terms of awareness of exactly what individuals and their families are forced to go without (Scott *et al.*, 2003: 40). Key areas are identified to include the negative effects of being a lone-parent student upon ability to afford to give gifts, socialise, and pay for children's activities, day trips and holidays. Children feature repeatedly in their parents' discussions of finances, with meeting their needs being paramount. While necessity dictates that children must sometimes go without materially, parents go to substantial lengths to ensure that they themselves go without in order to provide adequately for children. Nevertheless, Scott *et al.*'s conjecture that the basic needs that lone-parent students struggle to meet for their families may include adequate clothing and a proper diet (2003: 40) was confirmed by this research. Alongside describing buying clothes in charity shops because new clothes could not be afforded, more worryingly, lone-parent students describe feeding the family healthily to be a major challenge. Additional documented symptoms of limited finances include having trouble meeting the cost of course fees, travel to university, lunch at college, books, and Internet access (also identified by Scott *et al.*, 2003: 25). Research has found up to 67 per cent of lone parents studying full time in Higher Education to report not buying books they need because of not being able to afford them, compared to 37 per cent of all full time and 30 per cent of all part-time students (Callender and Kemp, 2000: 58). Research has further found 76 per cent of students from classes IV and V, and 77 per cent of lone parents to attribute a negative effect on academic performance to financial difficulties, compared with 53 per cent of students from classes I and II and 57 per cent of students in a couple with children (Horne and Hardie, 2002: 91). Further difficulties affording toys and entertainment for children (also Callender, 2002: 90) render it clear that lone parents' HE engagement frequently involves financial sanctions, not only for themselves, but also for their children (Scott *et al.*, 2003: 7; Callender, 2000: 13). In addition to the negative impact of financial stresses upon academic performance extensively documented by this research, insight illustrates the way in which such pressures are further perceived by lone parents to impact negatively upon the attention they are able to provide for their children.

For more affluent parents, increased spending power to buy quality childcare, housing, food, leisure activities, school trips, holidays, financial investment for the future, and much more for their families, may be seen as just remuneration for being away from them at work. In contrast, for lone parents on low incomes, including many of those studying in Higher Education, the struggle to internally justify absence from children in order to complete their studies may be irreconcilable. Poor lone parents are more likely to have to squeeze domestic tasks into the limited time they do have with their children, being less able to afford to buy in domestic services and labour saving devices. Justifying the costs of this being worth the sacrifices demands great long-sightedness to persist towards the goals of developing financial means, self-esteem, and the ability to provide a positive role model for children. In times of material hardship, study pressure and hence family stress, the coinciding poverty of time and money in the present moment can prove too much for lone parents to justify continued engagement with their studies. However, trajectories in this research of leaving, but later returning to, Higher Education point to determination amongst lone parents to find solutions and ultimately achieve their study ambitions.

Finances are a recurring theme for lone-mother HE students, not only in terms of experienced problems, but also projected concerns for the future, with many experiencing money as the major source of worry in their lives. Money worries focus on childcare, course fees, housing insecurity, debts accrued by ex-partners, and lack of funds for social activities. Descriptions of the unrelenting nature of money worries are commonplace, as explained by Marcia:

> *I feel constantly anxious about money – just keeping on top of bills, not exceeding my overdraft.* (Marcia, age 43, one child aged 7, Year 3 BSc Clinical Nursing)

These financial worries often spill over into other areas of life, preventing lone parents from focusing adequately on studies and children:

> *I think worrying about money has really affected my ability to focus on my studies. Money worries definitely do give me sleepless nights. The worry also affects my ability to enjoy my course and has definitely spilled over into my home life with my son as I am not able to buy him or do things with him that I would like to.* (Lucille, age 25, one child aged 4, PG Diploma Law)

Facing the impossibility of solving their financial problems, some attempt to adopt more pragmatic approaches of choosing not worry about what they do not have, along the lines of the following reflection from Bex:

> *I feel like I haven't got the money so they can hardly come and take it back!* (Bex, age 34, one child aged 12, MA Primary Ed. with QTS)

Housing

Lone-mother HE students attest to the impact of financially informed housing problems, as also identified by Gingerbread (2007d). Insecure housing is a key consequence of financial hardship for lone-parent HE students, as well as a barrier to taking up or continuing study (Hyatt and Parry-Crooke, 1990: 12–13, 33; also Scott *et al.*, 2003: 7). Housing and living arrangements can be a particular source of stress, discussed by nearly three-quarters of lone mothers in this research; one frequent cause is ex-partners having built up mortgage or rent arrears in joint names. While homeowners worry about keeping up mortgage repayments, those living with family or in rented accommodation worry about the prospect of never being able to afford their own home.

Only two lone mothers in the research reported having secured university-provided family accommodation. For one of these, university accommodation had not initially been available and she had been forced to begin her degree living in temporary council accommodation with her baby daughter. Lone-mother HE students describe renting accommodation from private landlords, local authorities, housing associations, and family members and friends. Parents and ex-partners also sometimes act as guarantors for rented or mortgaged properties. Securing rented accommodation as a lone-parent student can be a challenge, as succinctly summarised by Lily:

> *I had dreadful housing/accommodation problems during my first year, but that was due to local estate agents not the university, but being a student and a single mother didn't help – I felt like I was public enemy x2!!!* (Lily, age 31, one child aged 4)

Financial constraints had led to several lone mothers of varying ages living with their children in their own parents' homes while they studied, and these arrangements had varying degrees of success.

Having children often leaves lone parents less geographically mobile compared to other students, indicating that they would not be willing or able to move house in order to attend university, often because of the need to remain near support networks. Those who do relocate indeed often report a detrimental impact on accessing help from family and friends. Lone-mother students with school-age children more often discuss not wanting to uproot their children compared to those with younger preschool children, identifying an onus on not disrupting children's schooling in pursuit of their own HE studies. Perhaps significantly, self-identified working-class lone parents are considerably more likely to say that they would not consider moving away from their present location in order to attend university. This may relate to the increased levels of extended family support also reported by those identifying as working class.

Lone mothers describe how struggling to afford adequate accommodation can compromise their ability to engage with studies:

> I have had to compromise my academic efforts to such an extent in order to keep a roof over my head that I will not achieve the grades I need to go on to a PhD, but the way the course has been structured I don't think I can do anything. (Michelle, age 35, one child aged 12, MSc History of Science)

Alongside the detrimental effect on studies of having to also participate in paid work to afford living costs, other lone mothers describe how being trapped in poor-quality accommodation through financial limitations further impacts on their ability to apply themselves to their studies. The experience of those dependent on social housing too often results in being consigned to rundown areas characterised by deprivation and social problems. Lone-parent students describe living in such conditions as depressing, and unsafe for children, further reporting experiences of victimisation by neighbouring youths. Such stressors can seriously compromise ability to study, as evidenced by the following:

> A lot of us mums on that estate were depressed, in abusive relationships, on the poverty line, etc.

> It was horrific at times, and we all tried to manage the best that we could. As soon as my daughter started school, I went back to education to get my degree and get out of the hell-hole we had been forced into. It was a difficult decision (have you ever tried to study, living on an estate where cars beep and rev their engines non-stop downstairs, music blares round the clock from most flats, dogs bark consistently, children scream for attention, the police thump and kick down your neighbour's doors at least once a month . . . it was very hard to concentrate on reading thick text books and constructing

> *5,000 word assignments, as you can imagine!).* (Beatrice, age 31,
> one child aged 8, Year 3 BA Education – Primary Teaching)

Being unable to afford to buy or rent property close to university contributes to problems around travel and transport. Almost one-fifth of lone mothers in the research discussed travel and transport issues, mainly detailing problems incurred in travelling to attend university. This sometimes involved making round trips of up to 80 miles to attend classes, sometimes involving children having to stay overnight with grandparents. Apart from resulting in unsettled children with disrupted routines, additional obstacles include rush-hour traffic jams, and the costs of petrol, parking and car maintenance or public transport. Foregoing travel problems is often an explicit motivation for choosing distance learning, with some describing making the move to distance learning after finding studying at a traditional university too challenging as a lone parent in terms of travel and childcare.

One lone mother described how her HE participation affected her living arrangements in terms of effectively prolonging her lone parent-hood:

> *My relationship has only developed since being at uni, but it is hard because we are unable to live together due to lack of money which would not be a concern if I was working! So that's kinda annoying!!* (Sophie, two children aged 9 and 10, PG Human Resource Management)

Positive effects of student finances

Alongside the documented negative effects of juggling limited financial resources, contrasting trends in lone mothers' narratives indicate that factors like having to budget, and 'going without', can also be experienced in beneficial ways. In particular, the need for frugality is frequently recast as a positive, encouraging simple living and ensuring that children learn the value of money and do not become spoiled:

> *So, do we go without? Of course we do – but I have a great deal of life experience, I am intelligent and resourceful, as well as extremely (boringly) sensible, so I create a family ethos around the things that*

really matter in life and find ways round the luxuries. My daughters have actually commented that they think they are much less spoilt and better balanced than most of their peers and put this down to the fact that they have to face hard facts, disappointments and have to pay for their own mobile phones from birthday/Christmas money. A view that seems to be seconded by their grandparents who have openly told me that the girls are the least spoilt and most considerate of all 13 grandchildren. (Gillian, age 48, two children aged 13 and 15, Year 3 BA Primary Education)

Lone mothers describe valuing the opportunity of the circumstances in which to encourage children to appreciate what they have and not to be overly materialistic. Such an approach may in part be informed by aspects of HE participation, including ideas learned on courses, particularly within the Social Science disciplines studied by many lone parents, as well as through discussion of ideas with other students. It may further be informed by the decision by some to leave employment in order to focus on their intellectual development, including the intrinsic, personal development orientations toward HE engagement that often motivate mature students alongside instrumental employment and income goals. The placing of a positive value on the life lesson of 'going without' materially is not indicated to be determinate upon self-identified social class background. It reflects more significantly the development of lone parents' learner identities, prioritising academic and cultural enrichment over material gain. Moreover, it reflects a general determination demonstrated amongst research participants to find positives in testing times.

Lone-mother HE students' narratives further indicate that, for some, single status is experienced as an increase in financial resources, in contrast to the problems often inherent in being economically dependent on a partner (Jackson, 2004: 52). While lone parents are extensively shown to be financially underprivileged compared to partnered student parents (Callender, 2002: 91), they may, nevertheless, benefit from being masters of their own modest means. Thus, even if they feel downtrodden by the system as lone parents, they are more often free from the financial control of a partner. Although some lone parents do report new and ex-partners controlling their finances, there are also strong affirmations of the advantages of financial autonomy.

CHAPTER SIX

Juggling childcare

The previous two chapters identified the key stressors affecting lone-mother HE students' engagement with learning as they attempt to juggle complex and stretched equations of time and money. In the course of this discussion, concerns around childcare are identified as forming a core element of the challenges faced, in which issues around apportioning scant resources of time and money are crystallised. Existing research has identified lack of available childcare to be the largest barrier to lone parents accessing education and training, due in part to the absence of another parent to share caring responsibilities with (NUS, 2009: 14). Childcare is one of the key areas in which lone-mother HE students identify that they perceive their lives would be easier if their parenting circumstances were different. Levels of childcare use and satisfaction for this group invariably depend on managing a trade-off between time and money. Access to funded or affordable quality childcare, that children go happily to and parents feel happy using, is paramount to lone parents' successful participation in Higher Education without damaging family life and personal well-being.

Nearly half of lone mothers in the study discussed their use of formal childcare provided by their HE Institution or independent providers. Formal childcare is provided by: crèches and nurseries for preschool children; breakfast, after-school and holiday clubs for school-age children; and childminders and au pairs for both. The inflexibility of nurseries and crèches in terms of opening hours, and the comparative flexibility of childminders, is a recurrent theme amongst lone-parent HE students, informed by the particular childcare needs often engendered by HE participation, as discussed later in this chapter. No lone parents in the study reported employing a nanny to care for their children, and one lone mother had experienced an au pair resigning because the lone parent's long working days informed childcare demands that were deemed too heavy.

Seventy of the 77 lone mothers raised childcare issues, making it clearly one of the most important. The few who did not discuss childcare had children who, although still legally dependants, as teenagers were old enough to look after themselves out of school hours. It is impossible to overestimate the importance of childcare for lone parents; that it emerged as such a central theme concurs with academic, policy and service-provider consensus on primary issues facing UK lone parents. Cost and availability of good-quality childcare have been identified by several commentators as a key barrier for lone parents (Klett-Davies, 2007: 49; Jenkins and Symons, 2001: 137; Kiernan, Land and Lewis, 1998), and interest groups including Gingerbread, the Centre for Economic and Social Inclusion (CESI), Working Links, Work Directions and the Single Parents' Action Network (SPAN) agree that childcare is one of the pivotal issues affecting lone parents' ability to successfully manage paid employment with family responsibilities (SPAN, 2007). Lack of adequate childcare is similarly identified as hindering educational participation (Shaw and Woolhead, 2006: 178; Meredith-Lobay, 2004: 17). The Dearing Report found 48 per cent of lone parents to be dissatisfied with childcare provision for students, compared with 40 per cent of couples with children (Department for Education and Employment, 1997), and childcare problems have been identified as one of 'the most common reasons for leaving courses prematurely', alongside lack of time and money (Reay, 2003: 312). It has suggested that in terms of informing lone parents' engagement with paid work, childcare should be understood as a 'constraint' requiring constant renegotiation in light of changing situations, rather than as a 'barrier' that can be overcome once and for all (Work Directions, 2007). This is similarly relevant to understanding the ongoing demands of negotiating childcare for lone parents participating in Higher Education.

Even when satisfactory childcare structures are in place, unanticipated complications like children's illness continue to throw routines off kilter and threaten educational commitments. Commentators have highlighted the importance of onsite (or at least geographically convenient) childcare provision in enabling lone parents to participate in paid work (Cohen, 2007). The need for more consistent availability of institutionally provided or at least locally available childcare can be extended to the childcare requirements of lone-parent students. Ideologically, there is a need for HE Institutions to more consistently acknowledge the constraints posed by routine childcare responsibilities, availability of provision, and sick children, and to ratify these in institutional policy and practice.

Not wanting children to spend 'too much' time in childcare is a repeated reported barrier to lone parents' engagement with employment and learning (Hinton-Smith, 2007b: 2; Hinton-Smith, 2007a; Bradshaw and Millar, 1991: 33). This stands in notable contrast to the broader trend supported by successive government policies, toward even mothers of younger children, and particularly lone mothers, being in employment, hence necessitating the buying-in of childcare. The evidence from this research demonstrates that children's needs are the utmost concern of lone parents. It has been observed that while well-paid parents can afford high-quality care, those out of work often consider the devotion of their own time and efforts better than any childcare they are likely to be able to afford, and that in order to be sufficiently attractive to lone parents, any job must be satisfactorily rewarding to compensate for being away from children. Further, for lone parents to take up work, children who have already been separated from one parent, must also be separated from their other parent for extended periods. This means that while work can undoubtedly offer long-term monetary, social and emotional rewards, it can also exacerbate risks to family cohesion and income security. It has been stressed that lone parents often prefer to test out childcare arrangements before they take up work, but are not always able to do so (Ford, 1996). These observations around childcare considerations informing lone parents' engagement with paid work are equally relevant to understanding circumstances facilitating HE participation, particularly given that lone parents' move into Higher Education often necessitates immersion in unfamiliar childcare arrangements for their children.

One in eight lone parents in this research described their children being unhappy with existing childcare arrangements. This confirms evidence from Gingerbread that this is a common childcare concern (2007f: 13). Such problems were reported by parents of children unhappy at nursery aged from babies through to young teens whose resentment of babysitters thwarted their parents' hopes of a social life. The childcarers with whom children express dissatisfaction include non-custodial parents, extended family, friends and childminders alongside formal group childcare settings. (Issues in informal childcare provision for lone-parent students are discussed in detail later in this chapter.) Dissatisfaction with childcare arrangements can understandably leave lone parents feeling guilty, and sometimes results in curbing of participation in academic and other activities to avoid or minimise reliance on childcare. Significantly, all of the lone mothers researched whose children had disabilities reported childcare dissatisfaction because their children were unhappy with the arrangement. For example, one lone parent of a child with Down's Syndrome ultimately left her course because childcare arrangements were not working out, while another with a severely autistic child similarly struggled to make satisfactory childcare arrangements:

> *On occasions when I have had work due to be submitted and*
> *desperately need some quality study time to complete it I have asked*
> *a friend of mine to try to have him. He finds this on the whole very*
> *difficult and because of his disability I try to insist on paying her.*
> *Sometimes she accepts the money and sometimes she doesn't.* (Ruth,
> age 47, two children aged 9 and 12, Year 3 BA Social Policy
> and Criminology)

These experiences support evidence that parents of children with disabilities are particularly negatively affected by lack of appropriate childcare (Every Disabled Child Matters, 2011).

One-third of lone mothers in the research discussed the impact of their access to childcare on their ability to socialise, conveying that in the context of the limited childcare resources often entailed in lone parenting, the more important demand of study inevitably takes precedence over socialising. Lone mothers frequently report their ability to socialise to be minimal because of relying on informal childcare networks to facilitate it – most prominently family. Several key strategies emerge as significant for lone parents in overcoming childcare limitations in order to allow social contact; one common approach is to meet friends to socialise during children's school day, while another is to socialise with children. Lone mothers describe either taking children out socialising with them, or inviting friends to their home to socialise, although these strategies are not always experienced as ideal, and can have their own drawbacks and limitations:

> *Being a single parent means that socialising has mainly meant having people over to my house which is fine when its old friends, but does mean that it is more difficult to socialise with less well known people who otherwise you might go for a quick pint with.* (Bex, age 34, one child aged 12, MA Primary Education with QTS)

Childcare costs

Formal childcare is invariably discussed by lone parents in relation to its high cost, informing inevitable limitations on the extent to which it can be relied on to meet childcare needs. Half of the lone mothers researched discussed the cost of provision, making it one of the most salient recurring childcare issues. This corroborates existing evidence that the cost of childcare is an important issue for lone parents (Klett-Davies, 2007: 49; Shaw and Woolhead, 2006: 178; Jenkins and Symons, 2001: 137; Kiernan, Land and Lewis, 1998; Bradshaw and Millar, 1991: 45). This is likely to be nationally specific, given that UK parents bear some of the highest childcare costs in the world (OECD, 2011). Indeed, lone parents frequently raise the issue of the substantial surplus they are required to pay even when childcare assistance is provided by the UK Government, acknowledged by critics, including Gingerbread, to be a major problem. Even after government subsidy, UK parents have been documented to contribute on average 75 per cent of the cost of formal childcare, compared to an average of 30 per cent across Europe (Gingerbread, 2007e: 3). This is set to become an increasing challenge for parents of dependent children, including lone-parent students, as changes in the 2011 Welfare Reform Bill are predicted to lead to up to a tenfold increase in childcare costs borne by some families (Family Action, 2011). Lone mothers describe experiencing additional problems meeting the cost of travelling to and from childcare by public transport or car.

The cost of childcare emerges as an equally pressing concern for lone-parent students self-identifying as middle class and working class. Many discuss the childcare support they receive either as part of their Tax Credit entitlement or student funding, with frequent accounts of delays in payments from both sources leaving individuals unable to pay providers, sometimes for months, resulting in worries about losing childcare places. One lone mother resorted to taking out a bank loan to temporarily cover the shortfall while her childcare support entitlement was assessed. Another recurring theme around childcare cost is the need to shoulder additional expense from limited budgets to pay for children to stay late in the afternoon beyond the end of the standard session when academic timetables demand this, or paying for full-day sessions and holiday cover even when children are collected early or not in attendance for prolonged periods. Lone-mother HE students frequently recommend that there should be childcare fee remissions for students over academic vacation periods when they do not need to use childcare.

University crèches are frequently reported to be prohibitively expensive, alongside additional problems of sessions having to be booked and paid for in advance, and not corresponding with lecture times (also Jackson, 2004: 52). Research by the UK Government in 2005 highlighted that problems with cost and availability result in two-thirds of parents relying on family and friends for childcare, and the worry that childcare arrangements do not fit in with working hours (Ward, 2005b). Lone-parent students' utilisation of informal childcare is discussed further in the following section.

For lone mothers studying in Higher Education, the key documented shortcoming of informal childcare is that the cost is not financially supported by the UK Government. While both Working Families Tax Credits and student grants can include childcare subsidy elements, lone-parent students comment on the restriction that this assistance may only be used to pay formal childcarers. The UK Government's requirement that childcarers be registered in order to qualify for assistance with costs prevents lone parents from obtaining assistance in paying family members, friends and neighbours to childmind, thus potentially depriving them of the opportunity for children to be cared for locally and by someone they know and feel comfortable with. Extension of financial support to informal care arrangements is a key recommendation by both lone parents and lobby groups representing families, including for example Kinship Care Alliance.

Given lack of resources to remunerate informal childcare, lone-parent students describe feeling obliged to offer reciprocal childcare arrangements. This can be particularly challenging, and provides an additional source of stress for time-stretched individuals already managing heavy schedules of study, employment, children, domestic and other responsibilities single-handedly. Several described feeling aggrieved that this burden was aggravated by having to reciprocate by caring for others' children in return for informal childcare received. Lone-mother HE students' experiences support the need for informal childcare provided by friends and family to be eligible for government subsidy, given its unique potential to provide the affordable, trustworthy and flexible out-of-hours childcare often vital to improving opportunities through HE participation.

Informal childcare

Lone mothers studying in Higher Education frequently discuss childcare in the context of informal provision by family and friends, chiming with evidence from Gingerbread that lone parents frequently prefer to use informal, family-based childcare (Gingerbread, 2007f: 2). This is perhaps inevitable given the UK's high childcare costs, and, in practice, most lone parents describe relying on a combination of formal and informal provision. As with broader issues around time, and lone-parent students' experiences as a whole, access to a robust informal support structure is central to determining the success with which individuals are able to weld together study requirements and childcare availability. Existing commentary on lone parents and employment has emphasised the role of informal networks in providing flexible childcare to cover shifts, weekends or irregular hours, as well as the inevitable times of children's illness (Ford, 1996: xiii). The irregular and out-of-hours childcare that lone parents frequently need often cannot be met by the non-personalised childcare provision of nurseries and childminders (Gingerbread, 2007f: 13). These demands are also particularly relevant to lone-parent students' ability to meet the 'Bachelor Boy' demands of Higher Education. Informal childcare is frequently discussed in the context of 'out-of-hours' cover: early mornings, late nights and overnight stays to cover late and early lectures, exams (sometimes scheduled for evenings and Saturdays), and clashes between university terms or semesters and school or nursery holidays. Those undertaking nursing training with shift work placements, or Open University students with residential summer schools, both groups in which lone-parent learners proliferate, have to manage additional out-of-hours childcare requirements in order to meet their course commitments. Postgraduate students describe the need to call on informal childcare assistance from family in order to attend conferences requiring overnight stays away from home. Informal care is additionally used to cover evenings out with friends or partners, and in-patient hospital stays.

A frequent problem indicated by lone-parent students is children not being accepted at school or nursery when ill because of contagion risk. Unless informal childcare can be found to cover these times, lone-parent students are left with no choice but to miss university and paid work. For many this contributes to what Christie *et al.* have called a 'semi-detached' relationship to HE Institutions (2005: 27). Such childcare needs are unavoidable, but cannot be covered by formal childcare. Access (often short notice) to alternative arrangements is pivotal to facilitating HE participation, and whether lone parents share their home with other adults is a strong determinant of childcare access (Jenkins and Symons, 2001: 128, 130). Most lone parents in this research did not have the financial means for a nanny, or a spare bedroom for an au pair, to facilitate more flexible formal childcare arrangements. Hence, apart from one family who did have an au pair, the rest of those who did share their homes with other adults were living with friends, grandparents or lodgers. Lone parents' experiences indicate the need for development of cost-effective solutions, including institutional support in facilitating student childcare networks and cooperatives.

The importance of family and friends in providing childcare for lone parents has been highlighted by other commentators (Polakow *et al.*, 2004: 2; Scott *et al.*, 2003; Millar and Rowlingson, 2001: 239; Hyatt and Parry, 1990: 18). Use of informal childcare provided by family and friends emerges as the most commonly recurring childcare theme, being discussed by over half of lone mothers researched. Lone-parent students' own parents provide the bulk of informal childcare; with wider extended family also contributing, including siblings, aunts, nephews, grandparents and older children. Friends, neighbours, non-resident parents, new partners, and former families-in-law provide further help. This is one of the few areas in which there is a discernible social class relationship, with those self-identifying as working class four times as likely as those identifying as middle class to describe receiving practical help with childcare from wider family beyond their own parents. There is no discernible difference in the frequency with which the parents of working-class and middle-class participants are reported to provide assistance, with just over half of each group describing receiving such help. In the face of the inadequacy of formal childcare provision for meeting irregular and out-of-hours study needs, the help provided by family centrally informs the ability to participate in Higher Education as a lone parent for many, as the following indicate:

> *Tutorials are a problem. This year, they are in [. . .], so I know I*
> *won't make any of them, I don't think, unless my Dad can help out.*
> *I'd really like to go to at least one if I can manage it.* (Nicky, age
> 37, two children aged 8 and 10, BA Health and Social Care)

> *Re. childcare, I am lucky that my mum lives about 1/4 mile from me*
> *and is retired and happy to collect madam from school, etc. I have to*
> *say that I couldn't do any of this without her. There is no way that*
> *I could work full time and study as well, unless it was one module*
> *per year perhaps!* (Marcia, age 43, one child aged 7, Year 3 BSc
> Clinical Nursing)

Depending on local HE Institution access, subject, institution choice,
and offer of a place, entering university can mean a substantial change
of geographical location; and for lone parents this means uprooting the
family from informal networks of support. Even if lone parents' own
parents are supportive in principle, evidence indicates that in practice
they are often prevented from providing considerable practical assistance
by living too far away, working full-time, suffering ill health, or being
otherwise engaged with care responsibilities for other grandchildren. The
importance of the childcare safety net provided by family is made clear
by the negative impact its absence can have, as the following indicates:

> *Childcare has to be my biggest worry. My parents have been ill*
> *recently so I had to rely on friends more and more.* (Rita, age 36,
> four children aged 5–10, Year 2 Primary Education)

Apart from the importance of informal networks in providing free and
out-of-hours childcare, lone parents frequently prefer such arrangements
because they minimise upset to children by allowing them to be cared
for in familiar surroundings, by trusted carers with whom they have close
existing relationships. This is particularly relevant given that children
in lone-parent families have frequently already undergone significant
disruption to their lives through family breakdown (Gingerbread, 2007f;
Ford, 1996: 199). One lone-parent student who used au pairs described
her motivation for doing so as wanting to allow her children to be cared
for in their own home; few however had the resources to afford this
relative luxury.

Research into the role of family and friends in providing support to German, Swedish and British lone parents of different social classes has identified that, while the help of family is important for all lone parents regardless of country, social class or ethnicity, it is particularly prominent for working-class and black lone parents. Further, while a range of family members and friends are important for providing financial, emotional and practical support, the help provided by grandmothers is identified as particularly significant by both working-class and middle-class lone parents. The help provided by immediate family, including grandmothers, is particularly important for English and Swedish lone parents compared to their German counterparts (Duncan and Edwards, 1999: 99–102). This may in part stem from cross-cultural variation in pressures caused by a decreased formal safety net (UK) and increased expectations for mothers to return to the labour force (Sweden). One Swedish lone mother in this research described the significant role in her life of considerable practical childcare assistance from parents, extended family, friends and a Swedish network in the UK, as well as financial help from parents. Another British lone parent reflected that:

> Research on the economic advantages of a grandparent living in
> the vicinity of the children – and able to provide childcare – is very
> interesting. Perhaps the British grandmother is the only reason so
> many single parents can manage? (Beth, age 33, one child aged 8,
> Year 2 PhD Archaeology)

In the UK, over 40 per cent of all mothers have been reported to use grandparents, usually grandmothers, for at least some childcare (Land, 2007). UK grandparents in particular provide extensive childcare assistance for lone parents. This contrasts with France, where grandparents provide more financial assistance, but less childcare. The comparative lack of childcare assistance from French grandparents is notable given the country's relatively high employment amongst lone parents. However, it can perhaps be understood in the context of the country's comprehensive preschool provision, which prioritises lone parents (Millar and Rowlingson, 2001). The one French lone mother in this research enjoyed both financial and childcare assistance from her parents, although the pattern amongst participants as a whole was to emphasise practical over financial help, chiming with documented trends.

For many lone-parent students, networks of friends are additionally vital in providing informal childcare support. Such arrangements frequently come into their own as children grow older and increasingly independent:

> *My son is now enjoying a vastly improved social life as he goes to friends twice a week, rather than afterschool club every night (which he isn't too keen on). I would say he seems happier and doesn't care that I don't pick him up from school every day. He seems to have grown up a lot and just wants to play with the other boys in the street. This is very liberating for me as it means I can get on with my life without feeling like I'm neglecting him.* (Anne–Marie, one child aged 1, Psychology)

The childcare contribution made by non–resident parents centrally informs lone parents' ability to take up and stay in employment (Millar and Rowlingson, 2001: 237). The majority of non–resident parents of children in this research lived in the UK, often within reasonable travelling distance or even very locally. The distance between the homes of children in lone parent families and non–resident parents is identified as pivotal in determining level of contact (Gingerbread, 2007d: 15). Lone–parent students use the regular or irregular childcare provided by children visiting non–resident parents as an opportunity to study or socialise:

> *[My daughter's] Dad also provides support without realising it when he takes [her] out for a few hours after school.* (Marcia, age 43, one child aged 7, BSc Clinical Nursing)

The potential of such support is, however, frequently impeded by acrimonious relations with non–resident parents. Because children's contact time with non–resident parents often essentially constitutes study time for the resident lone-parent student, failure to honour visitation arrangements impacts on ability to fulfil study requirements. While 13 lone mothers described how their ex-partner helped or supported them, 54 complained about lack of support. The high level of dissatisfaction is perhaps to be expected considering that these represent partnerships that have broken down. These dissatisfied lone mothers stressed that they would like the non–resident parent to have more contact with their child or children, in order to allow them more child-free time for study, paid work or leisure.

A passive approach to co-parenting by non-resident parents can however be seen as an advantage in enabling resident parents to control decision-making, including around childcare issues:

> *The good thing with [my daughter's] Dad though is that he completely trusts me and doesn't question my decisions, for example changing nursery to make things easier for me.* (Carys, age 31, one child aged 1, Year 2 PhD Sociology)

There may also be an unexplored element of lone mothers preferring not to receive help from ex-partners, particularly given that these arrangements carry the baggage of failed relationships, and that help is often reported to come 'at a cost' or be unreliable, as Carys also indicated:

> *As I don't have any family here and my only friends who used to do some babysitting have moved away, the only person I rely on for that is [my daughter's] Dad. On the one hand, it is good that he is helping out, but on the other hand it also means that I am very dependent on him . . .*

In addition to the more than two-thirds of lone mothers in this research who complained about unsatisfactory arrangements negotiating child-care responsibilities with their ex-partners, several had zero support because non-resident parents either lived abroad, had serious psycho-logical problems that left them completely unable to participate in their children's lives, or were legally barred from contact. These lone mothers were particularly dependent on the informal support that networks of family and friends could provide.

Demographic differences in childcare issues

That lone-mother HE students indicate broadly the same childcare problems, with the same frequency, indeterminate of social class identification, is indicative of a trend shown by this research toward lone-parent status to a large extent trumping class as a unifying determinant of experience. This may be largely because, regardless of whether some lone parents may have enjoyed relatively privileged upbringings, affluent jobs or marriages, while these factors unarguably have the power to soften the hardship of lone parenthood, individuals are nevertheless all

133

thrown into the same boat of managing children and study, with the ensuing constraints on juggling limited time and financial resources. The shared circumstances of lone-parent students may mean that even the most relatively privileged are largely unable to lighten their burden by buying in domestic services in the form of nannies, au pairs and cleaners. This resonates with existing research on the educational participation of mature women students with children, including Scott, Burns and Cooney (1998: 250), and Reay's observation that:

> *Ironically, in the normative, nuclear, two-parent, middle-class family, 'the everything' becomes the responsibility of the many as sufficient economic capital allows for the delegation of both childcare and housework. Cleaners, nannies, childminders and tutors are routinely employed to lessen the load on mothers . . . Only in poor families like those of the lone mothers in this study does 'everything' become an individual responsibility as the old safety net of the welfare state is stripped away.* (2003: 312)

The only identified class difference in childcare use shown amongst lone-parent students − that those identifying as working class make fuller use of extended family support − may indicate the sociological stereotype of close-knit working-class communities, or simply that with fewer financial resources to draw on, poorer students are forced to call on free childcare from family and friends. This evidence of variations in use of extended family support affirms the continuing relevance of earlier findings that extended family childcare support is central to the lives of BME and working-class lone parents, while middle-class lone parents describe more loose-knit and friendship-based social support networks (Duncan and Edwards, 1999: 97–102).

Evidence emphasises the significance of contrasting European and Anglophone welfare regimes in informing lone parents' experiences (Klett-Davies, 2007; Millar and Rowlingson, 2001; Duncan and Edwards, 1999). While this research is focused on lone parents studying at UK HE Institutions, participation by lone parents with international family backgrounds and those who perceive their experience of lone parenting to be affected by the influence of the non-resident parent's cultural background, indicate the relevance of contrasting expectations of educational participation and family responsibility in informing negotiation of informal networks of support. Carys reflected on the difference she experienced between her own current circumstances as a lone parent, and her childhood growing up in a Scandinavian country:

> *I guess in a way, it is easier for me to look after [my daughter] if she is ill being a student than having a normal job. I can take days off and then work more in the evenings as I did when she had impetigo. It is hard but manageable. It would be more difficult to take time off with a normal job. My mum was also working when I was little, but at the time working parents could make use of 'sick-mums' – a childminder who would come and stay with the child at home when you went to work. Where I live SPAN (Single Parent Action Network) has organized a similar scheme.* (Carys, age 31, one child aged 1, Year 2 PhD Sociology)

Another lone mother similarly conjectured contrasts in expectations around lone parenthood and HE participation between Scandinavia and the UK:

> *My tutor has been really supportive, and helpful. I think I could go to her to explain my absences from seminars etc. when other lecturers tell her. My tutor has just been to Norway and she says the universities are much more geared up to mum's studying there, and you are more unusual if you don't have a baby at university! She said it made her realise how against mothers the British university system is.* (Mandy, age 26, one child aged 8, PGCE)

Beyond observed international and social class variations in childcare expectations, further differences include those between distance-learning and traditional-contact students. Perhaps unsurprisingly given the different requirements of their engagement with HE learning, and with childcare availability and priorities identified as frequently informing decisions to study by distance learning, lone-parent students on traditional contact courses focus on problems with formal childcare, while distance learners more frequently discuss their lack of 'babysitters'. It would be expected that, given the limited and irregular childcare requirements of distance learning, this group would be less likely to have formal childcare arrangements in place.

The most salient difference in lone-parent students' childcare experience pivots on number and ages of children. Although documented changing patterns in women's employment trajectories may lead us to anticipate parents with primary care duty to be increasingly willing to enrol preschool children in childcare, previous research with lone parents identified nearly three-quarters as citing children's ages to centrally inform willingness to engage with education or employment (Hinton-Smith, 2007b: 2). This corroborates earlier evidence indicating the age of the youngest child to be a major determining factor in limiting lone parents' desire not to work, with many lone parents of young children indicating that they would choose not to work even given access to adequate childcare (Ford, 1996: ix; also Bradshaw and Millar, 1991: 33). While some lone parents may reject study in favour of being with children, for others it is actively chosen as a relatively manageable alternative compared to paid work, offering increased flexibility, and hence more easily reconcilable with the responsibilities of lone parenthood.

Perhaps unsurprisingly given the increased domestic responsibility associated with each additional child, evidence indicates mothers with only one child to be more likely to succeed in completing their studies than those with two or more children (Zachry, 2005: 2571). Further, younger women with younger children have been found to be more likely to leave a course prematurely because of problems combining study with domestic responsibilities. This is attributed to an increased load of household work associated with young children (Scott *et al.*, 1998: 233). Given the assumed decreasing care burden of children as they grow older, it may appear somewhat anomalous that lone parents of preschool children are significantly less likely to discuss issues around fitting their parenting and study responsibilities together than those with school-age children, and that those with younger children also report fewer childcare problems and greater satisfaction with childcare arrangements. This can be seen as indicative that parents of preschool children often have an advantage over those with school-age children in having more comprehensive childcare provision in place, meeting study needs more effectively through covering early morning, after-school and school holiday childcare requirements, rather than settling for informal ad hoc arrangements with school friends, or leaving children unsupervised.

Lone parents of school-age children continue to face the considerable challenge of making study or work and childcare hours 'fit', but for older children, parents face different problems. Lone mothers describe how older children can assert their will by refusing childcare arrangements (also Ford, 1996). In such cases student parents resort to fulfilling study or work commitments by fitting work in when children are at school, working at home, or leaving children alone to care for themselves (also Christie *et al.*, 1995: 20). Lone parents' trajectories indicate, however, that, to an extent, having older children who are sufficiently independent to be left alone to care for themselves for fixed periods while their parent is at university does free these parents from some of the stresses of arranging childcare, allowing them to concentrate on their studies more effectively. These advantages include children being old enough to travel home from school alone by bus or foot and let themselves into the house with their own key, or walking to the home of a grandparent or other family member to be cared for there. Such arrangements are most frequently utilised for children aged 12 and above, although some are as young as nine. Children being able to take care of themselves in this way was always discussed by lone mothers in the research in positive terms, although it can also leave parents worrying about children travelling home alone or left at home unattended while they attend university. Lone parents indicate such arrangements to be not ideal, but nevertheless frequently a necessity given their circumstances:

> *[University location] is a long way from my house . . . and my son is in the house for about half an hour on his own before I get in (he is 11 years old and comes home from secondary school on the bus) which is not excessive but is still not ideal.* (Michelle, age 35, one child aged 12, MSc History of Science)

Lone-parent students with several children of varying ages frequently face considerable challenges in having to simultaneously meet their children's diverse specific needs through different childcare arrangements, often providing varying cover and at divergent locations (also Scott *et al.*, 2003: 30).

Juggling childcare and university

Lone mothers indicate that experiencing frequent mismatch between childcare availability and their specific childcare needs as HE learners often impacts profoundly on their ability to study successfully and engage fully with the wider life of university:

> *Much of my experience has been made harder because of financial*
> *difficulties and lack of childcare (or relief from looking after children)*
> *as I am currently completing the 2nd year of my PGCE (in service).*
> (Zeena, age 36, two children aged 14 and 16, Year 2 PGCE
> Secondary)

More than a quarter of lone mothers researched described the impact of childcare upon their HE studies. For some this means having to miss classes when childcare cannot be found or when children are ill, or that private study can only be undertaken during school hours. Others describe making more permanent study decisions based on childcare availability, for example, choosing to enter Higher Education once their youngest child reaches school age. That this is recognised as a key moment at which many lone parents reengage with education is significant in light of 2011 changes to the group's benefit entitlement, requiring them to move to Job Seeker's Allowance when children reach age 5. This preclusion of educational participation acts to close the door to education for lone parents at precisely the moment at which it is opening for many. Other ways in which childcare issues inform the parameters of lone parents' HE participation include choosing distance learning in order to minimise the demand studies make on time, childcare and travel, as indicated by Nicky:

> *I like studying with the Open University because it's so much*
> *easier. No worry about childcare while I go to classes, except the*
> *odd tutorial, as it's all marked from home.* (Nicky, age 37, two
> children aged 8 and 10, BA Health and Social Care)

Some lone parents relocate to live closer to family in order to access informal childcare support while they undertake their HE studies, while others cite the importance of remaining close to such an existing support infrastructure as a barrier to relocating to attend university. Hours of childcare provision and travelling distance between childcare and university emerge as centrally recurring childcare problems for lone-parent HE students. Many find it as problematic that crèches and nurseries open too late and/or close too early to cover their lecture or exam needs, resulting in stressful, rushed journeys and missed university contact time. As one pointed out:

*The nursery is on campus and is used by loads of lecturers, so I
would have thought they would realise that evening exams don't suit
people with children.* (Daisy, one child, Year 4 First Degree)

Those using childcare providers not located near their university
describe the negative impact of time spent travelling on their ability to
cope with daily schedules (also Cohen, 2007). This can mean up to two
hours travel each way by public transport through busy city centres, and
can lead to missing university contact time as well as feelings of a more
general wasting of precious time.

The fit between hours of childcare provision and university times
varies significantly between types of provision, and centrally informs
childcare decisions. Some lone-parent students choose private nurseries
over their university's crèche because of a mismatch between crèche
opening times and contact hours. This lack of match between childcare
needs and availability can oblige parents to make complex arrangements
of family or childminders delivering children to and from nursery or
school, and covering additional childcare needs. Although solving a
dilemma, this also creates its own further problems, with lone-parent
students often discussing the stress caused by balancing such complicated
webs of arrangements alongside work and study. Delegation of childcare
does not necessarily buy freedom from the distraction of worrying about
whether children are safe and well cared for, as the lone parent remains
responsible for coordinating and managing the smooth operation of
such complex plans.

The net result of childcare problems can be a restricted ability for
lone-parent students to participate fully in the life of university, with
ensuing social and academic consequences. Lone-parent students on
postgraduate courses frequently report that childcare problems compromise their studies, including their ability to monitor science experiments out of nursery hours, or to complete residential fieldwork
away from home. For undergraduate students, participating in group-
project assignments or independent study groups can be hindered
by childcare availability. Feeling unable to spare valuable childcare
time for extracurricular events can result in forfeiting participation in
curriculum-enriching university activities like DPhil seminars and
Mature Students' Groups. Such inability to participate in the social life
of university can profoundly impede integration for a group who are
already substantially isolated by their circumstances. This is particularly

worrying given the documented impact of social integration upon both academic attainment and retention (Hussey and Smith, 2010: 159; McShand, 2004; de Jonghe, 1973: 245). As one lone mother remembered of her initial transition to university:

> *The first week was very challenging, I was most anxious about childcare issues and couldn't even begin to think about meeting people or getting drunk in the student union!* (Anne-Marie, one child, Year 1 Psychology)

Lone-mother HE students' childcare experiences are not restricted to lamenting deficits of adequate provision; they also highlight the positive potential of childcare in paving the way for engagement with HE participation, as illustrated by the following reflection from Kristin:

> *At 17 I was pregnant by my 'one true love' who promised me he'd stay with me forever. He had had a breakdown and was sectioned at 16, I'd been with him since 12. I gave up my A-levels and was his carer (we'd been living together since before he was first sectioned). I was old and tired. At 18 I was on my own with a baby, bored, fed up and feeling less old but still tired, not to mention very, very, very poor (£36 income support a week!). I thought 'God there has to be more than this.' I tried everything to get in college but it was all too expensive, course fees, childcare. Then one day a women came to the local toddler group plugging this access to HE course as part of the 'let's rejuvenate and patronise poor villages' agenda. The European Social Fund would pay fees, childcare, perhaps even travel expenses; I signed up immediately.* (Kristin, age 26, one child aged 8, PGCE History)

This story shows the extent to which provision of adequate assistance with key facilitators, including childcare, fees and travel costs, is pivotal in mobilising lone parents' pre-existing motivation to reengage with education, and through doing so improve the futures of themselves and their children. The following section discusses the role played by universities in facilitating HE participation for this group through childcare access.

Universities' role in childcare provision

A quarter of the lone mothers researched discussed their university's role, or lack of it, in providing childcare; the majority of this discussion described negative experiences around lack of provision. Lone-parent students stress the need for HE Institutions to make increased childcare provision, including more facilitation of self-help childcare initiatives such as student-run playgroups and babysitting networks, and more campus nurseries. This user-identified need runs counter to the trend toward closure of campus childcare facilities, which the NUS have been involved in campaigning against since the 1980s (2007b: 2). Lone-parent students indicate further university childcare recommendations for increased HE Institution provision of weekend, half-term and holiday 'wrap-around' childcare for older children. Universities are criticised for either making no childcare provision at all, providing too few hours or places, or prioritising applications from staff over student parents. One DPhil student who moved to the UK to complete her studies and was disappointed to find that her university's nursery prioritised children of staff over students, expressed the importance of childcare provision for student parents.

> I know I have already told you about the nursery, but I just want to mention it again as I think good, affordable and flexible childcare is so important. And if the university can't provide it they should be better at helping students out in finding the information and facilities that they need. This is especially important if they have moved in order to be able to pursue their studies. (Carys, age 31, one child aged 1, Year 2 PhD Sociology)

In addition to provision of on-campus or off-campus university-run childcare facilities, some student parents use private nurseries not subsidised by their university, but either located on university campuses or having established institutional links. While it is far from ideal for lone-parent students to have to finance the high cost of childcare without institutional subsidy, these cases nevertheless demonstrate opportunities for HE Institutions at least to facilitate access to geographically convenient childcare for this group of widening participation students. Highlighting such possibilities is important given evidence that a substantial number of institutions are increasingly distancing themselves from responsibility for facilitating childcare access, largely through arguments that subsidies cannot continue in the increasingly cost-driven HE market. University managements' arguments against subsidy have focused on challenging the justification of investing funds in supporting what they argue is a small group of students. Exemplifying this, it has been argued from one of the UK's top universities that funds are better spent on resources benefiting the wider student community. Responsibility for managing university and childcare commitments is placed firmly with the individual rather than the institution, with the recommendation that students should be prepared for the pressures that families can create and how they can get in the way of university life, and should ensure that they have adequate funds to look after their families, and 'someone' (a partner is suggested) to look after their children when they are doing their academic work (Bonnet and Meredith-Lobay, 2004: 29). Such institutional assumptions of the ultimately irreconcilable nature of university participation and primary carer responsibility clearly problematise the position of lone parents. The following experience illustrates how universities' failure to engage with supporting childcare access can leave lone parents dependent on the complex patchworks of informal arrangements discussed earlier in this chapter, and the effect of this upon ability to fulfil study expectations:

> *I had to struggle completing them while trying to find childcare to cover the seminars and lectures I had to attend. I did approach the uni for help. They had no childcare facilities and could offer no help other than suggest I put an ad in the jobshop. I found this an absurd offer as it would mean finding the time to interview and then there is the issue of trust. In the end it took six different helpers, a variety of family, friends and babysitters to cover only the hours at uni!*
> (Patricia, two children, Year 1)

Further descriptions from lone mothers of the problems faced negotiating university participation within the constraints of heavy family responsibilities and limited childcare access, include feeling unwelcome to bring their children onto the HE Institution site, even having to leave children outside university libraries because of not having a pass for them (also Edwards, 1993). A recurring problem for those with children is not being able to go to the library to get books after lectures because of having to rush straight home to children (also Scott *et al.*, 2003: 29;

Gallagher *et al.*, 1993: 23). This inevitably disadvantages lone parents in that popular books recommended in the lecture have invariably been borrowed by other students by the time they make it to the library. Lack of childcare provision and administrative arrangements that take no account of domestic responsibilities can leave student parents feeling undervalued by their HE Institution compared to other students. For example, students with children report being told that seminar changes are only permitted for academic reasons, not for childcare (see Edwards, 1993: 86); and that only the student's sickness, and not having to care for sick children, excuses non-attendance or late assignment submission. One lone mother's use of an au pair when her children were younger had been motivated by the impossibility she found matching her university timetable with nursery provision:

> *If you had a problem, you had to deal with it yourself. very little leeway was given. This was one of the reasons I had an au pair, to help me with my changing timetable, as no [other] childcare provider would have tolerated it.* (Naomi, age 44, three children aged 13–16, Year 2 MSc Interprofessional Health and Social Care)

The response of university staff to the pressures faced by lone parents varies greatly, effectively leaving struggling students at the mercy of individual tutors' sympathy. While there are stories of sympathetic university staff who go out of their way to support and encourage their struggling lone-parent students, lack of sympathy from university staff over the difficulties of managing childcare with academic timetables is frequently experienced, as the following exemplifies:

> *So far I have not experienced any real problems apart from overhearing a lecturer complaining to a colleague that 'if parents couldn't arrange childcare over half terms, what is the point of them starting university?' Luckily for me I have a very supportive family who helped me out over half term.* (Stacey, one child, BA Sociology with Business and Management)

This illustrates once again the extent to which lone parents' ability to successfully negotiate the world of Higher Education so often hinges on the bank of informal support they are able to draw on. The insight below illustrates that lack of sympathy experienced by lone parents in Higher

Education is not restricted to their course tutors. As earlier indicated, student teachers and nurses, areas in which lone parents proliferate, face particular challenges in terms of securing childcare to meet their course commitments – difficulties that are not always treated sympathetically by the placement providers students must negotiate:

> *I'm on a teacher training course so will be on a school placement*
> *during May. It is in the same class where I was placed for a week*
> *in December. The class teacher told me I need to arrive in school at*
> *8 a.m. when I come back in May but this isn't feasible for me as it*
> *means childcare before AND after school. I can arrive at 8.30, which*
> *was the guide time college told us we should arrive. I've spoken to*
> *my personal tutor at college and she has told me it's reasonable for*
> *me to tell the school I can't arrive before 8.30. It's good to have such*
> *support from college to enable me to continue with my course. I think*
> *the class teacher was being particularly harsh as she knew I had a kid*
> *and she did the same course as me as a mature student with kids!*
> *Sometimes those people who should understand are the toughest.*
> (Eva, age 28, one child aged 9, Year 2 Primary Education with
> History)

While describing lone parents' problems managing university expecta-tions with childcare availability, this also illustrates the value of supportive staff in mediating difficulties and helping to make challenges surmountable. The following section completes this chapter by docu-menting evidence of lone-parent students' positive experiences in managing to fit together study requirements and childcare availability.

Satisfaction with childcare arrangements

Twenty-two of the lone mothers in the research described satisfaction with their childcare arrangements; the most important factors informing this were children's happiness, and flexibility of provision. Children being happy with childcare arrangements is the most salient factor in parents' satisfaction and ability to engage with their HE studies. While this is inevitably a priority for any parent, it is perhaps amplified for those whose children have experienced family breakdown, and separation from one parent. The significance of accessing childcare with which children and parents are happy for enabling HE participation underscores the importance of high-quality childcare provision to facilitate lone parents' separation from their children to engage with learning and paid work. The importance of children's happiness with childcare arrangements is discussed in relation to children of all ages, from babies to older schoolchildren, being highlighted by almost all those who report childcare satisfaction. Its salience in terms of facilitating parents' HE participation represents the flipside of children's dissatisfaction leading to parents' withdrawing from studies. The following comment crystallises this importance:

> *The kids however are having a great time! My son is at a fantastic nursery and they pick my daughter up from school as she is enrolled in their after-school club for older kids. They love it and to be absolutely honest I don't think I would have survived without this childcare.* (Christa, two children, Year 1)

While children's happiness emerges as overwhelmingly the major consideration in terms of informing childcare satisfaction, the second most prominent theme is the childcare provider, whether a nursery, childminder or other, offering flexibility in the care they provide. The importance of flexibility emerges consistently, with its significance in lone parents' lives encapsulated in the following comment from a lone parent of four-year-old twins:

> *One point which I will note this week, which has only occurred to me recently, my family had the sad duty of burying my great uncle last week and I did notice that, but for the kids being at preschool (and preschool agreeing to take the kids in ten minutes early) I wouldn't have had anyone to look after the kids – all family and family friends were at the funeral, so I would have either had to miss the funeral or take the kids along – which wouldn't have been appropriate! Anyway, as I say, the preschool where the twins attend every morning had agreed to take them a bit early as a one-off only.* (Sadie, age 27, 4-year-old twins, 3 LLB)

Such a sympathetic approach and willingness to bend the rules by childcare providers can make all the difference for lone parents juggling the heavy loads outlined throughout this and preceding chapters. It can be vital when the informal networks upon which so many lone parents rely cannot be called on for various reasons, including short notice or geographical distance. Others for example describe nurseries agreeing to keep sick children for several hours despite protocol, until their lone parent is able to collect them, when there is no one else to do so.

Also highlighted as contributing to childcare satisfaction is reasonable, affordable cost, although in the context of the study as a whole, dissatisfaction with high childcare costs emerged as a far more significant theme, as discussed earlier in this chapter. Demographic factors are significant in informing level of satisfaction with childcare arrangements; while satisfaction with childcare is expressed by lone mothers with babies through to much older children, those with preschool children are generally happier with childcare arrangements than those with school-age children. As highlighted previously, this may point to the more frequent establishment of comprehensive childcare cover for children who are not yet at school. Perhaps unsurprisingly, childcare satisfaction is expressed by half of lone-parent students with only one child, compared to a third of those with two or more children. This can be seen as indicative of the inevitable increased burden of additional children as discussed earlier in this chapter.

Of further significance, no lone-parent students also in full-time employment reported being satisfied with their childcare arrangements, compared to half of those in part-time work and two-thirds of those who were unemployed. This relative decline in childcare satisfaction according to level of paid work indicates a strong correlation between commitment-burden and the potential of childcare availability to satisfactorily meet needs.

This and the previous two chapters have introduced the three major interrelated areas of constraint centrally informing lone mothers' negotiation of university learning. The following chapter utilises these insights to explore in further depth how we can come to understand the holistic experience of this group's HE participation.

CHAPTER SEVEN

Understanding lone parents' experiences in Higher Education

Lone-mother HE students' lives in a wider context – the effects of family responsibilities on participation

It has been argued that the focus of educational policy frequently implies that education exists in a vacuum, independent of the rest of society, including family life (Leonard, 1994: 164). Institutional failure to sanction, or even acknowledge, the impact of wider life upon educational participation affects all students, but perhaps most of all those with primary care responsibility for dependants. This is identified by Merrill in her work on HE participation by mature students:

> *The mature student experience has to be placed within the wider context of their biographies. A study confined to participants' educational career at university would offer only a partial insight into the 'mature student experience' because 'as a student the impact of being a mother, wife and possibly employee [can]not be ignored.'*
> (Merrill, 1999: 204)

Previous chapters in this book have introduced the impact of key areas of life experience upon lone mothers' educational participation; this chapter locates lone mothers' HE learner experiences in the wider context of important features of their everyday lives. Having focused on effects of the intertwined yet distinct issues of access to time, money, and

147

childcare upon HE participation; the insights provided by lone-parent learners into their lives are brought together here to contribute to a more holistic understanding of how such HE students manage to fit together their two worlds of family and university, and the ensuing development of their identities as learners. In doing so, the chapter considers both positive and negative aspects of this developmental journey, and factors contributing to these.

The cumulative effects of being a parent impact strongly on individuals' ability to participate fully in the experience of being an HE learner; for lone parents, sole responsibility for these commitments magnifies this impact. While 'mature students' are frequently lumped together as a catch-all category of all those aged over 21, findings suggest that the lives of mature students aged 30–39 are dominated by responsibility for caring for their families, compared to younger mature students (Woodley and Wilson, 2002: 345). Pointing toward the strong impact of such responsibilities, in research with Access students, Reay found all of those who managed to complete their courses in one or two years not to have children, while those with primary care responsibility for children had all taken three to six years to complete their studies (2003: 303).

Beyond constraints placed by family responsibilities upon ability to participate in Higher Education at all, such commitments are evidenced for lone mothers to engender geographical constraints over which university is attended, corroborating existing research on mature students (Yorke, 2004: 106; Gallagher *et al.*, 1993: 36). Family commitments can frequently result in individuals finding themselves operating within narrow choices of HE Institution, sometimes effectively distilled to 'a choice of one' (Reay, 2003: 307). As such, lone-mother HE students can be seen as occupying a disadvantaged position in the 'education market place' (Zepke, 2005: 169). Lone mothers' narratives document the factors informing such constrained geographical mobility, including unwillingness to uproot families from homes, schools, non-resident parents and wider support networks. The perspectives of lone-parent students who do leave such networks behind to take up HE places, provide insight into negative ramifications. Problems centre on loss of support, as would be expected. This is one respect in which findings do point to the salience of social class, given indication by lone mothers identifying as working class that they would not consider relocating to attend university, while this was not identified as significant by any self-identified middle-class participants. This fits with the finding that lone mothers identifying as working class were four times as likely as their middle-class counterparts to report receiving support from extended family. While some argue that the increased importance in working-class families of extended family support, documented by Young and Willmott in their classic sociological study of *Family and Kinship in East London* (1957), has lost relevance in the context of increasing geographical mobility, reported social class differences in the role of such support by lone mothers in this research points toward its continuing relevance.

A further feature of geographical constraint emerges in the stories of lone mothers who choose not to uproot their families, but instead undertake gruelling travel arrangements to attend their nearest HE Institution as what Christie *et al.* term 'day students' (2005). While used by Christie *et al.* to denote students who attend university daily rather than living in university accommodation, 'day students' also pithily captures the experience of lone-parent students, who fulfil the role of HE learner by day, but must often cast it off upon leaving university in the evening to focus their attention on being care-giving parents. The difficulties for lone-parent students, as mature students more broadly, in relocating or travelling to access their nearest HE Institution or appropriate course, substantiate concerns as to the barriers facing such non-traditional students in making the transition from locally available FE colleges to one of the smaller number of (perhaps less) local HE Institutions, bolstering calls for increasing franchising of HE courses to FE colleges (Wisker, 1996: 4). Acknowledgement from the Equality Challenge Unit (2007) that part-time students continue to be prevented from fulfilling their aspirations by a lack of HE courses available in the evenings and sufficiently locally, indicates that this problem remains insufficiently addressed. The unequal spread of university place offers in a marketised HE sector that sees the most valued young, privileged applicants offered places at a number of institutions, while less valued non-traditional applicants may be lucky to receive a single offer of a place, exacerbate the problems of limited geographical mobility already faced by mature learners, and particularly lone parents.

Government emphasis on the need for evening and weekend courses to meet the needs of older students who need to balance work, study and family has been criticised by the Open University. Pro Vice-Chancellor, David Vincent has suggested that such an outdated solution has been replaced by the opportunities afforded by Internet and DVD-based learning (Shepherd, 2007). In the context of rapidly democratising affordability and access to PC hardware and the Web, for many non-traditional HE learners, including lone-parent students, such ICT-mediated distance learning provision may indeed offer increased accessibility compared to out-of-hours face-to-face provision, with its accompanying requirement for out-of-hours childcare, already documented as being so problematic for lone parents. The volume of lone-parent students who contacted the research website for this study evidenced the groups' high level of online activity, supporting the relevance of online engagement for facilitating lone parents' HE participation.

Fitting together different worlds

Much existing commentary on the fitting together of the worlds of family and university presumes a gendering of experience based on the premise that it is women who care for children. For example, research has suggested that returning to study frequently engenders a radical change in way of life for women with families, entailing stresses that men do not experience (Edwards, 1993: 9); that male PhD students do not see domestic aspects of their lives as relevant to their studies, while women make connections (Wisker, 1996: 6); and that the perceived incompatibility of educational participation with parenthood results in more educated women delaying childbearing and being most likely to remain childless (Sobotka, 2006: 183). In this latter respect, students with dependent children, including lone-parent students, represent something of an anomaly in seeking to reconcile and simultaneously straddle these two perceptibly incompatible worlds. Just as concurrence between this research and existing literature on mature women students illuminates the prevalence of many facets of shared experience between lone and partnered mothers engaged in HE learning, it is similarly important to acknowledge that in the context of changing ideals of fathers' participation in childrearing, many partnered student fathers may also be increasingly affected by the impact of their domestic childcare responsibilities on ability to participate in HE learning within outmoded traditional expectations of unfettered commitment. Identification of such shared facets of experience explicates the broader relevance to all students with care responsibilities of the gendered contention that, despite more than equal numbers of women in Higher Education and a host of equal opportunities policies, universities continue to fail women by expecting them to fit into a male academic mode (Jackson, 2004: xi).

It is argued that 'whilst the main problem facing school leaver students is *fitting into* university, mature students' chief difficulty is *fitting* university *in*, given their higher life loads' (Scott *et al.*, 1996: 235). Lone mothers' reflections show them to be only too aware of their deviation from an assumed model of ideal studentship. Frequently sure of their potential to do more than well if only they could devote all of time to studies, such learners are often mobilised by determination to prove themselves as good as younger students.

Evidence nevertheless demonstrates the ongoing demands of juggling the commitments of two apparently opposing worlds of family and university to remain definitive of HE experience for lone–parent learners. Edwards has asked of mature women learners:

> How do women, crossing the boundaries between the spheres as they
> have always done, deal with such ideological tensions between the
> two? Do they build connections and interdependencies between . . .
> education and family in such a way as these are not separate – as
> their feminine psyches would seem to lead them to do? Or do
> they keep a strict boundary between the two, as the public/private
> dichotomy would have it, not letting public world demands affect their
> family life? (1993: 30)

Such questions around how to manage the reconciliation of home and university are evident in the trajectories of lone mothers, for whom the tensions can result in being left with the feeling of a life split in two between being a student and a parent, or of effectively being forced to deny parts of their lives in order to participate in university, as Jackson has also found with regard to mature women students generally (2004: 45). Individuals describe symbolically marking the division between the two divergent worlds of their experience through external indicators, including dressing differently for home and university (also Leonard, 1994). The dichotomy between the masculinised public sphere and feminised private realm of the home is central to understanding the relationship between university and family in the lives of mature learners including lone parents. It is suggested that while women carry their private identities and concerns into the public world of paid work (and university), both men and women perceive a gulf between these two worlds that should be kept that way, with public world identities and concerns to be kept out of the home as much as possible and home being maintained as a private haven (Edwards, 1993: 32). The mutually conditioning causation between the two ideologically separated domains has however been extensively documented by feminist commentators (Wisker, 1996: 6). This includes the assertion that the ideological division between the public and private spheres is in fact a false one, as argued by Hannah Arendt (1958). Indeed, as Wisker has argued:

> *Apart from the middle-classes, women have always had a split day and world between home and work, and overemphasizing the public/ private dichotomy can operate against them to produce a rhetoric of inability as well as one of inequality.* (1996: 6)

Lone-mother HE students' narratives illustrate however that the physical meeting of university and family life can feel strange, with individuals sometimes reporting extreme strategies to keep the two worlds from clashing, like writing essays in the car park or in the middle of the night (see Wisker, 1996: 8). For those juggling childrearing with studentship, the reality is often that at home the family does not care about the new ideas igniting a learners' interest at university, where tutors and fellow students are similarly uninterested in stories about the children at home. Individuals must thus censor themselves to avoid breaching the boundaries by ensuring that their talk about their experiences does not stray across into the wrong context (see Edwards, 1993: 74).

In terms of potential for reconciling these two distinct yet central facets of experience, some individuals perceive making time for study as taking time for themselves, and hence taking away from others, so that studying at home means not being available to family, and family and university must therefore ideally be kept separate. However, for others who perceive the two spheres as more interconnected, time at home studying does not seem so much like time taken from families (Edwards, 1993). Far from the dual burden of responsibilities representing the educational disadvantage it is often assumed to be, Wisker has advocated the benefits to learning of connecting personal and academic lives:

> *The knitting of experience and academic disciplines and the knitting of life and study are essential in many . . . students' lives. The*

cohesion and coherence of the two helps produce a framework for learning and development. (1996: 14, 43)

Although the ideal of interweaving study and family life may sound desirable, the practice can be stressful. Evidence suggests that, despite their best efforts, individuals can frequently be left feeling deficient in meeting either set of requirements, and rarely feeling 'on top of' studies. It is suggested that for many students with family responsibilities, both their studies and their families are always in their thoughts, it being impossible to keep domestic life out of the academic environment, with responsibilities like shopping to do, children's pick-up times, and whether children are happy with their childcarer, always on parents' minds (Edwards, 1993: 68). It is similarly difficult for such students to cut back on the demands made by their university, as essays must be handed in and exams sat at particular times. Lone mothers' narratives demonstrate that such cutting back is nevertheless frequently unavoidable in times of crisis, regardless of the stress or consequences. The net result is that, whether they prioritise family or study, learners with primary childcare responsibilities are often left feeling uncomfortable. They want to fulfil everything as both areas of commitment are so important, but this appears impossible to achieve no matter how hard they try.

The stress of managing studentship with family life can, unsurprisingly, impact detrimentally on retention, and some lone mothers in this research reported leaving courses prematurely due to the constraints of juggling study with parenting alone. Students' lives outside university are evidenced to be a key reason for students leaving HE courses prematurely, with part-time students showing a greater propensity than their full-time peers to be affected by extra-institutional matters. Relevant factors include problems coordinating childcare arrangements, lengthy travelling times to tutorials, and lack of institutional flexibility over attendance, resulting in damage to relationships with family and partner (Yorke and Longden, 2004). Recurring themes in this research indicate the salience of all of these factors in the lives of lone-parent students. Level of attendance and hours of study are shown to be central to academic success (Laing *et al.*, 2005: 172–173). This too is relevant to lone-parent students, for whom parenting demands frequently compromise ability to fulfil university expectations of attendance and private study, regardless of best efforts.

Institutional and individual staff support

A key area informing lone parents' experiences in Higher Education is the level of support they experience from their HE Institution, as discussed in Chapter 6 in relation to childcare provision. The sympathy and flexibility of HE Institution policies and practices are evidenced to centrally inform lone mothers' broader ability to successfully integrate HE learning into the framework of wider lives and responsibilities, as the following indicates:

> *I think my experience has been made by the people I have met and the uni I go to being so accommodating.* (Charlie, age 29, two children aged 8 and 9, Year 2 BA Developmental Psychology)

This resonates with findings identifying support from academic staff as pivotal to HE completion by mature women students with children (Scott *et al.*, 1996, 233). In particular, relationships with personal tutors have been found to be centrally important in providing instrumental, informational and appraisive support (Wilcox *et al.*, 2005: 707), playing a central role in students' decisions over whether to continue with HE courses (2005: 716).

Over three-quarters of lone mothers who discussed their HE Institution's perceived attitude to lone-parent students experienced this as being negative. This included overtly negative attitudes, alongside reports of institutions offering no special interest or treatment to lone parents. Reports of institutional cultures of negative attitudes toward lone mothers are more frequently attributed to more prestigious traditional universities, exemplified by the following:

> *[My university] does have a student bursary fund for childcare. However, it is administered individually by the colleges and some do not participate. The amounts available rarely exceed around £1,000 for an academic year, which is obviously nowhere near enough. The attitude of the university is summed up in the recent article in [the university's] magazine where a senior staff member specifically commented that funds for student childcare was not money well spent and that those with children should consider options other than [this university].* (Beth, age 33, one child aged 8, Year 2 PhD Archaeology)

In contrast to the pervasiveness of perceived negative institutional attitudes to lone-parent students, more than 85 per cent of all lone-parent students researched described experiences of feeling supported at their HE Institution, compared to just over half describing experiences of feeling unsupported. This reflects that many lone mothers' positive experiences of feeling supported at their university come from individual staff, while overall institutional cultures are frequently experienced as negative. Discrepancies between numbers of lone-parent students describing feeling both supported and unsupported by experiences at their university reflect the presence of change over time informed by the longitudinal research design, and that the same individuals encountered experiences at university of feeling both supported and unsupported.

Significantly, all but one of the distance learners researched described feeling supported by their university, compared to four-fifths of those studying on traditional contact courses. Corroborating this trend, just under a quarter of distance learners complained of feeling unsupported by their HE Institution, compared to almost half of those studying on traditional contact courses. These trends exemplify a documented increased willingness amongst HE Institutions delivering provision part time and distance learning to acknowledge the needs of the mature student demographic who form the bulk of their clientele (Woodley and Wilson, 2002: 330). Research shows that for mature students, considerations of being tied to a geographic locality, family and employment responsibilities, and limited financial means are often motivations for part-time over full-time study (Brennan et al., 1999: 13–14). The validation of mature students' experiences by such part-time and distance learning providers catering to their needs, contrasts with more traditional HE Institutions that continue to value the ideal of the young student free from the constraints of external responsibilities. That learners perceive the benefits of a more 'student focused' approach amongst HE Institutions oriented to serving the needs of mature, part-time and distance learners has been indicated by students on a large scale through National Student Survey (NSS) results (Unistats, 2011). The Open University, with its high proportion of mature students attracted by focus on part-time distance learning, with online teaching delivery and out-of-hours contact timetabling, has consistently achieved NSS overall student satisfaction scores, placing it in the top three institutions since the survey began in 2005 (OU Senate, 2010). Similarly, Birkbeck College, nearly all of whose students are part time, has formerly been ranked top in the country (Shepherd, 2007). The Open University's Vice-Chancellor has attributed this success to pursuing a student-focused approach and 'constant focus' on student support, assessment and feedback, as well as peer mentoring and small class sizes facilitating personal interaction between staff and students (Lipsett, 2007a).

Beyond this key difference in student experiences of HEI support between distance learning and traditional contact students, this research identified little difference in satisfaction with support according to other factors – including, for example, social class, the age of lone parents and their children, number of children, employment status, or full-time or part-time study. Lone parents with only one child, those with only school-age children and those who are not in employment are marginally more likely than their counterparts to indicate satisfaction with the support they receive from their university, perhaps reflecting their less challenging circumstances.

A recurring theme in terms of what kinds of support from universities helps most is the willingness of individual staff to bend rules and make special concessions in recognition of lone parents' extraordinary circumstances, as Carys explained:

> *The administrative staff in my department are always very helpful.*
> *For example, they always get me a special parking permit which*
> *PhD students are not normally entitled to. This is because I have to*
> *leave my daughter at nursery in another part of town and then come*
> *in to university to teach at 9 in the morning.* (Carys, age 31, one
> child aged 1, Year 2 PhD Sociology)

Frequently described examples of such rule bending include: allowing students accompanied by small children to queue jump registration; and providing advance access to timetables; and first choice of seminar times. Lone mothers additionally describe appreciating being permitted to: sign up to seminar groups via email rather than in person; leave lectures and seminars early to get to childcare providers on time; and submit assignments late when circumstances beyond their control prevent them from completing them on time. Further concessions include allowing mobile phones to be kept on in lectures in case of emergency, and students leaving seminars to return calls from childcare providers, as explained by Carla:

*All the staff seem very understanding and helpful, e.g. it's site policy
that mobiles are switched off inside the building. However, after
asking what emergency contact number I could give my nursery, the
teaching staff have agreed I can leave my mobile on as long as it is on
silent, so I have my phone on vibrate, and I have spoken to nursery
and they are going to text me rather than ring if anything is wrong.*
(Carla, two children including one aged 1 year, Degree Year 1)

The positivity of students' experiences juggling Higher Education with
lone parenthood often depend pivotally on the individual staff they
encounter, with a recurring theme being that supportive staff can often
act unofficially as mentors toward lone-parent students. One lone parent
described her HE Institution, as a culture of 'female members of staff
who want their female students to do well', further describing that:

*I was introduced to my personal tutor very early on and I was
fortunate in that she was/is a lesbian who is on a mission of making
sure all women are treated at least equally and who also bent over
backwards to make sure I was ok and not having any problems with
the male teaching staff!! Seriously, she was a Godsend as she still
remarks today on how I used to sit in lecture halls looking like I was
thinking that I didn't belong there – and I was! She was a huge help
to me, she was the approachable wise owl that I knew I could count on.*
(Gloria, age 39, three children aged 12–17, PG Diploma HE)

Evidence of such female support does not, however, mean that female
staff are uniformly found to be more supportive than their male
counterparts. Lone mothers also describe encountering supportive male
staff and unsupportive women at university. Regardless of the gender of
staff, the key to their level of sympathy for the circumstances of lone-
parent students is often seen as being whether they have sufficient shared
experience to empathise with the challenges their students face, as the
following perspectives indicate:

*I do not have great words to say about [my] university. Some lecturers
are great and some are not so great! I feel that single parents are
looked upon as a burden. Some of them do not realise how difficult
it is to study and to be a single parent and chose to ignore our needs.*
(Greta, two children)

> *My lecturer has been understanding as he has two young children as*
> *well, so I'll say that I think that he has been lenient towards me, but*
> *has been very harsh on other students.* (Maria, two children, Year 2
> BA History and Archaeology)

Lone mothers studying toward postgraduate research degrees berate
supervisors for lack of contact and failure to read work promptly. For
undergraduate and postgraduate students studying on taught courses, the
previously discussed timetable issues of late availability and out-of-hours
scheduling are central to informing lone-parent students' assessment
of the degree of supportiveness offered by their HE Institution. The
difficulties caused by timetable issues can be exacerbated by negative
staff attitudes toward flexibility, with unwillingness to reassign students
to more manageable lecture and seminar times:

> *I spoke to all my tutors about this before and they were all really*
> *helpful, except one, who said that if I wasn't prepared to come to*
> *all the lectures then I shouldn't take that course. This was despite*
> *me explaining that it was due to no one to look after my daughter.*
> (Andrea, age 23, one child aged 1, Year 2 BA Development
> Studies)

As observed in Chapter 4 in relation to lone-parent students'
experiences of juggling their stretched time, frequently perceived failure
of universities' institutional cultures to acknowledge the significance
of students' care responsibilities for their educational engagement, and
HE Institutions' responsibility to mediate this, emerge more broadly as
problematic. Findings consistently iterate that consideration needs to be
given to making university life more family-friendly. Yet lone-mother
students repeatedly describe university staff as conveying explicitly or
implicitly that the needs of student parents are not a consideration, and
that such students' inability to meet set conditions is the problem of the
individual and not the institution. Lone mothers describe encountering
contradictory attitudes from some HE staff, that while students may be
congratulated for successfully negotiating their multiple commitments,
concessions will not be made, as summarised by Bex:

> *I think there is a strange attitude that combines a 'well done' attitude*
> *with a 'but don't think we will make any allowances because you*

knew what you were taking on' attitude. (Bex, age 34, one child aged 12, MA Primary Education with QTS).

Recognition by some university staff of the increased self-discipline and commitment to studies required for lone-parent students to succeed in Higher Education can have further positive consequences for some, as Cheryl explained:

I have now worked on two research projects through the summers and this will look very good on my CV. I am sure I was given this opportunity because I am older and demonstrate commitment. (Cheryl, age 31, one child aged 4)

While the majority of lone mothers researched indicated feeling supported by staff at their university in the challenges they faced negotiating Higher Education, it is significant that the support participants describe disproportionately focuses on informal support received by individual members of staff, rather than on family-friendly institutional policies. This iterates findings pertaining to childcare highlighted in the previous chapter, as to the problematic extent to which vulnerable widening-participation students appear subject to the whim of individual tutors' benevolence. While the majority of tutors may respond favourably to lone-parent learners' needs, the danger of being confronted by those representing the unsympathetic minority continues to threaten to undermine the fragile load such learners juggle. Lone mothers' narratives in this research corroborate Gallagher *et al.*'s charge that the lack of support encountered by students with children from some staff is 'alarming' (1996: 251). In this research lone mothers drew on their negative experiences to recommend that staff, including personal tutors and student services personnel, should be more supportive, respond to emails more promptly, and not break appointments. While a sympathetic response from individual HEI staff can radically ease lone-parent students' troubles, its discretionary nature can also inevitably leave students feeling that key determinants of their experience are at the whim of individuals. This indicates the need for a distinction between informal and formalised support from universities, with emphasis on building supportive principles into formal structures. In the interests of students and sympathetic staff alike, the warning that 'it is often the case that the pastoral aspect of tutoring tends to be left to the same few staff who feel they can cope with it' (Gallagher *et al.*, 1993: 59), is important in highlighting the inadequacy of relying on individual good practice. To rely on individual staff to support vulnerable students merely adds to the workload of already overburdened staff in feminised pastoral support and teaching-heavy roles carrying relatively low pay and status. Students thus 'rely on the goodwill rather than duty of universities to enable them to meet their study obligations when . . . "problems" arise' (Cappleman-Morgan, 2005: 9). Hence it is impossible to guarantee the level of support that students will receive from staff, instead relying on individual temperaments, and exonerating from responsibility those staff who favour the 'Bachelor Boy' ideal of university participation.

Transition to university

It has been suggested that for women with families, returning to study means a radical change in way of life entailing particular stresses that men do not experience (Edwards, 1993: 9). Managing the transition to becoming a university student emerges as a key theme for lone-mother HE students, highlighted as significant by almost half. Individuals describe feeling 'apprehensive, 'disorientated', 'frightened' and 'scared', but also 'excited' by their initial experiences of university life. The most commonly reported basis for the negative feelings is being unprepared for the workload and finding life 'hectic'.

Those who had recently attended FE college as a route back into Higher Education reported that this had prepared them well and minimised transitional problems. Reports by some participants that they owed their HE engagement to the availability of Access routes, chimes with findings that without the support of Access tutors, mature learners often feel that they would not have had the confidence to apply to university (Leonard, 1994: 168). There is often a view in Higher Education that mature students coming through Access courses are frequently better prepared for university life, including academic expectations around, for example, self-directed study, seminar presentations, and essay structuring and referencing, compared to traditional A-level entry students. While this may well be the case, it provides a deceptively incomplete picture. Mature Access route students who have had a long educational gap, whose previous educational experience may well therefore have been very different, and who both this research and existing literature have demonstrated may lack confidence and feel isolated, embark upon university life with specific needs for managing the transition successfully. Lone parents often relay that they would have liked more help with the transition from FE to HE, validating recommendations for preparatory modules to assist students in successfully making this step (Knox, 2005: 103).

Those citing problems adjusting often see educational gaps as a contributing factor, and the unfamiliar 'unstructured' and self-directed study regime compared to school or college can pose a further transitional challenge. Routines requiring moving between paid work and study or study and work placements for university courses pose a challenge as lack of repetition can make it difficult to 'settle in' to a pattern. Long university holidays contribute to the feeling of inconsistent routines. The key theme in terms of settling into new routines for university student life for lone mothers is childcare. It is important that while lone mothers are adjusting to new routines as HE learners, their children are undergoing the same process as they settle into new childcare arrangements, which they are sometimes not necessarily happy with, as well as being woken earlier in the mornings to fit in with their mother's new schedule.

The transitional phase of becoming a learner 'is not a straightforward one of simply shedding old identities and donning unproblematic new ones, but is instead a period of reflexivity and risk, confusion and contradiction' (Brine and Waller, 2004: 97). Chapter 5 highlighted the financial 'risk' that HE participation can represent for non-traditional students including lone parents. The potential risks however extend beyond monetary resources. Alongside economic and material risk sit risk to personal relationships and class identity, and the risk of academic failure. Lone parents' narratives evidence that HE engagement may involve risking existing housing arrangements, support networks, friendships and paid work, in pursuit of a long-term goal that may not come to fruition and repay the hoped-for dividends. Brine and Waller suggest that 'twin images of opportunity and risk shimmer, like a hologram, constantly changing through the process of reflexivity, as identities of the self are framed, contested and reframed' (2004: 103). Individuals must carry out a self-reflective assessment of the balance between risk and opportunity, treading a tightrope between the two. Brine and Waller further suggest that to not return to education would have 'enabled the [student] to believe that [they] *could* have succeeded, but to try it and fail is far more damaging [emphasis in original]' (2004:

103, 105). Mature students are indicated to have an increased fear of academic failure compared to their younger peers, partly because of the high-risk investment required of them and partly because of poor previous learner identity. The significance of development of a learner identity is discussed in detail later in this chapter.

One lone parent's reflection in this research:

> *The transition from college to uni was both exciting (no one in my family had ever been to uni before) and completely terrifying.* (Gloria, age 39, three children aged 12–17, PG Diploma HE)

illustrates the 'risky business' that HE engagement can be for mature students who shoulder sole responsibility for their children's well-being, and have no bank of previous family experience of university from which to draw belief in its plausibility. Although this research did not reach back to catalogue FE learner pathways, testimonies provided by lone mothers as to chance factors informing their enrolment in university, and the educational trajectories of their peers and families, resonate with findings that many mature students with family responsibilities ultimately 'fail' to make the transition from Further Education to Higher Education because they perceive the associated risks to be too great (Reay, 2003: 303, 306, 312).

This research discerned no impact of age, or length of time out of education upon lone-mother HE learner's apprehensions and experiences around the transition to becoming a university student. Those in their early 20s appear as likely as their peers several decades older to perceive their distance and isolation from traditional entry-age students. The following reflection encapsulates several key transitional themes:

> *The transition back into education was a bit tricky, not just because of being a single mum, but because I had been out of education for about four years. It took a while to get used to it again and to the fact that so much of the work has to come off your own back! Not like school at all!* (Andrea, age 23, one child aged 1, Year 2 BA Development Studies)

Regardless of whether they had been out of education for one year or 20, the process of adjusting to university life was most marked for those studying on traditional contact courses, who were three times as likely to discuss the impact of their transition to university compared to distance learners. Similarly, full-time students are significantly more likely than part-time students to identify an impact of HE engagement upon their daily lives, discussing settling into new routines that can pose challenges – particularly in terms of (lack of) time. The few comments made by part-time students around the impact of university participation upon daily life were predominantly positive. These differences are arguably to be expected given the increased impact of physically attending university in terms of altering everyday life. What those studying by traditional contact had to say about their transitions and initial acclimatisation to university life was overwhelmingly positive. This contrasted with the trend in the smaller number of described experiences of the transition to university made by distance learners. The latter group predominantly reported either that there had been no significant transition to university or that it had been negative in some way. Those distance learners who did describe embarking on Higher Education as being a transitional experience discussed it in terms of adding a further commitment to the juggling equation or returning to education after a long gap, rather than having feelings about the university or course itself.

There was no discernible pattern in how frequently and positively lone mothers described their transition to university according to full-time, part-time or unemployed work status. In each group, there was a spread of participants reporting ease, difficulty, excitement, apprehension, or no tenable transition at all. Charting the transition to university was also one of the few areas in which self-identified social class background appeared to impact saliently upon experience. Participants identifying as working class were twice as likely as those identifying as middle class to discuss their transition to university. However, there was no discernible variation in the experience of transition to university reported by different social classes. In each social class group, those who discussed transition to university were divided in terms of whether they found it easier than they had expected, or reported negative reactions, including that they initially found university 'frightening', 'hard', 'tricky' or 'a shock'. The salient point, then, is that individuals from working-class backgrounds were significantly more likely to perceive the move to university as representing a 'transitional' moment in life worthy of noting in discussion, whether this was fundamentally positive or negative.

Lone mothers' narratives illuminate the extent to which changing routines engendered by the transition to university are experienced as challenging, not only for research participants, but also for their children, particularly where preschool children were involved. While there is no discernible difference in patterns of how easy and positive participants find the transition to university depending on how many children they have, significantly, a pattern does emerge for those with preschool children, for whom reflections on their experience of the transition to university are predominantly negative. This experience of university frequently contrasts sharply with an initial attitude to university of excitement. Heather explained the stresses of adjusting to university life as a lone mother of a still relatively young baby:

> *I think overall [my son] adapted better to the new routine than I did. I was completely exhausted in the first week and overwhelmed with the change from motherhood to student. It was a bit of a culture shock and sometimes I wonder if I'm doing the right thing. As [my son] is in full-time childcare I really don't see him that much and the weekends can be dominated by chores.* (Heather, age 30, one baby, Year 2 BA Urban Studies and Planning)

Additional barriers: health, illness and disability

Beyond the responsibilities of caring for very young children, a further salient factor compromising lone mothers' abilities to engage fully with their HE studies is the poor health or disability of themselves or their children. Health issues emerge as a major source of worry, with half describing their own or their family's health problems. Lone mothers' experiences as HE learners document two-way causation between ill health and inability to manage university studies, with the stresses of managing university as a lone parent causing illness, as well as vice versa. Health problems and disabilities are more prevalent amongst both mature students and lone parents, compared to the traditional entry-age student population. The impact of ill-health and disabilities upon lone-parent students' ability to successfully manage university participation that is indicated by lone mothers' narratives, is problematic in terms of the individualising of shortcomings for which institutions have responsibility in facilitating access and support, particularly for widening participation students. The paradigm of individual responsibility for learning experiences (Bostock, 1998: 226) enables HE Institutions to blame mature learners, and students with SEN or disabilities for 'failing' to successfully manage Higher Education (Jackson, 2004; Quinn and Allen, 2010), when more onus should fall upon HE Institutions to facilitate participation. This resonates with insights from the social model of disability, with its emphasis on the responsibility of institutions to remove physical, social and cultural barriers in order to create environments that facilitate participation by diverse individuals, rather than problematising the perceived failings of individuals who deviate from narrow expectations of 'normal' participation (Oliver, 1996; Shakespeare and Watson, 2002; Barnes and Mercer, 2009).

In addition to the mutual causation between study stress and health, some individuals indicate perceiving their circumstances as lone parents to have a detrimental health impact, as exemplified by Zeena:

> *I think the sheer physical effort of going it alone (running a home, kids, work) can wear you down physically.* (Zeena, age 36, two children aged 14 and 16, Year 2 PGCE Secondary)

Attempting to juggle insufficient time and money is frequently reported to impact detrimentally on lone mothers' health, with individuals frequently describing lacking the time and money to look after their own health by cooking nutritious meals, although many discuss the importance of feeding their children well. Another related theme is those feeling their health to be compromised because lack of financial resources, time or childcare prevents them from exercising as much as they would like to. These orderings of priorities illustrate the frequent relegation of care of the self to the bottom of the priority list resorted to as a means to managing irreconcilable deficits of resources (as discussed in Chapter 4). In terms of their own health, lone mothers' priority is frequently restricted to worrying about what would happen to their children if anything serious happened and they were not able to care for their children independently. For some, this vulnerability was realised, forcing them to call on various combinations of friends, family and formal social service provision. One lone mother described refusing reconstructive surgery after breast cancer because she felt that as a lone parent she could not justify what she perceived as the unnecessary risk to her life of a non-essential surgical procedure.

Children's health and behavioural problems are indicated to pose significant hindrances to their lone parents' HE participation. Those with school-age children are more likely to describe health problems, including their own disabilities, compared to those with preschool children. This may indicate the combination of health problems and responsibility for younger children to have a prohibitive effect upon educational participation. Alongside the inconvenience of normal childhood illness, keeping lone parents away from studies and paid work, individuals often describe how more serious physical or mental illness amongst dependent or adult children, ageing parents, siblings and ex-partners can temporarily replace other priorities, including fulfilling study commitments.

Almost a quarter of lone mothers researched described the impact of their own or their children's SEN, disability or long-term illness. Several suffered from more than one serious medical condition, or had more than one person in the household suffering from serious conditions. The most frequently discussed and less debilitating conditions reported amongst lone-parent students and their children included hyperactivity, dyslexia, dyspraxia, dyscalculia and attention deficit hyperactivity disorder (ADHD). These are less likely to be reported as impacting detrimentally on ability to study, particularly where families have been able to secure adequate support from local authorities. In contrast, more serious conditions are understandably far more likely to impact seriously upon individuals' ability to manage their heavy responsibilities as lone parents, students, and frequently also employees. The following illustrates the direct impact of managing children's disability upon lone parents' ability to participate fully in university studies:

> *As I am a lone parent and also have an autistic son who is 11 I have never attended any tutorials, etc., with the OU.* (Ruth, age 47, two children aged 9 and 12, Year 3 BA Social Policy and Criminology)

Among the more serious reported health conditions impacting negatively upon educational engagement included children with Down's syndrome, and lone parents with arthritis, chronic fatigue syndrome (CFS), fibromyalgia, mobility problems due to the legacy of previous injuries, and multiple sclerosis (MS), one sufferer of which had become dependent upon a wheelchair for daily life.

Lone-parent students with chronic disease or disability in the family are more likely to study in Higher Education via distance or part-time learning pathways, pointing to the additional constraints that ill-health can place upon participation. The documented lack of suitable and affordable childcare provision for disabled children is also relevant to facilitating participation in education as well as paid work for the parents of disabled children. Persistent difficulties accessing adequate support from local authorities emerge as a recurring theme amongst families with particular needs stemming from disability or chronic illness. One lone-parent student who had chronic MS, and who also worked as a Disability Employment Adviser, was able to provide a professional perspective on some of the difficulties and discrimination faced by individuals, alongside her personal experience:

> *Having a disability and having faced redundancy means reshaping.*
> *My part-time work now as a disability employment adviser brings*
> *me into contact with a range of clients, some women with children*
> *also having to re-skill. It seems a common pattern, and disabled*
> *adults face particularly hard barriers in accessing selection for posts.*
> (Veronica, age 41, one child aged 10, Year 2 PG Diploma
> Management Studies)

Alongside the documented constraints placed on participation in HE learning and paid work by illness and disability, lone-parent students additionally describe the negative impact of their own or their children's disabilities or ill health constituting an additional barrier to social contact. As Veronica explained: 'the MS is the major block to getting out and about, particularly in the evenings, i.e. meeting or socialising, and I tend just to have very occasional dinners with friends here'. While socialising may seem a less serious activity to be impeded by illness or disability compared to access to work or education, lack of social contact can have a serious detrimental effect on health and well-being, informed by the essential isolation from support of many lone parents' circumstances. This is discussed further later in this chapter.

Stress

Three-quarters of lone mothers researched described the stress, pressure, nerves, anxiety or worry they experienced juggling HE participation with other commitments as a lone parent. The diverse sources of stress described were largely peripheral to the process of HE studentship itself, and yet greatly inform individuals' ability to give adequate attention to studies. Prominent sources of stress include: ill health; debts; estranged family relationships; worries over children's educational progress; and whether to formalise relationship breakdown with divorce. The worries that preoccupy lone-parent students are often described to cumulate from a combination of concerns, as encapsulated below:

> *There has been a kind of domino effect of stress and worry in my life. It builds up and one thing inevitably has an effect on another. Issues can come together and compound the stress and worry caused by one disadvantage or another. It really is hard to pick out the main stressor.* (Ruth, age 47, two children aged 9 and 12, Year 3 BA Social Policy and Criminology)

Sources of stress and worry frequently focus on what might happen in the future rather than what is happening at the present time, as expressed below. However, despite not yet having materialised in the present, such stresses nevertheless impact in very real ways on lone-parent students' levels of health and well-being:

> *Constantly worrying about what MIGHT happen, which is what most worry is about – the unknown! There are things that need to be planned for in advance; applying for loans, arranging placements, how to fit in assignment work, keeping ahead of the need for clean underwear!!! But once I have done what I can I step back and get on with something that needs doing NOW, rather than wondering if the loan will be approved, or whether I have passed/failed an exam.* (Gillian, age 48, two children aged 13 and 15, Year 3, BA Primary Education.)

> *Will I be able to continue to afford my mortgage? How will I pay my ex-husband his share of the house when my son reaches 18? Will I end up with a shopping trolley and a doorstep as my only 'home'? (That's on really bad days!) Will I be brave enough to do something different with my life when I finish my degree?* (Samantha, age 47, one child aged 11, BA Humanities)

At the extreme end of described experiences of stress and depression, six lone mothers discussed receiving counselling (usually provided through their university), since they had become students, while three had been prescribed antidepressants, and four had experienced nervous breakdowns. Approximately one-quarter of the lone parents' researched reported suffering depression. This fits with ONS statistics that one in four British adults experiences at least one diagnosable mental health problem in any one year (Mental Health Foundation, 2011). The role of HE participation in the lives of those lone mothers reporting suffering from depression is indicated to be widely divergent. HE studentship could represent either cause or cure, as demonstrated by the following contrasting perspectives:

> *I think the main reason I'm feeling depressed a lot of the time is because I feel so isolated, from other students because I have a child and from other mums because I'm at uni all week.* (Daisy, one child, Year 4 First Degree)

and

> *Being a student is cool! It can be very hard work sometimes, and can get stressful, but it's stopped me from feeling depressed and lonely!* (Nicky, age 37, two children aged 8 and 10, BA Health and Social Care)

Loneliness and social contact

Loneliness and lack of social contact run centrally throughout lone-mother HE students' narratives, and the resulting sense of isolation can lead to unhappiness and depression. Unwelcome limitations on opportunities for social contact were discussed by over two-thirds of lone mothers researched, with this amounting to feelings of loneliness and isolation for over a quarter. Indeed, the majority of perceived problems of lone parenthood were seen to revolve around the 'aloneness', with one in six describing the problem of everything being down to them, with no one to share it with, including the following:

> *I think as single parents we do have more worries as we have to deal*

with absolutely everything on our own, from washing and shopping to ill children and the car breaking down. (Rita, age 36, four children aged 5–10, Year 2 B Ed Primary)

The following insight exemplifies how this sense of aloneness can manifest in concrete ways in the lives of lone mothers who are also struggling to manage HE participation:

My sons also have special needs: they have glue ear and have delayed speech. We have had problems with the childcare provider who did not/still does not fully appreciate their condition and they associate their behaviour as being naughty, not the fact they may not understand what is being said to them. I have been called up to the nursery on numerous occasions and they have referred my sons to the local SENco officer who has referred them to a portage service who deal with behaviour management at home and nursery, even though I have stated that there is no major issue with them at home. So initially I felt singled out as I believe that I am the only lone parent in the nursery and I felt at times bullied and pressurised by them to agree to these services as I was afraid they would ask for the boys to be removed from their care. I also have no partner or the children's father for support on these issues; therefore at times I felt vulnerable. (Tish, three-year-old twins, Year 3 BA Social Care)

These insights into the lives of lone-mother HE students build on themes around the frequent loneliness of lone parenthood (May, 2004: 396; Greif, 1992: 567), and work on mature students' distance from other students, and from social activities (Reay, 2003: 307; Leonard, 1994: 169; Edwards, 1993: 79, 96,102; Gallagher *et al.*, 1993: 33). The key recurring theme is that being prevented by family responsibilities from participating fully in the social life of university results in not being able to forge new bonds of friendship with peers, leading to feelings of isolation from other students. The following quote succinctly summarises the feelings that many lone parents studying in Higher Education describe:

As the course is so demanding I miss not being able to go out and have a drink with people. Although I love having my son, the constant pressure of having to work all day and then go home alone

170

*every night whilst others go out can get a bit much at times, it can
also mean that I feel excluded from conversations the next day.*
(Lucille, age 25, one child aged 4, PG Diploma Law)

Social integration into university life is far from a peripheral distraction
from studies; it is demonstrated to fundamentally inform students'
academic success and retention (Hussey and Smith, 2010: 159). Wilcox
et al. have suggested that inadequate attention has been devoted to
understanding the importance of making friends and developing social
lives at university in relation to successful completion, arguing that
equal emphasis should be placed on the role of successful integration
into the social world of university as the academic world. It is argued
that making friends and living arrangements are central to successful
university completion because they provide direct emotional support
equivalent to family relationships, and buffering support in stressful
situations (2005: 707). This is significant to lone parents' experiences as
university students, given that they usually live without other adults and
face substantial childcare constraints upon ability to socialise. Edwards
found the most valuable aspect of friendships that individuals had made,
or would like to make as students, to be shared understanding through
similar circumstances (1993: 96). Lone mothers' experiences relay
disappointment at university not having provided the social opportunity
they had hoped for.

While ability to access adult company is frequently severely curtailed
by lone-parent status, studying at university provides an envious window
into a sometimes illusive world of social opportunity. It is suggested
that the stereotypical idea of a student lifestyle, with its combination
of independence, dependence, leisure and academic work, is alien to
mature students, for whom being a student invariably means something
entirely different, with any sort of social life being sacrificed (Reay,
2003: 307). Contributions to this research indicate that for lone-parent
students, this contrast between ideals of studentship and their own lives
can be experienced particularly sharply, exacerbating the extent to
which individuals are left feeling like deviant tokens because of their
family responsibilities (Edwards, 1993: 102). This illustrates a theme
running throughout this research, that parallels between lone-parent
students' experiences and those of mature students more broadly,
indicate a primary difference in degree rather than in kind across many
facets of experience, with lone parents experiencing the same broad

171

predicaments, but frequently amplified by their status as sole carers.

Lone-parent students' reflections chime with existing findings indicating that mature students frequently feel acutely conscious of being older than most students, and that they often participate differently in seminars. This can lead to feelings of uneasiness between mature and other students (Leonard, 1994: 169). HE study is shown often to leave lone parents feeling more isolated than before, in sharp contrast to hopes of improved social lives. While family responsibilities can prevent mature students from engaging fully with university social life, study responsibilities can simultaneously compromise existing friendships (Edwards, 1993: 143). Lone-parent students' experiences as HE learners, however, indicate that such negative causation is only half of the story, with other lone mothers experiencing university as enhancing their social lives:

> *I've just come back from a manic weekend in London visiting me best mate [. . .] who funnily enough I met at uni. Actually thinking about it, for the purpose of your study, that has been one of the biggest bonuses [for] all the hard work – the great people I have met along the way, so it's not all bad eh?!* (Beatrice, age 31, one child aged 8, Year 3 BA Education – Primary)

This deviation from existing research on mature students with family responsibilities, in emphasising the potential of university to enrich lone parents' social lives as well as to curtail them, perhaps represents the significant absence of a partner and hence adult company at home. The impact upon social networking generally of being partnered, compared to being a lone parent, may affect students' motivation to engage with university social networks. It is perhaps unsurprising that the importance of socialising featured so strongly in lone parents' accounts. In contrast to partnered parents of dependent children, for lone parents without a partner, lack of social life can often mean lack of access to any meaningful, recreational social contact with other adults, as indicated by many:

> *I'm laughing as I feel like I've lost the art of socialising; I never socialise, hardly ever. I think I've been out with friends twice since October 2003; I find this very difficult. I miss it, but all my friends are married and move in dinner party circles, so that having no partner means I don't fit in!! So I don't get invited; if I know of*

a possible male suitor, suddenly I get invited again, but that small town mentality is draining . . . I would love to be socialising more often with a group of friends regularly, say a nice evening in the local. I'm not talking clubbing, I used to work in the music business, so I used to be out every evening in London and in America too, so being a single parent has had an enormous effect on my socialising . . . I don't want to get back to that, I would just like some nice company and conversation. (Danielle, age 33, one child aged 3, Year 3 BA History and American Studies)

Lone mothers frequently describe socialising as being restricted to the occasional work or university night out, particularly events like the Christmas 'Do'. Most social activity described focuses on meeting with extended family, and this is frequently perceived unfavourably compared to the social lives younger students are assumed to be enjoying. Traditional times of social activity, including festive periods and public holidays, are indicated to be seen as particularly lonely times for many lone parents, as children visit non-resident parents. In the context of constrained opportunities for face-to-face social contact, the opportunity provided by Internet forums and chat rooms for easily facilitating geographically dispersed virtual friendships and imagined communities of others in similar situations from the confines of one's own home, is an important resource for lone-parent students, particularly for those with limiting disabilities or ill health. This iterates the significance of online contexts in enabling social participation for lone parents, discussed earlier in this chapter in terms of the advantages of online HE learning provision.

Loneliness and access to social contact are shown to be highly contingent upon biographical characteristics, with factors including disability and geographical relocation having a particularly inhibitive effect. While no difference emerged between levels of loneliness and isolation experienced by lone-parent students of different ages, children's ages have a strong impact. Despite the increased childcare commitment associated with younger children, lone parents with older children are twice as likely as those with preschool children to describe feeling lonely and isolated. This may represent increased opportunities offered by caring for younger children, to meet other parents at parks, group activities and nursery settings. In comparison, parents who no longer escort older children to and from school, friend's houses, parks and activities may experience, alongside increased freedom, growing

173

isolation if this development takes place in the context of lack of alternative social opportunities. Alternatively, it may be that while lone parents with young children may expect substantial limits on their social lives in the immediate term, those with older children feel more disappointed with their level of social activity, given children's assumed growing independence. Similarly, only a quarter of lone parents studying via distance learning described feeling lonely compared to one-third of those on traditional contact courses. While traditional courses would be assumed to offer increased social opportunities compared to distance learning, it may be that distance-learning students' selected mode of study has furnished them with lower expectations of university participation providing them with a social life, and that they are consequently more satisfied despite sometimes experiencing relative isolation. This difference in experience may be further indicative of the level of shared experience between lone parents and the other learners they encounter on distance-learning courses. The limited social element entailed in distance learning may bring lone-parent students into contact with other learners in similar situations to themselves, compared to the sense of isolation that can be experienced as a lone parent amongst a mass of relatively responsibility-free peers. Nevertheless, some students studying by distance learning did describe feeling that their mode of study contributed to them feeling lonely and isolated.

Perhaps expectedly, an inverse relationship emerged between employment participation and feelings of loneliness and isolation, with over half of those not in employment feeling isolated, compared to considerably less than half of those in part-time employment and only one in seven of those in full-time work. This may represent increased opportunities for adult social contact provided by employment, and valued by lone parents who have no adult company at home. Similarly, unsurprisingly, lone mothers with two or more children are less likely to indicate loneliness and isolation compared to those with only one child, perhaps representing increased social contact in a larger family. Lone-parent students express that life can be lonely once children have gone to bed and there is no possibility of seeking out any further human company. Time and again it emerges as significant that lone-mother HE learners do not perceive their experiences of loneliness as resulting from a specific factor like parenthood, student or employment status, extended family relationships, or living arrangements, but rather from a deeper, underlying sense that their cumulative circumstances set

174

them apart from what they assume to be the norm. Alongside clearly observable demographic differences from other students, such feelings can be exacerbated by the approach taken by universities, as indicated by the following reflection on experience:

> *There appears to be little experience in dealing with single parents, which is a change from my undergraduate degree at [my university] (which had a lot of single parents) and I have had to search information out myself about any hardship funds or entitlements. No information was supplied at any stage of the enrolment process to my dismay. I think this has contributed to me feeling very alone on this course, although the other students and the staff are fine.* (Michelle, age 35, one child aged 12, MSc History of Science)

Unsurprisingly, lone parents describe feeling less isolated when they are able to make connections with other students who share similar circumstances with them in some way, as Stacey explained:

> *There is a high percentage of mature-students at my university, so I did not feel isolated.* (Stacey, one child, BA Sociology with Business and Management)

Another young lone mother described how she felt less isolated once she was able to obtain living accommodation for herself and her baby daughter on the university campus, explaining feeling that being able to access university accommodation as 'normal' students could, went some way toward overcoming the constraints informed by her lone-parent status.

Input from lone mothers around relocation to pursue HE journeys further illustrates the importance of perceived shared experience with others to informing experiences of loneliness or integration, as indicated by the following quote reflecting on a previous period of part-time postgraduate study after maternity leave:

> *Before going back to full-time studies I went to some mother and baby groups, but to be honest I never felt that comfortable. I always felt like an outsider, because of what I'm doing, because I don't have a partner or a husband and because of the fact that I'm not English.* (Carys, age 31, one child aged 1, Year 2 PhD Sociology)

Whether international or regional, experiences show that geographically relocating to attend university can particularly exacerbate feelings of loneliness and isolation for many lone-parent students.

The role of informal support

A key insight of lone mothers' narratives is to highlight the importance of informal support provided by extended family, partners, non-resident parents, friends and neighbours in facilitating HE participation. The significance of such support was discussed by nearly all, and emerges the single most important enabling factor for lone mothers engaging with HE study. The role of informal support networks has been discussed in Chapter 5 in relation to financial assistance, and in Chapter 6 in relation to childcare provision. In addition to childcare and financial assistance, lone mothers' informal networks provide essential moral support, even if this is given over the phone. Such support is highlighted as particularly important for lone parents, who often lack both a partner to share concerns with, and the childcare to allow them to socialise outside the home with friends or family.

Although a range of family members, including adult children, make study possible for lone parents, it is help from their own parents that is by far the most important. Time and again lone-mother HE students say that without the help and support of their parents it would not be possible for them to be at university, with the sentiments being typical of many:

> *If I hadn't have had a fantastic family to back me, I could never have completed my time at university.* (Shelby, age 32, one child aged 6, PGCE FE)

and

> *Unless you have family support as well as childcare I think it is impossible.* (Jada, age 35, one child, Nursing)

However, responses to mature students' studies from friends, family and partners can range from wholehearted support through to extreme hostility (Jarvis, 2003: 6; Wisker, 1996: 8; Leonard, 1994: 169), and this range of experiences is reflected amongst lone-parent students. That informal support is seen to be so pivotal in facilitating lone parents' HE participation has clear negative ramifications for those who are not able to call on such support, a fact that many indicated being acutely aware of:

> *I think there must be many single parents who haven't got a good support network who quit because the stress is too much or they feel guilty because what they are doing is affecting others around them.* (Francesca, age 34, four children aged 6–18, Year 1 BA History)

The importance of informal support indicates that informal networks may be plugging a gap due to inadequacies in formal support structures. Reliance on informal support networks raises specific concerns for those who relocate, leaving support networks behind in order to participate in Higher Education. This informs the recommendation that HE Institutions have a responsibility to provide more consistent and effective institutional support to students who need it, including mature learners with children, and in particular lone parents.

Having explored the key areas of hardship faced by lone parents in the immediate term as they negotiate their way through HE environments usually designed for other types of students with lives very different to their own, the remainder of this chapter now turns to examining the deeper, long-term effects that university participation has for this group.

Effects of HE participation for lone parents

Previous chapters preliminarily introduced the notion that, amongst the challenges, some lone-parent students describe experiencing benefits from the ways in which learning and family responsibilities come together in their lives in terms of apportioning time, financial resources, and childcare. Alongside the documented challenges, half of the lone mothers highlighted positive effects of their current situation as lone-parent HE students:

> *Although I may seem to have a negative view of uni, I can honestly say, so far I feel much more alive. I have been a single mum from day one, been at home with no real contact of non mums for two years, and now I feel so much happier. My mind is actually working again.*

177

I do feel that if I didn't have these feelings I would have quit the course already. (Julie, one child, Year 1)

Key perceived benefits include improved financial resources, time management skills and social lives, alongside holidays that fit with children's schooling, becoming more focused and determined, and widening horizons. While overtly flagged up as benefits of circumstances by some lone parents, these facets of experience are implicit in the accounts of nearly all.

While being a sole parent undoubtedly increases the burden of responsibilities upon an individual, Chapter 4 explored how it can also paradoxically allow more time for studies compared to being in a two-parent family, through increasing personal control over determining priorities. To this end, being a lone parent and university student is construed by some to provide a positive life balance:

I think if I had to juggle a partner and children I would struggle, as I only have to share my time with myself and my children, which, as they are both at a reasonable age, I can do quite satisfactorily. If I had no children it may be better, but I think I would then become bored with my studying. (Mikki, age 39, two children aged 8 and 14, Year 1 BSc Occupational Therapy)

Beyond the documenting of specific advantages, lone mothers' contributions to this research highlight how at a deeper level, alongside the considerable stress of juggling the demanding roles of lone parent and HE student, the same meshing together of contrasting experiences allows studentship to enrich the experience of lone parenthood, and vice versa. Despite the very real hardships faced, the two roles can in fact, paradoxically, also be perceived as offering a more balanced perspective and respite from each other, as indicated by many:

In some ways I think that studying for a degree and then PGCE in some ways balanced out the negative connotations that go with single parenthood – now people say to me how well I have done, how hard I have worked, etc.

I feel that studying has impacted very much on my free time as things

are never really finished – more could always be added which can be
a pressure. However, studying does remind you that there is a world
beyond your own immediate life. (Bex, age 34, one child aged 12,
Year 1 MA Primary Education with QTS)

Combining family responsibilities and education can be experienced as
more manageable than paid work because of increased autonomy, flexibility, and therefore physical availability to families. Being a student can
be more flexible than paid work in terms of managing children's illness,
childcare hours, and fulfilling other responsibilities like food shopping.
Edwards suggests that family life can be experienced as offsetting the
greediness of Higher Education, describing some individuals reporting
so voracious a desire to study that it can feel just as well that they have
families to stop them from going 'over the top', with family life providing a sense of proportion and reality (Edwards, 1993: 66, 76). Lone-
mother students' experiences in this research demonstrate that university
participation can similarly offset the greediness of family responsibilities. As well as counterbalancing one another, family responsibilities
and university can valuably inform one another. Home life can provide
valuable context in terms of concrete experience to inform academic
studies, and HE engagement also profoundly informs wider life, as is illustrated throughout the remainder of this chapter. Lone-parent students
acknowledge their current circumstances and paths leading to these as
contributing centrally to developing the confidence and commitment to
engage with Higher Education that they had not had when they were
younger. While being a mature student and lone parent can engender
insecurities in approaching HE, it can also inform enhanced confidence:

I find that, as a mature student I tend to be reasonably assertive,
which usually means getting better service! (And of course being a
parent I have totally lost the facility to become embarrassed in public
places!). (Rosa, two children, Year 1 MBA)

Students with high self-esteem are documented to experience greater
success in the academic setting, and it is suggested that one factor
informing this is that they more easily focus on strengths in other areas
of their lives when confronted with academic failure, thus suppressing
negative thoughts about immediate performance. This in turn leads
them to overcome failure more quickly than those who have low self-

esteem (Murphy and Roopchand, 2003: 245–6). These findings have transferable implications for validating potential attainment benefits of the ways in which lone-parent students combine family and university, by necessity remaining permanently grounded in the alternative source of achievement and validation provided by home life, with its potential to provide nurture at times of loss of academic confidence. The positive dimension to this life balance between studies and children is the key perceived benefit of their circumstances described by lone-parent students in this research, seen as providing a more 'well-rounded' experience than that of those who were *only* lone parents or *just* students. As one learner reflected:

> *My other responsibilities help to keep my studies in perspective.* (Gillian, age 48, two children aged 13 and 15, BA Primary Education)

While the longitudinal contact with lone mothers exposed the fluid, often contradictory, nature of experience, it also simultaneously indicated more permanent change in the broad direction of travel toward different lives that represent irreversible change:

> *I realised in my 30s I wasn't getting on. Financially I have always done well in work but academically I felt left behind, so three years ago started OU. There was a gap of about 18/19 years !! There was no transition. I have to say that was the best decision I have ever made, as usually I make bad ones.* (Josephine, one child, BSc Social Policy)

Both this study and existing commentaries emphasise the pervasive tensions between academic work and wider responsibilities faced by students with primary family responsibilities (Jackson, 2004: 52; Jarvis, 2003: 3). This research unearthed examples of both immediate positive benefits to lone parents' HE participation amongst the challenges, and long-term disadvantages amongst the gains. However, there is a clear weighting in experiences toward negative short-term effects of university participation, compared to more positive residual change. The following reflection illustrates both trends, counterbalancing immediate negative effects with deeper long-term implications:

*Being a student has changed my perspective on mothers. I feel
that when the children are at full-time school then the parents can
achieve their ambitions – there are no excuses!! I do feel, however,
that studying is quite isolating and does restrict my life as well as
causes extra stress.* (Connie, age 23, one child, Year 1 Business
Behaviour)

More than half of those who described the effects that HE study
had on their lives documented trajectories of permanent life change
engendered by engagement with learning. The contrast between
temporary negative and permanent positive effects illustrates the
trade-off lone parents must frequently make to participate in Higher
Education in terms of sacrificing the present in pursuit of securing the
future. This demonstrates the extent to which those lone parents who
ultimately succeed in completing their HE participation rely on a strong
willingness to defer gratification. It also, however, highlights precisely
the areas where better institutional support could make this trade-off
more attractive and indeed manageable for lone parents to embrace.

In 1976, Levin put forward four criteria for evaluating the equalising
influence of a nation's education system – equality of access, participation,
results, and effects on life chances. Woodley and Wilson have argued with
regard to mature students, that while there has been moderate research
concerning the first three criteria, there has been very little around the
effect on life chances (2002: 329; see also Wisker, 1996: 5). This relevance
remains the case, and extends to lone parents. Polakow *et al.*'s work on
lone mothers' HE access in the US context does however focus on this
area, suggesting that, although obtaining a degree holds benefits for
everyone, it can be particularly valuable for lone parents (2004: 115).
The US context of Polakow *et al.*'s work means that their observations
around lone parents' HE participation take place against the backdrop
of subjection to a particularly harsh welfare regime, with minimal
educational support. The relevance of this US experience is however set
to become increasingly relevant in the UK as the Government borrow
welfare lessons from the US in incentivising the two-parent family
model, decreasing out-of-work benefits, and extending work requirements for lone parents. Without built-in safeguards recognising and
supporting educational participation as legitimate work-related activity,
the application of such policy measures threatens to constrict lone
parents' ability to augment permanent change for the better in the lives

of themselves and their children through HE participation. Polakow *et al.'s* research has led them to make bold but justified claims as to the life-changing potential of HE participation for lone parents:

> *HE matters. For low income mothers with children, a college degree may be the only secure pathway out of poverty, ensuring access to economic self-sufficiency and family stability . . . The transformation from 'welfare mothers' to determined and capable student parents and activists mobilizing the resources of the communities in which they live, dramatically demonstrates how HE builds social capital in a previously stigmatized and disenfranchised constituency.* (Polakow *et al.*, 2004: 237)

Recognition that advantages of HE participation encompass deep individual, intergenerational, and societal benefits alongside financial gains is equally relevant to lone parents in the UK and indeed international context, as demonstrated throughout this book. It also chimes more broadly with findings that the benefits of HE participation for UK part-time students (of whom we know many are mature students with family responsibilities, including lone parents) extend beyond career to include increased community involvement, better health, and improvements to children's educational attainment (Woodley and Wilson, 2002: 338). In this research the most prevalent permanent changes described centre on developing confidence, an increasing value being placed on education, and becoming a better role model for children. Lone parents' personal development in these areas resulting from HE participation is further discussed later in this chapter. Lone mothers further document changes in broad life perspective and attitudes to others resulting from HE participation:

> *I would say definitely being a single parent has increased my confidence, it has also made me more understanding of people who live in poverty, and the struggles that mothers go through to make a good life for their children. I would be a lot less judgmental of other parents now.* (Rosa, two children, Year 1 MBA)

These findings complement existing evidence that mature students often experience altering political or religious beliefs (Merrill, 1999), and changing outlook in relation to social issues like racism and homosexuality, through meeting new people and making new friends at university (Edwards, 1993: 99). Lone mothers describe becoming more objective, questioning, open-minded, understanding of others and tolerant as a result of their studies, as explained by Shelby:

> *Being a student has changed me. I am better informed and tend to generalise less readily. I feel more educated and more politically aware, which in turn has unfortunately made me even more cynical! I do feel it has influenced my parenting style, in the sense that I see the introduction of wider experiences and the promotion of education as essential.* (Shelby, age 32, one child aged 6, PGCE FE)

Employment outcomes

The following reflection from Eva illustrates the way in which intrinsic and instrumental hopes from HE participation are frequently tightly woven together in the lives of lone-parent learners:

> *I think my being a student has enhanced our quality of life as I am more relaxed and fulfilled, so doing a better job despite perhaps not having as much money. I hope to finish my degree and become a teacher and be a good role model to my son, and hopefully he will finish his education without a break because I think it's easier than trying to go back to education after a long break. I'm hoping if I do qualify as a teacher and get a job that we will be better off and maybe I could buy a house.* (Eva, age 28, one child aged 9, Year 2 Primary Education with History)

However valuable intrinsic benefits of lone parents' learning are acknow-ledged to be, the significance of the impact on employment prospects cannot be ignored. It is this utilitarian agenda of potential impact upon earning capacity, rather than one of social justice or personal development, that largely informs both lone parents' motivations for educational engagement and policy justifications for supporting the group's participation in adult learning. The obstacles encountered by lone mothers balancing HE study with family commitments that are extensively documented in this book underline the temporary hardships experienced in the transitory intersecting of two competing main roles.

183

No doubt the progression onto managing the roles of employee and lone parent after HE completion brings its own unique problems, as demonstrated by the testimonies of those lone mothers in the research who were: already juggling employment alongside study; who graduated and commenced graduate employment while the research was in progress; and the future projections of those for whom it was yet to come.

It is recognised that women can perceive education as a solution to the exploitation and contradictions they experience at work and in the family when they are discontented with domesticity and working for low wages (Merrill, 1999: 110; Pascall and Cox, 1993: 5), and the importance of education in leading to better job opportunities for women has been identified by feminists since the 19th century. Education is seen as particularly central to assisting women in (re)finding a place in the public world after periods of childcare (Edwards, 1993), and for middle-class women at least, education is seen as representing access to the public world of professions and economic independence.

In the context of the previously discussed relative lack of research documenting employment outcomes for lone-parent graduates, data pertaining to HE learner groups in which lone parents proliferate is relevant. Findings have indicated that Open University and other part-time mature graduates earn more than other graduates (Woodley and Wilson, 2002: 335), with the majority of graduates from part-time HE courses reporting significant increases in income and that completion of studies contributes to positive career changes (Brennan *et al.*, 1999: 6). Similarly, research has indicated that the majority of mature university graduates feel that their degree has improved their job prospects, with full-time graduates aged 25–29 and over 40 the most likely to say that their degree has led to a satisfying job (Woodley and Wilson, 2002: 337–338). This is relevant to understanding the impact that sole responsibility for a young family may have on lone mothers' employment expectations and outcomes from HE participation, given that students with responsibility for young children are likely to be heavily represented amongst the 30–39 age group who indicate experiencing the least favourable employment outcomes from HE participation.

Nevertheless, some research has documented high levels of employment after graduating amongst lone parents, with moderate to high occupational status and job satisfaction (Burns and Scott, 1993: 39), and lone mothers with degrees are shown to be significantly more likely to be employed than their less educated counterparts:

It is clear that lone mothers with work experience during lone motherhood are more likely to be employed . . . So too are those with vocational and educational qualifications, notably those with public sector professional qualifications (nursing, teaching, etc.) and those with a degree especially. (Jenkins and Symons, 2001: 140)

OECD figures have shown that although the UK has had by far the highest HE fees in Europe, even prior to the drastic increases announced in 2010, 'students investing in HE in the UK can expect a much higher return in future earnings than their counterparts in most other western countries' (Bawden, 2006). This includes lone parents, for whom research indicates HE completion impacts positively upon wage level (Horne and Hardie, 2002: 70; Jenkins and Symons, 2001: 129).

Lone mothers' contributions to this research cast light on hopes and expectations for the future resulting from HE participation, including hopes that increased earning potential resulting from HE qualification will lead toward an enhanced quality of family life. While this thread represents a central motivation for initial HE engagement and persistence in the face of challenges, there is, however, a concurrent trend of a wavering of lone parents' confidence in the positive effect of HE participation upon employment potential, as they move toward and beyond completion of their studies. This is notably apparent amongst the substantial number pursuing teacher training courses, for whom the clearly associated vocational orientation of their studies inform highly instrumental, career-oriented HE motivations:

To tackle your final point about whether my reward reflects my efforts, well, I guess if I had managed to get a full-time teaching position then, yes, I would say it would have been worth all of the effort, but as yet, things are still a little precarious and as such I'm not entirely sure. On one level it was definitely worth the hassle, i.e. personal development, etc., but the amount of debt that I now have really does need to have some financial reward associated with it and, as yet, I don't have that, so I suppose the jury is still out on that one! (Gloria, age 39, three children aged 12–17, PG Diploma HE)

Such disappointment around the ultimate fruits of lone parents' labours in Higher Education may be more pervasive than recorded, given that most of the lone mothers had not yet completed their studies and commenced job hunting. It may alternatively indicate low self-confidence informing unduly pessimistic expectations of employment potential amongst some lone-parent graduates – expectations that are subsequently superseded by more favourable outcomes.

By far the most salient factor influencing the employment outcomes that lone mothers experience from their HE participation is the impact of their family responsibilities. This concurs with existing findings on factors affecting the graduate employment outcomes of mature women learners who make up the bulk of those students with primary family responsibilities. Relatedly, male graduates from part-time courses have been found to report enhanced career development and income gains resulting from HE participation compared to women (Brennan *et al.*, 1999: 9). Such divergence of experience represents much broader persistent gender trends in that women's consistent out-performance of men in education does not translate into greater equality in employment (Taylor, 2007: 36), with women continuing to earn substantially less than men for undertaking the same work, despite several decades of equal opportunity interventions.

While it far from accounts for the totality of gender inequality in the workplace, the uneven domestic responsibility borne by women, and by lone parents, is a key factor in the unequal spread of remuneration for paid work, and mediating the extent to which individuals' experience enhanced employment outcomes as a result of their HE participation. Having children (and being their primary carer) is consistently documented to have clear opportunity costs to career progression (Sobotka, 2006: 183; Joshi, 1998), and family responsibilities are shown to affect mothers' employment decisions, whether lone or partnered (Bradshaw and Millar 1991: 47). Lone mothers' trajectories in this research tally with existing findings that mature graduates with dependent children are particularly likely to take time out of the employment market after graduating in order to care for their families (Woodley and Wilson, 2002: 333). The most pervasive explanations for British lone mothers' persistently low employment rates have been lack of affordable childcare, disincentives in benefit entitlement, and lack of suitable jobs (Jenkins and Symons, 2001: 121; also Edwards, 1993:147).

Lone mothers' plans for life beyond graduation frequently do not prioritise career ambitions, as has also been highlighted with regard to mature women students generally (Edwards, 1993: 3). Such 'choice' can perhaps be cast more positively as representing the balance of priorities they juggle. In many respects the similar pressures experienced by partnered primary care-givers can be seen as being redoubled in the case of lone parents. Although the evidence may demonstrate that parents with primary family responsibilities benefit less from their HE studies than other graduates, it is important to locate this within the context of lone parents' unique position of dual interests and responsibilities, meaning that, unlike other graduates and workers, or even partnered parents, they cannot orientate themselves as exclusively toward either work or family, even for short periods. The relative advantages of HE study experienced may be a satisfactory, if not ideal, outcome. Indeed, an important contribution of lone mothers' insights in this research has been to show that many reflect that, on balance, their HE studies have been worthwhile even if they have not resulted in hoped-for enhanced financial circumstances.

Existing research on mature women students has found that only a minority succeed in entering the type of paid work that they had hoped to and saw as a suitable reward for their HE participation. Lone mothers in this research indicated that for many of them also securing graduate work can be a case of doing whatever fits in with family responsibilities (see Edwards, 1993: 149). This resonates with existing findings that working-class women in particular are often expected by their families to return to low-paid feminised work upon completion of their degrees (Taylor, 2007: 47). Evidence that many women continue to 'choose stereotypically feminine courses of study and aim for traditionally female job areas which are of low status and poorly paid' (Burns and Scott, 1993: 40) remains stubbornly persistent, with such 'choice' recognised to operate within the determining and frequently narrow constraints of structural inequalities around gendered expectations of domestic responsibility and vocational aptitude.

The large proportion of lone-parent students in this research whose HE courses were training them as teachers, teaching assistants or nurses demonstrates a disappointing continuation of the same trends noted by earlier studies. HE subject 'choices' documented by lone mothers in this research will largely channel them into traditional gendered roles in the public world, leading them into traditional women's work in the caring professions, including as play leaders, teachers, untrained social workers, clerical or administrative workers, or in management posts in training agencies. Going into a career in teaching is often seen as a 'fall-back' option rather than a main ambition, useful when opportunities are limited and childcare needs must be considered. While parents who are primary carers for young children describe selecting such career directions for their perceived enhanced flexibility over alternatives, in doing so they accrue ensuing disadvantages in terms of pay and work conditions (Edwards, 1993: 7, 148). In addition to the financial implications, over-participation in such feminised caring work by lone parents contributes toward a double burden of overstretched emotional labour as theorised by Hochschild (1983), dominating life both at home and work.

This chapter has highlighted that lone mothers' choices of HE Institution and hence course can be curtailed by lack of geographical mobility relative to other students. While lone-parent graduates' employment options are shown to be frequently constrained in terms of career direction, this is compounded by similar restrictions on geographical mobility, as has been documented to be the case for mature students as a whole (Gallagher *et al.*, 1993: 36). Such constraints conspire to consign lone parents to a disadvantaged position in the context of an education and employment marketplace whose goal 'is to create efficient "autonomous choosers": people who have marketable skills for the market place culture and use them to exercise choice' (Zepke, 2005: 169).

While lone motherhood engenders its own distinct effects upon individuals' HE participation, beyond the well-documented parallels with students with childcare responsibilities more broadly, many of the group's experiences of disadvantage and inequity in the learning process and employment outcomes can also be seen as being exacerbated by their position as mature students in education, and in employment economies that place a premium on youth. Age is acknowledged to be a significant determinant of the extent to which individuals benefit from their degrees in terms of employment (Brennan *et al.*, 1999: 11), with mature graduates from full-time courses experiencing disadvantaged employment outcomes compared to their younger counterparts (Woodley and Wilson, 2002: 335). Lone mothers indicate acute awareness of the barrier posed by their age in relation to career prospects, as Merrill has found also to be the case with mature women students in general (1999: 190).

Ageism has been blamed for substantially decreased labour force participation amongst mature graduates from both full-time and Open University courses three and a half years after graduation, which is particularly marked for those aged over 40. Mature students have also been documented to be substantially more likely to be registered as unemployed and seeking work, indicating that age differences in employment levels cannot be wholly explained away in terms of older graduates taking time out of paid work in order to focus on family, continuing education or other avenues. Older graduates from full-time courses are further indicated to be additionally more likely to face job insecurity in terms of being employed on temporary contracts (Woodley and Wilson, 2002). Lack of HE career guidance for mature students is berated as often being 'too little and too late'. Given the importance of carefully tailored careers advice for mature students in the context of often 'chequered career histories' it is suggested that it could usefully be targeted at the pre-entry stage (Gallagher *et al.*, 1993: 59). Such provision may be particularly useful for those lone-parent students and others who at the point of HE course selection, steer their futures toward the feminised caring employment trajectories discussed.

Concern around 'whether or not mature graduates engage fully in the labour market' has been couched in terms of potential lack of return on investment, both for society and individuals (Woodley and Wilson, 2002: 333). The following sections of this chapter, however, testify to the substantial social and individual gains implied in lone parents' HE participation, beyond instrumental employment outcomes.

Positive effects of lone parents' HE participation on parenting and children

Children of lone parents are indicated to be at increased risk of academic failure (Lipman and Boyle, 2005: 1451). In contrast, daughters of lone parents who work are more likely to do well at school and less likely to become lone mothers themselves (Shaw and Woolhead, 2006: 178). One of the key potential net gains of investing in supporting lone parents to fulfil their potential through HE participation and gain independence from the state, is the 'spill-over' effect in terms of encouraging both present and future generations to participate in and value education. Therefore, lone parents can be seen as holding the key to influencing the attitude of future generations to education, work, and state dependence through acting as role models for their children (Horne and Hardie, 2002: 71; Scott *et al.*, 1996: 234). The potential to steer social values and behaviour in these areas is a holy grail pursued with, so far, limited success by consecutive governments.

Positive effects of lone mothers' HE participation upon their children's

189

lives emerged as centrally significant in this research. The importance of this perceived impact is demonstrated by it being the most frequently cited area of effect on lone parents' HE engagement upon wider life, being discussed by nearly half the participants. The effects described encompass both temporary and permanent impacts, and divide equally into positive and negative effects. The major negative effect perceived is having less time for children while studying, demonstrating the previously discussed trade-off between temporary negative and permanent positive effects of lone parents' HE participation:

> *How will my higher ed. affect [my son]? [He] can see that education doesn't stop when school ends. It's a good model to see parents having to put in hours which aren't connected to jobs. But it has its cost too, and it's usually time with [my son] which goes.* (Veronica, age 41, one child aged 10, Year 2 PG Diploma Management Studies)

The most salient positive effects upon children that lone mothers identify as resulting from their HE participation are achieving the means to provide better financially for their families, becoming a better parent, providing a positive role model, and encouraging children to have ambitions. Parents' educational participation is evidenced to provide important parenting skills that impact fundamentally on children's academic performance independently of socioeconomic status (Duckworth, 2005: 240), attesting to the significance of positive intergenerational outcomes from lone parents' HE participation despite employment outcomes not always being favourable.

Some lone mothers describe taking older children to university as an introduction, hoping this will encourage them to choose to study at university one day, and it is further seen as beneficial that parents studying in Higher Education can share the study process with older children, particularly those studying for GCSEs or A-levels (also Edwards, 1993). Parents' studies have been elsewhere indicated to positively influence language and reading interactions (Eccles and Daris-Kean, 2005: 192–193). In terms of fostering such results, this research suggests the importance of time spent helping children to learn, and critical discussion of current affairs as a family. Lone mothers describe feeling that their children are better informed because of family discussion of social issues being studied at university. In addition, some describe being more aware of how they bring children up, especially daughters, in

190

terms of sexual stereotypes and assumptions (Jackson, 2004: 57; Edwards, 1993). Findings in this research resonate with observations that benefits to children of parents' engagement with learning include:

> *That they were better able to help their children with their school work, to offer better advice about difficulties with homework and to be more understanding of the problems their children faced as students. They also remarked that their children, especially their daughters, were more serious about their studies and more motivated to continue their education as a result of the role model the mother had provided.* (Scott *et al.*, 1996: 234)

In addition, lone mothers exploit their new-found confidence, critical engagement, awareness and research skills to achieve goals for their children, including, for example, fighting to achieve a specific school place for a child.

Confidence and self-esteem

Lone mothers' narratives illuminate the lack of confidence and self-esteem that many bring to their engagement with HE learning. Key factors contributing to this include the breakdown of often controlling relationships, and the stigmatised status of lone parenthood that they have experienced. The impact of long educational gaps, and perceived failure in initial education are identified as further key contributors (see Crossan *et al.*, 2003: 60; Weil, 1986), with Brine and Waller suggesting that mature students frequently return to education with 'weak or bruised identities' (2004: 103). Being encouraged educationally by parents and school during childhood is seen as being central to informing outlook and success in adulthood (Crompton and Harris, 1999: 143).

Existing commentators on the educational participation of mature women students have indicated the relevance of low academic confidence (Murphy and Roopchand, 2003: 247, 256; Rich, 1985: 27; Spender, 1981, 1982). Feelings of inadequacy, fraud and fears of being 'found out' as not being as capable as other students are a recurring theme in lone mothers' narratives (see Jackson, 2004: 50–51, 169; Wisker, 1996: 9). Further, the persistence of such feelings of intellectual inadequacy amongst those who had progressed to postgraduate level, including some who had made the step into paid research or teaching while they completed their postgraduate studies, resonates with Clance's documentation of the fears of perceived 'impostordom' frequently described by women academics (1985).

Research, however, indicates the strong effect of educational participation upon adult learners' confidence and self-esteem. While findings suggest HE participation contributes to personal development for three-quarters of learners, this is indicated to be particularly marked for mature students (Woodley and Wilson, 2002: 338). In addition to the long-term benefits to family quality of life fostered by HE engagement, rich intrinsic personal benefits in terms of developing confidence and self-esteem are shown to be centrally important (see Horne and Hardie, 2002: 69; Hyatt and Parry, 1990). This can mean that the net gains of educational participation make it worthwhile for lone parents, even if anticipated employment and financial outcomes are not realised, as discussed earlier in this chapter:

> *I don't feel like I've wasted my time, even if it doesn't work out because it's shown me that anything is possible. I'd always thought I was restricted in my options because I was a single parent, whereas now I've made a huge life change and things are okay, so I know I could potentially do anything.* (Eva, age 28, one child aged 9, Year 2 Primary Education with History)

An important related theme is the sense of 'pride': HE participation goes some way toward lifting the stigma that commentators acknowledge to be associated with lone parenthood (see Freud, 2007: 53; Polakow *et al.*, 2004: 237). Lone mothers frequently iterate their acute awareness of the often-stigmatised social status of lone parenthood:

> *Basically (and I'm talking about lone mothers here) we do an outstanding job, don't shirk our responsibilities, forgo all sorts for the benefit of our children and work ourselves into the ground. For this we get condemned and pressurised into adding to our workload by having to take up paid employment as we are a drain on the State or whatever. Makes my blood boil : 0).* (Ruth, age 47, two children aged 9 and 12, Year 3 BA Social Policy and Criminology)

Experiences of bearing such stigmata as lone parents are counterbalanced by perceptions of the vindicating potential of educational participation, leading to individuals feeling more 'equal' and respected by society in general, and others that they meet, as described by Beatrice:

> *When some people realise that I'm a student teacher, their reaction towards me immediately changes. I thought I was imagining it, but now I don't think I have been. It's not everyone, but it's very noticeable in the way some people treat me. A particular kind of respect enters their eyes, and they suddenly become more interested than they originally were. Is it that they no longer see me as just another black, single parent, probably sponging off the State, with a string of worthless 'baby-fathers' behind me?* (Beatrice, age 31, one child aged 8, Year 3 BA Education – Primary)

The extent of such feelings may at least in part be culturally specific, given the documented prevalence of such a stigmatised model of lone welfare-dependent parenthood in Anglophone countries compared to continental regimes (Klett-Davies, 2007: 12–13). The assertion that it is largely the potential to provide for one's family independently that leads to increased confidence and self-esteem for lone parents engaging with education (Shaw and Woolhead, 2006: 178) underlines that apparently instrumental and intrinsic effects of lone parents' HE participation cannot be easily separated.

The increased self-esteem and confidence that HE participation can develop for lone mothers is indicated by their narratives to greatly inform academic experience. This is of important significance given evidence that academic confidence in Higher Education impacts centrally upon attainment levels (Woodfield and Earl-Novell, 2006:356). Individuals' developmental journeys, drawn out by the longitudinal perspective, describe the process of growing confidence and self-esteem as leading toward increasing self-recognition of academic ability. This academic development appears most pronounced for those in their first year of HE study. The following quotes from one lone mother at the beginning of her HE learner career, document such a journey of personal development:

> *I started university on the 20th of September of this year. I found the Induction week to be terrible. I felt very concerned that I had chosen the wrong course. I felt like I was being bombarded with information overload. It was a very traumatic time. I continued to feel terrible and*

just wanted to give it up. The course is very intense and the course is taught by PBL [problem-based learning] and practice placement and also reflective learning. These are all new to me. (Mikki, age 39, two children aged 8 and 14, Year 1 BSc Occupational Therapy – October)

Eight months later, her responses demonstrated her academic confidence to be growing stronger, although still fragile:

The stress for deadline is mainly my fault as I panic about each assignment even though I know I can do it, but most of the time I don't believe in myself enough to put pen to paper early enough. (Mikki – May)

A month later, while the pressure was obviously still significant, the same participant's outlook on her ability to cope with her studies had become markedly more positive:

Your timing was just right, the reason for the delay in replying to your e-mail was that I had two assignments and a viva to revise for. Ha Ha. One of the assignments I had started in advance and was fairly confident, but then had a viva to revise for and assignment due the day after, which was quite hard going as it is also half term for both children. I feel fairly confident in writing my assignment now and also with the viva, but I have had to put everything and everyone on hold. (Mikki – June)

In addition to educational effects, the consequences of increasing confidence and self-esteem engendered by HE participation upon lone mothers' intimate relationships are significant, illustrating the complexity of impact. Relationships are an area in which Higher Education can have a contradictory effect, with negative and positive repercussions interwoven. While some lone mothers shed light on the positive impact that HE participation can have on enhancing the quality of intimate relationships, the emergence of tensions in existing relationships resulting from individuals' personal and intellectual development is also apparent (also Jones, 2006: 496). Lone mothers convey experiences of discord between unsatisfactory relationships and developing student

194

identities, including studentship, eventually coinciding with decisions to make a formal and permanent break from relationships:

> *I can say that me becoming a student was a catalyst in the*
> *breakdown of my marriage. He encouraged me to study but didn't*
> *like that I became confident again and more like the person I was*
> *before he controlled me.* (Rita, age 36, four children aged 5–10,
> Year 2 B Ed Primary)

It is suggested that it is often only when partners refuse to share education with mature learners that inequalities in the relationships became transparent, and the first year of study is seen as a crucial period for relationship breakdown for mature students (Edwards, 1993), as they develop new self-esteem, expectations, and sources of validation.

Lone mothers' reflections indicate their immersion in HE learning as informing both optimism around the potential for a more free and equal imagined future with a new partner and, contrastingly, reluctance to re-engage with intimate relationships. For some, single status can come to be perceived as a central pillar of the strong new self:

> *Being a single parent has taught me to be more emotionally objective*
> *– not constantly being caught up in someone else's mind games has*
> *left me free to see my real feelings and deal with them more honestly,*
> *as well as make my own decisions and deal with the consequences*
> *whether they turn out to be good or bad.* (Gillian, age 48, two
> children aged 13 and 15, Year 3 BA Primary Education)

The effects of growing confidence and self-esteem resulting from educational participation extend beyond intimate relationships, with lone mothers indicating positive effects throughout diverse areas of their lives:

> *I feel more confident in my abilities in the commercial environment,*
> *and able to stand outside my own company and take an objective*
> *view. This is purely thanks to the course. Understanding how business*
> *works means feeling part of our local network. There's huge value in*
> *that.* (Veronica, age 41, one child aged 10, Year 2 PG Diploma
> Management Studies)

> *Attending university has given me the confidence to question a*
> *diagnosis that I have MS, as although I appreciate we are all different*
> *and experience different symptoms and maybe my positive outlook*
> *helps, having seen a consultant privately, [as] my doctor would not*
> *refer me on the NHS, I am going to have a scan on my lower back.*
> (May, four children aged up to18,Year 2 Social Sciences and
> Human Biology)

These examples capture practical applications of lone mothers' growing confidence and self-esteem resulting from HE participation, in
concrete dilemmas in their lives in the areas of academic work, relationships, paid work, and health. A coexisting current in descriptions of
developing confidence and self-esteem describes changes in individuals'
core sense of self-worth that inform concrete manifestations of confidence, reflecting deeper, inner change in self-belief and outlook, as the
following exemplifies:

> *Being a student has changed me. I question a lot more. I can see a*
> *lot more and understand more. I always questioned everything before,*
> *but I am now more informed. I feel like I am doing something with*
> *my life. I am working towards a goal and I am happy with myself for*
> *that.* (Josephine, one child, BSc Social Policy)

Lone mothers describe feeling more 'worthwhile' and 'valuable', with
one describing experiencing learning as a 'voyage of self-discovery'.
This evidenced personal development function of HE participation
is particularly relevant given the discussed loss of 'me time' and compromising of care of the self frequently experienced to result from the
heavy investment required of lone parents to participate in Higher
Education, given their limited resources of time and finances. Lone
mothers' testimonials as to the positive intrinsic benefits of HE participation
suggest that, while the additional time commitment may leave them tired,
and going without exercise, socialising, watching television or reading for
pleasure, it simultaneously constitutes an alternative mode of caring of the
self, or 'me time'. Some consequently explicitly associate their study time
with attending to their own needs, rather than the needs of others, and the
following is one of many examples of the experienced potential of HE
participation to mediate some of the negative aspects of lone parenthood
in the immediate term, in advance of future anticipated income potential:

Student life can be tough, but is a massive improvement to being on the dole; more women should be encouraged to study while bringing up their kids. There is nothing more miserable than staring at the wall all day till the children get home. (Michelle, age 35, one child aged 12, MSc History of Science)

Identity

Evidence of deep and permanent change in the lives of lone mothers resulting from HE participation to a large extent represents individuals' development of a learner identity, which extends into informing expected roles and experiences in wider life well beyond the context of the classroom (see Crossan *et al.*, 2003: 61). This new-found identity is integrated into lone mothers' core sense of who they are, including their values, aspirations, behaviours, tastes, and priorities. This affects not only their own lives, but also the orientation of core values toward their children, with ensuing intergenerational implications, including developing a culture of valuing learning within families that can permeate generations. The following reflection illustrates one mother's increasing identification with the idea of herself as a learner, something that she had previously seen as alien to her own experience:

One thing that I have learnt is that a degree may change some people in some ways, yet fundamentally it doesn't matter whether someone has a degree or not as long as they are kind, generous people. But a degree doesn't teach people to become this, it has to be there initially. So maybe all the times I've thought I'm not good enough or clever enough, it was just me taking the wrong perspective; at the end of the day it is what is in a person's heart that matters. I don't think I'm better than anyone else because I now have a degree. (Jennifer, age 44, four children aged 10–20, Year 3 BA Education Studies and History)

It is suggested that the learning career can be seen as an aspect of identity formation that is particularly transformed through exposure to more diverse forms of social interaction, new events and changing circumstances (Crossan *et al.*, 2003: 57). The establishment of consensus over study requirements and behaviour can contribute to the formation of group learning identities within cohorts of mature learners, and the formation of such subcultural groups by mature students can in fact be seen as essential to 'surviving' at university. Lone-parent mature students frequently represent a dominant subculture within the wider mature student subculture, and the presence of other mature students experiencing the same problems and self-doubts can vitally help to alleviate anxiety, with mature students becoming 'a microcosm within the world of the university' (Merrill, 1999). Among the most significant reported positive effects of lone mothers' HE participation is: a change in broad life perspective: becoming more objective, questioning, and open-minded; understanding of others and tolerant. This is all representative of the development of a learner identity contributed to by mixing with a more heterogeneous and politically tolerant population and learning to be a critical thinker (Kaufman and Feldman, 2004).

The return to education as an adult learner does not represent the start of an individual's learning identity, but a reconstruction of earlier experiences of childhood education (see Brine and Waller, 2004: 102; Komulainen, 2000: 449). In particular, lone-parent students' childhood backgrounds, as introduced in Chapter 3, indicate how attitudes to education are often shaped by factors including attitudes to gender, class, ethnicity, and assumed 'place' in the world. Further origins of an individual's learner identity can also be found outside the formal education system (Weil, 1986: 224), for example through community education, and self-help, consciousness-raising or political groups (1986: 226). It is significant that lone mothers as young as their early 20s are as likely as much older students to indicate the gap they perceive between themselves and traditional entry age students, pointing to the salience of lone-parent status, and suggesting that it is this lone-parent status and/ or the presence of an educational gap, rather than its length, that creates the feeling of distance.

Our social identities impact upon the opportunities available to us (Parr, 2000: 34). It is suggested that university lecturers, like school teachers, frequently make assumptions about the characteristics of an ideal student, and that non-traditional students often do not conform to this model (Merrill 1999: 180). 'Learner identity conflicts' can be caused by university tutors' assumptions about gender, race and class (Weil, 1986: 231). This dovetails with Goffman's observations around 'spoiled identity' (1963), whereby others are able to use their power to shape our identity, then treat us according to the label attached, and is particularly relevant to understanding lone parents as a stigmatised group. The following excerpt illustrates how acceptance of a lone-parent identity, with its associations of lack, failure and stigma, can contribute to an erosion of other incompatible aspects of self-identity:

> *Would I change anything? That's a really painful question. Before [my son] was born I had a really hectic social life and loads of friends. Staying in on either Xmas Eve or New Year's Eve was absolutely unheard of. I had good enough clothes and wore make up in those days and looked after myself exercise-wise and such. With the combination of [my son's] disability and lone parenthood everything I ever was has been eroded away. Sometimes I don't even feel like a shadow.* (Ruth, age 47, two children aged 9 and 12, Year 3 BA Social Policy and Criminology)

Through engagement with HE learning, a stigmatised lone-parent identity can be trumped by an emergent learner identity, and subsequently a graduate identity. Lone mothers' narratives chart the ways in which they actively interpret their identities and 'work on' their lives and biographies (Crompton and Harris, 1999: 133). It is suggested that 'the self of mature students is partially stripped on entry to a university and their identity rebuilt as they progress through their student career', leaving them changed persons (Merrill, 1999: 128). Being a student can engender uncovering the 'real' self that life has suppressed (Pascall and Cox, 1993: 120). Engaging with education means learning a new role (Merrill, 1999: 127), and mature women learners have been found to be particularly concerned with the impact of education upon the self and the way that self is subsequently presented to the world – not in terms of achieving a status role, but in terms of their concrete interactions with other people. Metaphors of growth, extending, stretching and expanding horizons are both hoped for and realised, alongside a sense of the inevitability of change, given the deeply penetrative nature individuals perceive of the educational participation (Pascall and Cox, 1993).

A range of personal circumstances affect the extent to which individuals are willing and able to immerse themselves in university networks; there are hence varying extents to which learner identity may become a core part of self-identity, either within the learning context, or beyond. Lone mothers describe how factors including age (see

Merrill, 1999: 153), nationality, and sexual identification can contribute to a perceived lack of shared identity with other students, and ensuing heightened sense of isolation. Much relevant work on mature students' development of a learner identity focuses on the salience of gendered experience, and adult educational engagement and the ensuing develop-ment of a learner identity can inform radical reconstruction of dominant identities of gender and class (Merrill, 1999: 204). This includes, for example, the way in which university life can give women 'time and space in their lives to develop, and change their self and identity', and that in doing so they redefine themselves as women, no longer wanting to be dominated by domesticity (Merrill, 1999: 205). This research has illustrated the ways in which HE engagement can represent the search for a new or reshaped identity, and to assert some control over the way in which that identity is defined. Individuals' narratives similarly indicate how individuals who, having strived for many years to achieve some independence, autonomy, power and self-identity outside the home, choose to use Higher Education as the vehicle with which to achieve this (see Parr, 2000; Merrill, 1999). While the process of this metamorphosis can be wrought with anxiety, for others, returning to learning as an adult can be experienced as a more harmonious, organic development, a natural progression as they move on from the childrearing era of their lives toward the world of work (Pascall and Cox, 1993).

While some of the lone mothers researched re-entered education to commence a full-time degree after a long break, thus representing a radical shift in identity, others had been studying continuously for a number of years. For many, part-time adult continuing education, including non-accredited courses, further education and Open Uni-versity modules, had been part of their lives over a prolonged period. Similarly, some students had been studying slowly over many years, which could contribute to a sense of fragmented identities, and lack of formation of a distinct learner identity, despite, perhaps, nearing completion of a degree or even having embarked upon postgraduate study.

That lone-parent learners indicate feeling less isolated at university when they experience others around them as sharing similarity with themselves demonstrates the extent to which feeling 'at home' at uni-versity is contingent upon a match between facets of the dominant student identity and one's own self-identity. This is especially significant in terms of some aspects of self-identity, including social class. It has long been argued that individuals from middle-class backgrounds feel like 'fish in water' in Higher Education (Baker, 2005), and that university serves to 'certify' students from middle and upper-middle-class backgrounds for privileged social and occupation positions in the world (Kaufman and Feldman, 2004: 464). Given the documented overrepresentation of both lone parents and mature students in socioeconomically disadvantaged positions (Taylor, 2007: 35; Althaus, 1996: 285), lone-parent students may have a tendency to feel more like fish *out of* water at university, impeding formation of an inclusive learner identity. The perceived placing of a negative value upon working-class status at university may contribute to the proportion of lone parents indignant at being asked how they identify in social class terms, and unwilling to define themselves in this way.

It is argued that social class networks inform experiences of identity and belonging for lone parents (Duncan and Edwards, 1999: 97). While social class is inevitably pivotal in determining experience, this research indicates that in many respects, lone-parent status trumps social class as a more salient facet of identity for lone-mother HE learners, as highlighted in Chapter 4. Findings, however, also revealed areas in which social class patterns do appear significant in the development of a learner identity. Significantly, no self-identifying working-class lone-parent students discussed whether they felt that they fitted in at university, potentially representing lower expectations of 'fitting in' at university as what may be assumed to be essentially an institution of class privilege. Further, lone-parent students identifying as working class emerged as twice as likely to feel as though they had made major life changes to become an HE learner, indicating that university participation continues to constitute a bigger deviation from the norm for individuals from working-class backgrounds. For lone-parent learners from working-class backgrounds, the move to university therefore emerged as significantly more likely to represent an important transitional moment in life, whether this was experienced as being fundamentally positive or negative, and even if this further distance travelled in adjusting to university still left them with a decreased sense of fitting in compared to their middle-class counterparts.

The unique combination of being both HE student and lone parent, also mediated by further individual demographic characteristics, can be seen as causing a crisis of self-identity, a feeling of slipping between distinct groups, and consequently finding common ground with none.

Managing the development of a learner identity as just one aspect of a multiplicity of roles (Merrill, 1999: 128) results in the need for constant compromise, and often a fragmented experience (Pascall and Cox, 1993: 127). This sense of fragmentation of life can be exacerbated by the way in which mature students can feel forced to choose to compromise existing relationships in order to focus their limited resources upon their HE participation (Brine and Waller, 2004: 108).

There is a substantial tradition of sociological work investigating identity in education. While some commentators theorise how facets of identity are intermeshed (Francis, 2001: 157), lone-mother HE students' accounts of how home and university coincide in their lives also demonstrate the coping strategy of keeping university and home/family separate (see Christie *et al.*, 2005: 14). This is illustrated by the way in which almost a quarter of those researched chose not to inform tutors and fellow students of their parent status. This demonstrates the desire to establish a student identity, but also the understanding that this may best involve denial of a key aspect of their non-HE experience and identity. Francesca's view on this was typical:

> *I don't say to everybody that I am a single parent, as I try to not let that fact get in the way, it would be as though that is an excuse, which is silly, but I try to juggle everything without having to apologise for not doing something because of family commitments.*
> (Francesca, age 34, four children aged 6–18, Year 1 BA History)

This decision to withhold wider identity from others at university exacerbates lone parents' sense of isolation, although this research none-theless conveyed greater fluidity between facets of self-identity compared to that documented in existing commentaries. The concept of a fluidity of roles that seep into one another, whether or not this is desirable or intended, seems fitting given both the everyday stories told by lone-parent students, and the conceptualisation of university and family as greedy institutions, with their insatiable demands creeping forward and defying boundaries.

Some commentaries employ individualistic explanations to provide typologies of coping approaches for managing the student role alongside other responsibilities. For example, Christie *et al.'s* typology divides widening participation HE students into three groups: those who feel that they are missing out on full engagement with their studies because of other responsibilities; pragmatists who understand that university cannot take over life; and those who seek to keep home and university separate (2005: 14). Each of these categories applies to some of the lone-parent students who contributed to this research, as does Klett-Davies' typology of lone parents as strugglers, copers or pioneers (2007), and Crompton and Harris's categorisation of some types of women juggling dual commitments of children and full-time work as 'maximizers' (1999: 143). What the longitudinal perspective of this research adds to such typologies (usually based on one-off interviews) is to illuminate how individuals move between strategies over time, so that, depending on recent events, a lone mother may be a pragmatic coper one month and a pessimistic struggler the next. Such fluidity in accounts does not however undermine the underlying pattern of more deep-seated and non-reversible identity transformation, with the move toward becoming a learner for lone parents therefore often representing something of a 'two steps forward and one step back' scenario. Merrill suggests the alteration of attitudes, values and behaviour entailed in the transition to developing a learner identity to mean that individuals can never 'go back totally to the person they were before entering university' (1999: 183). The magnitude of this shift has led commentators to employ vivid metaphors of education for mature returners as being 'like a midwife easing the birth of this genuine yet suppressed but resourceful self' (Komulainen, 2000: 454), 'the new self that . . . rise[s] from the educational baptism' and becoming a 'new person' (Pascall and Cox, 1993: 94).

Lone mothers describe experiencing regret and sadness at the end of their degrees that their time at university is soon to be over. Worries around 'what next?' as individuals travel toward and beyond completion of their studies, anticipate the creation of a void in need of filling once university participation comes to an end, illustrating the way in which leaving university marks another transition and turning point, and the need for a new identity to be found. This exemplifies the extent to which HE learning becomes integrated into lone mothers' daily lives and self-identities, and demonstrates that HE engagement represents much more than an instrumental drive to secure a more financially prosperous future. Merrill suggests that student identity can become such a dominant part of mature learners' life stories, that individuals can become 'institutionalised', to use Goffman's terminology (1999: 197).

The increased prevalence of the 'what next?' sentiment amongst full-time students in this research indicates that HE study becomes a more integral aspect of self-identity for this group compared to part-time learners.

The future

> *I did start the semester really positive – 'final year' – light at the end of the tunnel and all that, but now I feel like at this rate the only degree I will get will be a posthumous one . . . ! . . . I just want the course to be over. I just want a peaceful life! Am I striving down this career path at the expense of my son? Will I ever actually get my foot on the property ladder? I know that I am juggling three balls and I cannot do it much longer without one going 'belly up'.*
> (Lucy, age 34, one child aged 5, Final year LLB, November)

> *Hi there and sorry for not replying to some of your previous mails – I was studying hard for my final exams and graduated on 26th July with a 1st class degree!!! I came top in the whole year and won a prize for that too. I feel like a new person – with renewed confidence and an exciting future ahead.* (Lucy, one month after graduation)

Although most of the lone mothers did not complete their HE studies during the time in which they contributed to the research, most of them did discuss effects they conjectured or at least hoped would occur in their individual and family futures. Many indicated holding only minimal hopes for the future, explaining this to be a learned defence mechanism against being disappointed when things go wrong. However, while there were exceptions, thoughts on the future were by and large positive, projecting that what lay ahead as a graduate must constitute an improvement on the past and present as a lone parent. Much discussion of the future focused on employment, being discussed by over half of lone-parent students researched. Over a quarter of the lone mothers were either already teaching or hoping to use their HE qualifications to begin a career in teaching. These included one who hoped to teach abroad and a small number teaching in Higher or Further Education, but the majority were training to teach full time in UK primary and secondary schools. This attractiveness of teaching as a graduate profession, particularly for those with financial family responsibilities to meet, is likely to be affected by cuts to teacher training funding, including the abolition of bursary packages announced in 2011. Other professions being entered by substantial numbers of lone-mother graduates in this research include nursing, law, psychotherapy, government, and the arts. Beyond projected and realised employment outcomes of HE engagement, others described hoping that as children grew older and less dependent, opportunities for extending their horizons would increase, opening up time and freedom to pursue travel, volunteering, and geographical relocation, as indicated by Kiera:

> *I feel pretty much settled in my choice of career, but I hope as the*
> *children get older to realise my ambition to travel the world. I'd*
> *like to take a career break and maybe do some voluntary work or*
> *something like VSO. I suppose it all depends on the finances and*
> *mortgage.* (Kiera, two children, Year 1 PG Cert. Managing
> Health and Social Care)

Several older lone mothers perceived themselves to be in a more vulnerable, precarious position, worrying about not having a pension, or that age would be a barrier to realising their employment potential in the future:

> *Those things I don't remember mentioning before are the 'future'*
> *issues. Other than that my fears for myself are that my (extreme!)*
> *age will be a barrier to getting a job.* (Gillian, age 48, two children
> aged 13 and 15, Year 3 BA Primary Ed.)

Further study features strongly in the future plans of lone-parent students, with a third discussing their continuing studies after the current academic year, and a quarter planning to undertake further study after completion of their current course. This is illustrative of the identified way in which one course frequently leads to further educational engagement for mature students (Hyde, 2007). Such prolonged educational engagement amongst lone mothers can be contextualised by their indicated recognition that it is frequently easier to manage study with lone parenthood than employment (also Klett-Davies, 2000: 60). Lone-parent students' planned continuing educational participation can often involve moving from a traditional HE Institution to distance learning for completion of studies, in order to fit in more easily with other commitments; a change that some had already made.

One in nine of the lone mothers planned to complete a teaching qualification after their current studies. Others planned to train in law or nursing, or complete an alternative further professional, vocational or academic postgraduate qualification after their current course of study. Such plans for further study are frequently explained in terms of recognition of the need for further qualifications in an increasingly competitive graduate labour market:

> *It will provide entry to a profession, but post-grad qualifications will*
> *be necessary in order to earn a reasonable amount. What I mean is*
> *I could become an unqualified social worker and earn thousands less*
> *for doing the same job and I would also be required to get the actual*
> *social work qualification. It would be the same case if for example*
> *I wanted to work on a youth offending team or in probation. Even*
> *in housing I would have to take more 'professional' qualifications.*
> *In fact a lot of the courses I have done are very similar to those of a*
> *social work course, but I'd still have to repeat it all. It seems that there*
> *are now 'professional' qualifications necessary to obtain almost any*
> *job, whether it is working in a nursery, an estate agents or whereever.*
> *So whatever job I do end up in I am looking at having to continue*
> *studying whether I want to or not. In my position as a lone parent*
> *with a disabled son that isn't good news. But it's the way it is : 0).*
> (Ruth, age 47, two children aged 9 and 12, Year 3 BA Social
> Policy and Criminology)

Others projected that they may be hampered from pursuing their post-graduate study ambitions by financial constraint:

> *Won't be any financial benefits from completing the studies, wanted*
> *to go on to be ed psych, but training can be self supported (12K)*
> *and hours are office hours, and my son is still at school, so ambition*
> *in that area is on hold.* (Juliette, age 45, one child aged 12, PG
> Diploma Psychology)

Lone mothers' further study ambitions are indeed indicated frequently to prove more problematic to realise than ideally hoped for. Continuing informal feedback from some after the research ended attests to ongoing struggles to achieve graduate employment. For example, one Art graduate who had hoped to earn a living as an artist in residence was working as a teaching assistant, while another participant's DPhil progress had been delayed considerably by financial need forcing her to take on two part-time jobs once her research funding ended. The research illuminated that perhaps the most notable recurring cloud on the horizon is the thought of having to repay debts accrued while studying, including student loans. This concern will become realised at an earlier point of many lone-parent learners' educational trajectories as new legislation increases the consistency with which part-time students are eligible for student loans, but simultaneously renders them liable for repayment from three and a half years after commencement of their course – half way through many of the part-time degrees that have disproportionately attracted mature learners including lone parents, given their perceived compatibility with family and employment responsibilities. This is likely to impact further upon employment and future study choices upon graduation for lone parents.

In today's knowledge economy the value of postgraduate study is increasingly recognised. Given the hopes of some lone mothers to pursue postgraduate study, and their fears that financial barriers would prevent this from being possible, further analysis of motivations for continued educational engagement is needed, as is exploration of whether lone parents are able to realise these ambitions to extend their studies, and the barriers they face in doing so. University vice-chancellors have acknowledged the importance of ensuring that non-traditional students have access to postgraduate study, and that it does not remain the domain of the well-off (Brown, 2007).

One in seven of the lone mothers described hoping that their completion of HE studies would benefit their children by facilitating provision of a more materially comfortable lifestyle. This included, for example, hopes that increased income would facilitate dreams of home ownership, as well as improving family quality of life, including allowing more holidays and other treats for children:

> As regards our quality of life – at the least I hope I will be able
> to keep paying the mortgage (we love this house), run the car and
> be able to carry on as we are with, perhaps, the addition of proper
> holidays and save enough to replace essentials and have a few

> *luxuries. At best it would be nice to feel financially secure and be able to have enough to go on adventurous holidays, maybe indulge hobbies, etc.* (Gillian, age 48, two children aged 13 and 15, Year 3 BA Primary Education)

For some lone-parent students it is important that HE completion is perceived as enabling them to provide a better childhood for their children than their parents had been able to give them. A further theme is that of hoping to have more time for their children in future, either because of no longer having to study, or for those training as teachers, because of working days and terms that are anticipated to fit with children's school lives. Hopes for children are a key area of hopes for the future, discussed by a third of lone mothers researched:

> *As I have all girls, I've been very keen to let them know that they must equip themselves with skills and knowledge so that they do not have to rely on anyone else to survive; I'd hate for them to have confidence and issues that I had and still have.* (Gloria, age 39, three children aged 12–17, PG Diploma HE)

Despite themselves having risen to the challenge of participating in Higher Education as a lone parent, lone mothers often indicate the hope that their children will learn from witnessing their experience, not to have children young or alone, and to go to university before settling down with responsibilities, while it is perceived to be possible to immerse oneself more fully in enjoying the experience:

> *I would not really encourage [my son] to do what I have done, because although I have made some friends through university I think it would have been more fun if I had gone before I was a parent. Really, though, it is highly unlikely that he will ever be a single parent as a boy, but I would still say go to university before you have children. But if you haven't got around to it then still go anyway!* (Bex, age 34, one child aged 12, MA Primary Education with QTS)

Beyond this, lone parents hope that their success at their studies will make their children proud of them, and the overwhelming perceived benefit of their HE participation upon their children's futures is to act as a positive role model to encourage children to strive to fulfil their own academic potential. Despite not being directly questioned about it, almost a third of lone-parent students researched indicated hoping that their studies would inspire their children in their own educational journeys, to study to the best of their abilities and develop an intellectually inquisitive approach to life:

> *To me it is important that I set an example to [my daughter] through what I do and I did not feel staying at home on benefits would do that. I think that by going to university instead and hopefully becoming a teacher I can show her that, despite the odds, she can achieve what she wants.* (Lily, age 23, one child aged 1, Year 2 BA Development Studies)

This chapter has placed mothers' experiences as university students within the contexts of their wider lives and developing self-identities, as they progress through their HE learning journeys toward and beyond graduation. The final chapter summarises salient factors in determining the potential for lone mothers to participate successfully and fully in HE learning, identifying good practice and making recommendations for future development.

CHAPTER EIGHT

Conclusion: looking forward

The insights of this book have been contingent upon the window provided by lone-mother HE students into twelve months in their personal journeys of walking the tight rope between raising their children alone, while making moves toward realising their own personal and career goals through university participation. This research has sought to shed light on the unique Higher Education journeys of those students who are bringing up children alone. While this group may share many facets of identity and experience with other groups, including lone parents generally, university students as a whole, and other particular marginalised groups in Higher Education, this book has sought to demonstrate how the combination of particular perceptions, problems and priorities affecting this group constitute a distinct experience contingent upon lone-parent HE student status. While illuminating the existence of a cohesive shared experience of key concerns amongst lone-parent HE students, this research has simultaneously highlighted the significance of intersecting variables in informing the lone-parent HE student experience.

Through the lens of HE participation, this book has explored patterns of how women combine home and study when they are parents. Most existing relevant qualitative research addressing the HE experiences of mature women students with children dates back to the 1990s. Alongside identifying points of contrasting findings, a key contribution of this research has been to highlight the extent to which findings of earlier studies often remain pertinent today, and the extent to which many of their recommendations remain largely unimplemented. This chapter summarises the most salient findings evidenced by the in-depth, longitudinal framework of this study, and channels recommendations for facilitating lone parents' HE participation.

What are the needs of lone parents?

Findings from this research iterate the recommendation that if governments are serious about widening participation and promoting lifelong learning, they must address the barrier faced by lone parents in balancing studying (particularly in the final year) with caring for children (Horne and Hardie, 2002: 69). The narratives provided throughout this research affirm that lone parents frequently make diligent HE students, whose fundamental need from the education system is the opportunity of a genuine second chance, or as Wisker has suggested, perhaps, their first real chance at engaging with education (1996: 3). The important question then becomes, *what are the material conditions and institutional assurances needed to make such a second chance a realistic opportunity?*

Given the substantial challenges faced in negotiating the university landscape as a lone-parent learner, adequately informed policy and support structures at both governmental and institutional level are vital if HE access for lone parents is to be anything other than a survival of the fittest struggle where only those with the strongest individual agency and informal support structures can succeed. This research has affirmed existing findings that HE Institutions can do better than they do presently at addressing the needs of non-standard students (Jackson, 2004: 28). The narratives of lone-parent learners also affirm as important that it is those universities particularly in the pre-1992 sector that need to change if they are to provide positive experiences for non-traditional learners including mature working-class students (also Reay, 2003: 301, 311; Polakow *et al.*, 2004: 117–127). Lone mothers' experiences underline that changes needed to contribute to facilitating participation by students with family responsibilities are not all financial (also Wisker, 1996: 3). For example, the need for greater dialogue between HE providers and benefits agencies, as well as improving awareness amongst local authorities and housing associations of the needs and entitlements of lone-parent students, are key factors in supporting the groups' HE participation (Scott *et al.*, 2003: 9). The Dearing Report found 51 per cent of lone-parent students to be discontented with levels of awareness of the needs of students with family responsibilities, compared with 28 per cent of married or cohabiting students with children, and that 60 per cent of lone parents did not believe that enough support was given to mature students (1997). Fifteen years later, lone mothers' experiences in this research illuminate the negative implications of a continuing lack of awareness of lone parents' needs and entitlements.

Accessing advice and information

A key area of recommendations for improving services for lone parents is the need for improved information and advice (see Scott *et al.*, 2003: 10). It is argued that a paucity of easily available information leaves student parents disadvantaged by lacking awareness of entitlement to government assistance (Carlisle, 2005: 347–348), preventing individuals in need from benefiting from resources like hardship funds (Taylor, 2007: 41). Suggestions variously include: the need for universities to provide customer-friendly reception and information areas where parents with small children will not feel out of place coming for information (Wisker, 1996: 31); or providing information through community-based learning units, particularly for minority and deprived student populations (Scott *et al.*, 2003: 17). A 'one-stop-shop' model of HE provision for lone parents through community colleges, incorporating childcare, work placements, support services, financial aid, and coordinating local welfare officer referrals to the college, is documented to have been particularly successful in facilitating lone parents' HE participation in the USA (Polakow *et al.*, 2004: 149–170). In the UK, public-private welfare-to-work programmes serving lone parents report yielding positive outcomes through facilitating day sessions in local community centres on out-of-town estates, where lone parents can access training and employment advice without having to travel long distances to visit city centre agency offices. It is further suggested that in the UK, the role of NDLP advisers could be usefully expanded to provide lone parents with information and assistance accessing HE studies (Horne and Hardie, 2002: 71).

The project website for this research received emails from lone-parent students not participating in the study, who said that they did not know who to turn to for informed confidential advice (see NUS, 2009: 25). Other emails told of financial worries putting lone parents off applying for, or accepting, HE places. Work with the Government's Student Finance Policy Division as part of this research indicated the department's awareness of the problem of lone parents not knowing who to ask for advice as being a barrier to entering HE. Lone parents considering Higher Education are advised to contact Money Advisors at their HE Institution of choice before applying, but there is clear lack of awareness of the existence of such a service. Lone mothers' narratives document that they would like to see a streamlining of the student financing system, focusing on the key objectives of making it easier to understand and providing more information about childcare support. These priorities sit alongside corresponding calls for increased dialogue between Benefits Agencies and HE providers, as well as greater awareness amongst Local Authorities and Housing Associations, in order to make the process more coherent for users (Scott *et al.*, 2003: 9). However, government negotiation over transferring funding and policy responsibility for full-time HE students in receipt of DWP income-related benefits from DWP to DIUS was ultimately rejected as unfeasible (Prangley, 2007), further distancing the possibility of easing lone parents students' experiences of negotiating their two worlds of lone-parent welfare entitlement and HE studentship.

Calls from lone-mother returners to education for increased streamlining and communication between services correspond with observations of cumbersome bureaucracy for lone parents returning to work. Service providers working with the group have indicated that a change in financial circumstances frequently entails claimants completing up to ten separate, lengthy complicated forms, with staff errors often complicating the process further (Gingerbread, 2007b). In some cases staff at relevant agencies may require additional training in liaising with other organisations and providing accurate information. The information and support needed by lone parents wanting to access Higher Education comes from a range of sources including Benefits and Advice Agencies, LEAs, HE Institutions, Student Welfare, NUS and banks; but a gap is perceived in providing coherent advice on the complete picture as to the feasibility of HE studies and what choices to make prior to enrolment. For example, some lone parents have found themselves better off studying part time on benefits than full time on a repayable loan, although this can disqualify them from passported entitlements. This further indicates the unintended consequence of having rendered continued welfare dependency the most attractive option for many lone parents wishing to complete Higher Education. The proportion of lone-parent HE returners for whom studying on benefits is a viable option has decreased dramatically as the age of the youngest child at which lone parents are migrated to Job Seekers' Allowance (JSA), and hence required to be available for work rather than engaged in education, has decreased rapidly from 16 down to five over the three-year period from 2008 to 2011.

The difficulties lone mothers describe experiencing in securing adequate financial support and advice to assist their progression toward economic self-sufficiency through HE participation, suggest the need for government to take a longer-term perspective in investing in the future of lone parents and their children. This contrasts with what this research has shown lone parents themselves often perceiving as a 'quick-fix' policy approach to cutting unemployment figures by engaging lone parents with any work through minimal investment in learning and training. Lone mothers reveal negative experiences that the level of support provided by the New Deal for Lone Parents (NDLP) is, like support from HE Institutions, too often at the discretion of individual staff, being heavily contingent upon decisions by individual case workers (see Department for Work and Pensions, 2007). This is of concern given that NDLP advisors are argued to 'have little incentive to promote sustainable employment' (Gingerbread, 2007e: 10). With the focus being on cheap, quick solutions to joblessness, there is frequently strong resistance to providing funding for education and training beyond the most short-term, vocationally orientated, and cost minimal options. Claimant job placements achieved through low investment welfare-to-work programmes are shown to result in high levels of job churn, with claimants cycling between welfare dependency and temporary employment, frequently characterised by a downward trend toward lower pay jobs over time. Poverty levels remain high in such circumstances, despite the presence of intermittent employment, and the most vulnerable families are shown to be the most susceptible to downward churn over time.

The recommendation that the role of NDLP advisors be expanded to deliver more support for educational participation may be unduly optimistic given the overriding agenda of minimum investment for maximum job placement outcomes recognised by service providers, policy makers, and lone parents alike. Further, the clear contemporary trend is away from, rather than toward, supporting educational participation for lone parents. As Gingerbread highlighted in response to the 2011 Welfare Reform Bill, the incoming work requirement for lone parents of children aged five attacks the precise time at which many lone parents capitalise on the opportunity provided by their youngest child's enrolment in school, to invest in their family's long-term future through returning to education themselves.

Individual agency and structural constraint

The documented lack of adequate support and advice facilitating lone parents' HE participation contribute to the climate criticised by the NUS, in which they suggest that lone parents must increasingly be determined and resourceful financial experts on managing their own Higher Education, in order to negotiate a complex and constantly changing system. This research highlights the importance of strong individual agency in determining the ability of lone parents to negotiate Higher Education successfully. While agentic arguments can frequently be politically aligned to the right in emphasising individuals' personal responsibility, lone mothers' trajectories in this research illuminated that it is the very presence of structural constraints that can render HE participation impossible for all but the most determined lone-parent students. This demonstrates the complex interplay between structure and agency explored elsewhere (Woodfield, 2007: 70; Cappleman-Morgan, 2005: 9; Merrill, 1999: 26; Crompton and Harris, 1999: 144; Procter and Padfield, 1998: 244). Crompton and Harris's assertion of the need for theoretical pluralism to acknowledge the coexistence of choice and constraint, cooperation and conflict, individual and group dynamics, with regard to exploring women's employment and family lives (1999: 128) is equally relevant to understanding the HE participation of lone parents. In the context of deep social inequalities encountered by lone parents, individual agency becomes pivotal, and it is frequently those individual lone parents exhibiting the highest levels of both agency and informal support networks who succeed despite the hurdles. This has worrying implications for those most vulnerable lone parents with the least resources to call upon.

Institutional factors

One of the key areas of recommendation for ways in which lone parents' HE participation can be better facilitated is in changes for which individual universities themselves are responsible. That universities need to demonstrate greater commitment to meeting the needs of (lone) parent students has been repeatedly voiced and evidenced throughout this research. Chapters 4–7 introduced some of the ways in which the policies and practices of HE Institutions serve to help or hinder lone parents' experiences as university learners, while Chapter 7 also underscored that too often lone-parent students' experiences of support in Higher Education are determinant on nuances of individual staff, departments or institutions, rather than being indicative of uniform standards of conduct. In this way the research highlighted the need for family-friendly practices to be embedded more strongly in policy, rather than leaving widening participation students most in need of support subject to a lottery of experience. There are questions around the level at which recommendations for HE sector policy change should be implemented. Opportunities for improved delivery of provision may variously be addressed at a range of levels, from (but not reliant upon) good practice by individual staff, departments and HE Institutions, through to broader policy by government, unions within the sector, and umbrella bodies, including Universities UK, The Office for Fair Access (OFFA), The Higher Education Funding Council for England (HEFCE), and the Higher Education Policy Institute (HEPI).

In terms of support provision from HE Institutions in particular, factors contributing greatly to facilitating lone-parent students' participation are frequently cost-neutral or minimal, hinging pivotally on altering perceptions of how students with family responsibilities manage the balance of study and home life, and questions of legitimacy around this. Lone mothers highlight examples and deficits of institutional good practice that extend beyond their identities as lone-parent students; for example, those with disabilities also assert the need for universities to increase their support for disabled students. In addition, many of the issues highlighted hold much broader relevance beyond addressing the needs of lone parents, frequently representing good practice in catering to the needs of all students, or at least for non-traditional student groups, including mature, working-class and BME learners. The growing importance of institutional recognition of the multiple responsibilities juggled by many HE students is evidenced by the impact of successive university fee rises over the last 15 years. Given that part-time employment is increasingly a requisite of affording HE participation for many students, regardless of whether individuals have dependants, HE Institutions can no longer legitimately expect their students to prioritise university over competing commitments as they once could.

It is suggested that the need for increased support from HE Institutions for lone-parent students stretches back into the pre-enrolment stage. For example, Wisker has argued that as part of the HE admissions interview:

> *Women with domestic responsibilities should be made aware of the possible ways in which they can combine [their] responsibilities with study: the flexibility of modes of study, the availability of concessions (which could enable them to take part in courses for which they have to pay fees, without feeling they were taking money out of the family food allowance).* (1996: 31)

Lone mothers suggest that more help is needed to ease the transition from Further Education to Higher Education, particularly for Access route students. Evidence indicates the benefits of preparatory modules to assist students in successfully making the transition from FE to HE, with implementation of such programmes shown to result in positive outcomes (Knox, 2005). Such intervention may be particularly beneficial for lone-parent students, given their frequently low confidence levels, as discussed in Chapter 7. However, indication of the benefits of pre-engagement with prospective widening participation (WP) students runs counter to contemporary developments in HE policy. While the Aimhigher scheme, which ran from 2004 to 2011, supported school-leaving and mature WP students through activities including pre-entry outreach work; the National Scholarship Programme (NSP), replacing Aimhigher from 2012, includes no outreach element. This is despite guidance to universities from OFFA advising on a focused WP strategy on outreach work rather than bursaries, given that the latter have been shown not to affect students' HE choices (2010). Similarly, the government report, *Unleashing aspiration: The final report on the panel of fair access to the professions*, recommended the role of universities' engagement in pre-entry outreach work in promoting social mobility (Panel on Fair Access to the Professions, 2009).

Alongside the importance of easing the *transition* to university for mature students after an educational gap, lone mothers' accounts of their HE experiences identify key priorities for HE Institutions in facilitating their learning experiences *throughout* their journeys as students. These recommendations begin with calls that the termly registration process be made quicker and easier for those who have no choice but to bring young children along. While many HE Institutions have now acknowledged and addressed this concern through the introduction of online registration, evidence from lone parents suggests experience not to be uniform in this area as with many other aspects of the HE experience.

Campus services and facilities

The broad focus of recommendations for ways in which universities can contribute to improving HE experiences and outcomes for their lone-parent students are clustered in the two areas of academic delivery, and campus services and facilities. These areas are addressed in the following subsections of this chapter. In terms of campus services and facilities, lone parents' narratives contribute to understanding by pinpointing priority areas. Increased provision of suitable campus family accommodation is highlighted as a priority; and for one young lone mother of a baby in this research in particular, it was eventually securing low-cost, on-campus family accommodation that ultimately enabled her to continue with her course and focus on maximising her engagement with her studies. Other lone mothers describe resorting to living at home with their own parents while they complete their HE studies, due to a lack of suitable, affordable accommodation within travelling distance of their HE Institution. While potentially offering valuable support and informal childcare, these intergenerational households are also indicated to be invariably experienced as a source of stress, and these lone mothers often perceive that both overall quality of family life and their ability to focus on their studies would be substantially improved if they were able to secure accommodation for themselves and their children to live independently.

Other lone mothers who were able to secure on-campus family accommodation described experiencing that university campuses are nevertheless often not 'geared toward' families, once again testifying to the continued prevalence of the implicit 'Bachelor Boy' model of studentship in many universities. This lack of attention to their needs was felt particularly acutely by lone parents with younger children; for example, campus GP practices may not have access to health visitors. Other lone mothers with babies suggested that universities should be obliged to provide students with facilities for expressing and storing breast milk, as they would be obliged to do for breastfeeding staff.

A key priority in terms of vital extracurricular provision is the need for increased counselling provision (see Wisker, 1996: 7–8; Hyatt and Parry, 1990: 33; Edwards, 1993). Lone mothers' narratives highlight that more extensive access to counselling services is particularly important in light of evidenced issues around low self-esteem and depression resulting from facets of past experience highly prevalent amongst lone parents. These factors include negative initial schooling experiences and lack of family support for education in childhood, long educational gaps, and confidence-destroying past relationships. Individuals' experiences show that overburdened waiting lists dictate that even those suffering severe distress are frequently exposed to long waits for both initial assessments and access to regular counselling, which may also be inadequate in terms of number of sessions provided. Calls for increased counselling provision form part of the recognition of the wider need for improved pastoral care for mature learners throughout their university journeys. This sits uncomfortably with widespread losses to university student support services as part of the response to successive rounds of central HE spending cuts over recent years. It has been observed that counselling provision varies widely between HE Institutions (Gallagher et al., 1993: 59), representing another area in which universities' responsibility to students, and in particular WP students, should be ratified by minimum standards in directive policy.

Lone-parent students also recommend that it would be beneficial if universities were to take a more systematic and proactive role in instigating networking between students with parental responsibilities (see NUS, 2009: 39). While not a legitimate substitute for formal support, such peer mentor networks may provide a cost-effective and student-empowering means to plugging an identified gap in existing institutional provision. Such networks can be pivotal in alleviating the frequent loneliness of life as a lone-parent student discussed in Chapter 7, and can address a range of the key problem areas experienced by the group. These include, for example, providing opportunities for informal sharing of practical, emotional and academic peer support, babysitting cooperatives (see NUS, 2009: 66), and opportunities for home sharing, with all of the associated practical and financial benefits. For one student with Attention Deficit Hyperactive Disorder (ADHD), guidance from other students on how to revise had been vital, demonstrating the academic potential of peer support, alongside the social benefits. The success of an Open University Women in Technology (WIT) programme, in which students were supported by self-help and study-support groups to aid confidence-building and provide a safe environment to discuss concerns about skills and practice, provides further evidence in support of the potential benefits of such models (Wisker, 1996: 28). The Open University has attributed its successive high scores in the National Student Survey (NSS) in part to provision of student support groups (Lipsett, 2007b), and lone mothers in this research repeatedly described the importance of knowing of others in similar situations for both emotional and practical reasons:

> *I don't know many other students in the same boat – it might have helped to have other people you could share childcare burdens with. Maybe like a community of lift-sharers, only for children?! I think my fellow students see me as a bit mad.* (Michelle, age 35, one child aged 12, MSc History of Science)

The needs of dependants are identified as a key factor compromising the HE retention of part-time students (Yorke, 1999: 61), and up to 65 per cent of lone-parent students report having considered leaving their course (NUS, 2009: 3). It has been suggested that expanding access is pointless unless HE Institutions follow policies and practices, including provision of mature student support services and childcare facilities to meet the needs of these groups, and help ensure that they do not underachieve (Leonard, 1994: 174–175; also Wisker, 1996: 8). Indeed, Gallagher *et al.* argued that 'without basic childcare provision such as playschemes and crèche facilities, institutions are effectively closing their doors to many mature students' (1993: 58). Once again, a key contribution of lone-parent students' insights provided in this research has been to highlight, not only that recommendations made as long as almost 20 years ago remain largely unaddressed, but more pressingly, that contemporary policy development is leading away from such provision, including the trend toward closure of campus childcare facilities discussed in Chapter 6. Successive commentators on mature women students' HE participation have uniformly acknowledged the primacy of adequate childcare provision in facilitating access (see Edwards, 1993: 150; Wisker, 1996: 31; Merrill, 1999: 197), including Adrienne Rich in her recommendations for the 'woman centred university' in 1979 (Jackson, 2004: 127). Alongside institutional nursery provision and supporting student-run initiatives, further key childcare recommendations include the need for childcare provision on all sites of multisite institutions, employment of childcare coordinators, holiday playschemes, playgroups and subsidising networks of childminders (Edwards, 1993: 58). It is further suggested that student parents should be made to feel that, rather than stay away if childcare arrangements break down, they might take children into university (Merrill, 1999: 169), representing an aspect of the need for change in broader institutional cultures discussed later in this chapter.

Academic provision

Beyond the documented need for increased pastoral care and provision of services and facilities, the second major area of lone mothers' calls for greater support from their HE Institutions focuses on academic provision. The significance of academic delivery can be broadly divided into issues in three broad areas: around teaching timetabling; flexibility and support; and provision of remote access to services.

As Chapter 4 introduced, a key area in which lone mothers suggest that universities can support their prospects of successful HE participation is the various aspects of scheduling. These recommendations encompass areas from timetabling of teaching (also NUS, 2009: 22, 24; Scott *et al.*, 2003: 9) and exams, through to library opening times. One lone parent suggested that students should sign a contract with their HE Institution, setting formal parameters of commitment requirements negotiated as realistic, that students would be expected to meet, and that HE staff would not make demands of individuals beyond this. The student suggesting this perceived that this would protect students with family commitments from being stung with unachievable additional expectations, such as meeting other students outside formal contact hours to prepare group presentations, not factored into existing work and childcare arrangements. In addition, lone mothers suggest that timetables should be available in advance to those with family responsibilities, and should not be altered, and even that students with responsibilities should be notified of last-minute lecture cancellations via text message to save them unnecessary journeys and childcare arrangements. Timetabling suggestions frequently cluster around fitting HE contact time with childcare provision, and lone mothers' experiences illustrate the positive effect that sympathetic timetabling can have; for example:

I was able to obtain a timetable before other students because I am a parent and was therefore able to get my childcare in place before the start of term. (Jo, three children, Year 2)

Suggestions include that university hours should fit with school hours, that Open University tutorials should also be available during the day rather than just the evenings, and that university contact time should be crunched into two full days rather than being spread patchily throughout the week. While organisationally difficult for universities, the latter request is likely to gain strength as major fee increases can be expected to result in larger numbers of students managing increasing loads of part-time employment with their HE study, as well as remaining in the parental home and travelling substantial distances to study at university as day students, in order to avoid incurring living costs alongside hefty fees.

It is advocated that universities should ensure that exams fit with the opening hours provided by their own nurseries, and that library access should include weekend opening. Further suggestions allowing lone parents to schedule their study commitments to fit in with parenting responsibilities more easily include that university reading weeks should coincide with local school half-term holidays, and that reading lists and assignments be made available further in advance. Lone mothers also call for the following term's reading to be made available to them at the beginning of the holidays, and that assignments be set before the holidays – recommendations enabling time to work ahead and be prepared for unexpected hindrances like children's illness. While some indicate a preference for single rather than continuous assessment to reduce the pressure of constant deadlines; for others, coursework is preferential over exams in allowing study time to be spread out, and the need to rely on childcare minimised. One lone parent suggested that HE experience would be improved if academic timetables were constructed to divide seminars by age, with some seminar groups set aside exclusively for mature students to voice their opinions without feeling that they were dominating younger students. This chimes with Leonard's finding that mature students are often acutely conscious of their tendency to dominate seminar discussion, leading to feelings of uneasiness between themselves and other students (Leonard, 1994: 169). While mature student-only seminars may appear an attractive alternative to adult returners feeling alienated from the majority student body, they may however also act to further exacerbate the very feelings of isolation from other students they are aimed at addressing.

Support and flexibility

In addition to timetabling issues, lone-parent students indicate the importance of the support and flexibility they receive from their HE Institutions to facilitating their participation. Calls for increased flexibility by HE Institutions extend back to interviewing and admissions procedure timed to suit parents with children (Wisker, 1996: 31). For one disabled student, her university's provision of a home computer and an exam invigilator to allow her to sit exams in her own home facilitated her HE participation. Relevant tailored support identified by many lone mothers as contributing strongly to facilitating successful HE outcomes includes mock examinations to acquaint students who have lengthy learning gaps with educational procedure, more qualitative feedback on exam performance and partial essay drafts to aid confidence building, as well as increased assistance in setting up training placements, as frequently required for students studying vocational HE programmes from teaching and nursing, through to graphic design and journalism. Given that many HE faculties invest their time heavily in addressing these areas of recommended support, it can be surmised from students' contrasting feedback that these are aspects of experience in which the learning experiences and outcomes of WP students are highly dependent upon the motivation and resources of individuals, staff, departments and institutions.

In addition to addressing the support needs of specific groups of WP students, the blanket need for increased flexibility in HE provision emerges as pivotal time and again (NUS, 2009: 22, 24; Merrill, 1999: 197; Wisker, 1996: 7) as a key indicator of facilitating HE participation by students with family responsibilities. This includes calls for more flexible class times and deadlines, changing rules about borrowing library books, special permission to leave mobile phones on during lectures or seminars, and being granted assignment extensions when children are ill. Lone mothers further request license to change seminar groups where they clash with unavoidable commitments. Christie et al. emphasise that increased flexibility would contribute to HE participation not only by students with children, but for all mature students (2005: 23). As with other aspects of lone-parent students' experiences, the relevance of such demands increasingly extends beyond mature students, with students' growing reliance on part-time work to support their HE participation necessitating recognition by HE Institutions that individuals have both a need and a right to request more flexible seminar times. Therefore, the recommendations that increasing flexibility would represent acknowledgement by HE Institutions that mature students have other responsibilities (Gallagher *et al.*, 1993: 31), and that non-flexible courses that are inaccessible to students who have to work in term time amount to class discrimination (Taylor, 2007: 39), will be seen to be relevant to ever-increasing proportions of the HE student population.

Some trends toward increasing flexibilisation of HE provision are taking place as a function of the WP agenda, acknowledgement of the implications of changing student finances, and the increasing technologisation of HE provision discussed in the following section. However, developments are far from uniform across areas of identified need for change, or adoption by institutions. While many staff may perceive benefits, and resource costs may not be prohibitive, some changes may nevertheless require seismic shifts in institutional cultures, particularly in more traditional HE Institutions, as explored later in this chapter. It is suggested, for example, that increasing flexibility in Higher Education can in fact be seen as contentious in formally acknowledging the legitimacy of students' conflicting responsibilities. For academics who maintain an ideal of the academy as a bastion of 'Ivory tower' intellectualism, this may raise uncomfortable questions over whether such concessions will apply to all students or particular groups only, and fears of fostering laxness, declining standards, inequity amongst students, and abuse of the system.

Attesting to the importance of variation between institutional cultures, the following reflection bolsters the recommendation for increased staff training to address the way in which, in cultures built around the established norm of a privileged student population, lone-parent students' experiences of support for their circumstances can continue to be informed by the prevalence of implicit assumptions that students are not burdened by conflicting responsibilities:

> *In addition to an earlier email, I had a very interesting conversation*
> *with one of the professors yesterday. While discussing PhD options,*
> *I gave him a quick run-down of my circumstances – working part*
> *time (unlike anyone else on the course) and a single parent. He was*

visibly surprised and commented that it was good to know these things. I am finding that members of staff at [this university] are very helpful IF they know my circumstances. The problem is that there is no institutional set-up to inform them of these matters, unlike my last uni where the staff all knew or asked in the first few weeks to find out everyone's circumstances, it was openly dealt with. It is very difficult to have to inform people without sounding like you are asking for special treatment, and in my case it has taken almost two terms to do so. As students at [this university] tend to be wealthy (and not parents), the staff are simply not aware of the need to manage these situations. They need some form of training!
(Michelle, age 35, one child aged 12, MSc History of Science)

Remote provision

Provision of avenues for virtual contact with HE Institutions via the Internet are seen to be central to facilitating learning participation for many lone-parent students, with widespread calls for increased opportunities for independent study from home with online support, minimising the need to buy in expensive childcare. Additional elements of remote access to university highlighted by lone parents as facilitating their learning experience include: increased email contact with tutors; being able to sign up for seminar groups electronically; increased availability of videoed lectures online (also Christie *et al.*, 2005: 23); and remote online access to university library catalogues, renewals, reservations, and institutional electronic journal subscriptions.

The Open University's consistently high NSS outcomes (Lipsett, 2007a) point toward students' valuing of remote access as a core element of sympathetic HE delivery. The large proportion of lone-parent students studying with the OU in this research offer further indication of the benefits of the mode of study for this group of learners, both indirectly, through their numbers, and directly, through the feedback they provided. Remote provision clearly offers distinct benefits for lone-parent students who very frequently lack childcare and hence opportunity to physically attend university. Lone mothers studying through distance learning in this research (heavily represented by OU students), overwhelmingly report experiencing their HE Institutions as being supportive of their situation. Institutions providing distance learning do not however escape lone-parent students' recommendations for improvements in provision. One distance-learning student in this research perceived a need for increased online learning and test content to keep distance-learning students feeling more in touch with their course.

While the rapidly continuing technologisation of society as a whole informs the remote access needs of HE students with childcare responsibilities being increasingly met, evidence from lone-parent students indicates that there remains need for further development, and that some institutions have further to travel than others in facilitating remote access. Further, institutions' responsibilities to provide remote access to key services can be expected to become increasingly important to larger numbers of students, beyond those with childcare needs, as fee hikes resulting in more students remaining in the parental home and travelling to their HE Institution daily decreases physical access to campus facilities.

Institutional cultures – attitudes

The university learning experiences of lone mothers highlight the persistence of the default model of the 'Bachelor Boy' student endemic in Higher Education. In some cases, lone mothers' experiences indicate their HE Institution's rhetoric to profess far more positive attitudes to non-traditional students with external responsibilities than are borne out by practice. This discrepancy recommends the need to extend investigation of WP provision beyond analysis of formal policy, to incorporate insights from the subjective experiences of non-traditional students, as this book has done. Insights into timetabling issues; universities' refusal to be flexible around lone parents' needs; and the humiliation experienced by some lone parents in the process of applying for assistance from their HE Institution's Access to Learning Fund, as explored in Chapter 5, all underline the way in which HE Institutions implicitly chastise and punish lone parents for failing to comply with the model of the ideal university student, as primarily devoted to studies and living frugally on modest, but manageable, means. By default, lone parents have other responsibilities more important than their studies, and while they have higher incomes than other students, these are outweighed by their heavy outgoings, incurred through childcare and other childrearing costs.

Underpinning the calls for individual concessions and factors

226

addressing the needs of lone-parent HE learners discussed throughout this book, runs a thread of implied need for deep-seated change in institutional cultures, beyond curriculum and support developments, if the needs of non-traditional learners are to be truly embraced. Wisker has suggested that 'universities should be required to consider restructuring their provision to enable . . . students to combine family life with study' (1996: 6). It has been further suggested that the term 'widening participation' is in itself problematic in failing to convey an indication of the institutional change required to embrace the learning and associated needs of diverse students (Christie *et al.*, 2005: 6). In this, deficiencies in HE strategy resonate with those highlighted by the social model of disability, in erroneously assuming 'inclusion' to constitute bringing excluded individuals into the dominant framework, rather than problematising deficiencies in the framework that result in some individuals being left outside it (Barnes and Mercer, 2009; Shakespeare, 2006; Oliver, 1996).It is suggested that institutional cultures in Higher Education have failed to take the needs of the non-traditional students targeted by WP strategies as seriously as those of conventional 18-year-old students, leaving the former feeling unwelcome (Murphy and Roopchand, 2003: 256; Gallagher *et al.*, 1993: 22).

Participation in this research by lone mothers studying at HE Institutions representing the breadth of the sector, have furnished insight into the wide divergence in terms of receptiveness to the needs of non-traditional students, including lone parents. For example, while some universities permit no assessment extensions at all, others leave them to the discretion of individual staff. Such discrepancies raise important issues as to whether, and the level at which, such concessions are embedded in policy and practice. Lone-parent students' experiences clearly convey the need for the more traditional elite HE Institutions, most heavily invested in the ideal of the 'Bachelor Boy' model, to embrace lessons around facilitating access and participation from institutions with higher concentrations of non-traditional, part-time, and distance-learning students. Lone-parent students' in-depth narratives attest to the presence of substantial cultural differences in institutional attitude to the value and entitlements of WP students, including those with family responsibilities. This warrants the need for further investigation into such differences to build upon the insights of this research, and further, the need for deep-seated institutional change within the cultures of some of the UK's most prestigious HE Institutions. This affirms assertions that it is universities in the pre-1992 sector that most need to change if they are to provide positive experiences for non-traditional students (Reay, 2003). As one lone mother in this research reflected of her university experience:

> *I do have the feeling that more traditional (and prestigious)*
> *institutions like [University] cater less for the needs of students with*
> *different backgrounds. I might be wrong, but this is what I think.*
> *I know they have a lot of initiatives for widening participation,*
> *which is good, but there is little support for students who are parents.*
> (Carys, age 31, one child aged 1, Year 2 PhD Sociology)

In contrast to chastising, negative experiences of university participation described by some lone parents, others recount positive experiences of university lecturers who have treated them as equal adults, and validated the significance of their experiences outside university as parents. These experiences resonate with ideals of pedagogical practice developed in Women's Studies (Jackson, 2004: 127), and support calls for course provision and assessment that validate the embodied experience and material context from which mature students with children engage with HE learning (Wisker, 1996) – although in practice many students find this to be far from the experience of the HE teaching they encounter (Edwards, 1993).

Widening provision and informing choices

The final broad area of educational provision recommendations for meeting lone parents' needs in HE participation is in terms of widening availability. It has been argued that 'the model of the three year, full-time degree dependent upon two A-level entry frequently does not meet the needs of mature women, depending as it does upon mobility' (Wisker, 1996: 4). This is borne out by the heavy participation by lone mothers in part-time and distance learning pathways, as well as discussed problems of geographical access. Mature students who undertake Access courses in the hope of progressing to Higher Education are evidenced frequently to find the next stage in their educational development stifled by lack of a local university to attend. While it may be possible to fit Access study into daily routines of domestic and paid work, and still get home in time to collect children, transferring to study at degree level can entail travelling to the nearest university 50 miles away or more on an extended day, or several days a week. This experience has been described by lone mothers in this research, with its ensuing challenges in terms of time, childcare, and travel costs. Lone mothers' experiences in this respect bolster support for the franchising of HE courses to FE colleges. Franchising addresses not just the identified problem of distance, but as arguments presented above indicate, serve further positive functions in facilitating lone-parent students' higher learning experiences by tapping into educational cultures more attuned to their needs. That increasing development of university franchises has attracted mature students who are mainly women attests to the suitability of the mode for this group, and lone mothers in this research document HE learning journeys achieved through university courses franchised to FE Institutions. In addition, other lone mothers indicate perceiving that they would not have been able to access Higher Education at all without the opportunity provided by the Access route as an alternative to A-levels, resonating with the claim that 'the Access movement has been highly significant in returning mature women to education' (Wisker, 1996: 4), and this being particularly true of the Access to Social Work and Nursing courses (Jones, 2006: 485) which this research has shown to be strongly represented amongst lone mothers. The potential of vocational courses to provide lone parents with HE pathways that offer training subsidies and lead to relatively secure career outcomes has been endorsed by some commentators (Scott et al., 2003: 9), and is relevant to this research given the large proportion of participants studying vocational courses, including nursing and teacher training, largely reporting such subject choice to have been influenced by their lone-parent status.

The popularity amongst mature students, including lone parents, of FE and HE courses channelling graduates into careers as nurses, social workers, teachers and teaching assistants is not however unproblematic. While training for these professions may buy learners the relative security of regular work and income, it also leads individuals into careers frequently characterised by the same low pay, low-status, and high-stress caring work that also dominates their lives at home bringing up children. It is warned that while foundation degrees for nursing auxiliaries and teaching assistants do help those in low-paid, low-status jobs to gain qualifications, they are unlikely to enable individuals to move away from these traditionally feminised fields of employment (Jackson, 2004, 14). Access courses may provide locally available and otherwise accessible gateways to higher learning for traditionally excluded groups, including lone parents, but in feeding onto particular courses at particular universities, they can also limit participants' HE options. This indicates the need for widespread and robust availability of careers advice at all stages. Research from the NUS and the Confederation of British Industry (CIB) shows more than half of HE students to want more advice from their university around understanding employability (2011: 39); and the Government acknowledge providing more information on the implications of different FE and HE subject and institution choices as being central to improving social mobility for disadvantaged groups (2011: 45, 50). However, the replacement of Aimhigher with the NSP scheme discussed earlier in this chapter, with its ensuing termination of funding for university school-outreach work, undermines acknowledgement of this priority. BME students are more likely to attend FE colleges rather than sixth form colleges, compared to white and richer students. This, in turn, influences choices of HE subject and institution, and is ultimately indicated as a factor in lower levels of First classifications achieved by BME students at university (Connor *et al.* (2004). The relevance of this identified chain of causation can be extended to WP students beyond BME groups, including lone parents, who, as identified in Chapter 3, may also experience a comparative deficit of options, family experience and educational support to inform strategic choices around post-compulsory education. It is also nevertheless important not to lay responsibility for learning pathway, subject and institution choices with WP students themselves, as evidence also shows them to be disadvantaged by discriminatory admissions practice (see Burke and McManus, 2010), with 'high tariff' HE Institutions in particular long evidenced to show a bias toward 'traditional' entrants (Purcell *et al.*, 2009). This section of the final chapter has underlined that there are key areas in which both individual HE Institutions and the sector as a whole can make a range of improvements, recommended by lone mothers themselves as non-traditional HE students, in order to assist more proactively in facilitating the success of their HE learner journeys. The remainder of the chapter broadens the scope of discussion to include recommendations for provision of an improved service focused on wider funding and policy issues.

Key financial issues

Beyond recommendations for change from HE Institutions, their staff, and the sector as a whole, financial issues unsurprisingly represent a key area of identified need for improving lone-parent students' experiences of HE participation. Lone mothers' narratives iterate time and again how central accessing adequate support is to facilitating their HE participation, for example:

> *I have been lucky that my fees were paid for otherwise there is no way that I would have been able to attend.* (Marcia, age 43, one child aged 7, Year 3 BSc Clinical Nursing)

An overarching theme in much of what lone mothers have to say about their experiences of available financial support for their HE participation is the feeling that the system frequently acts as a disincentive. This book has explored in depth the journeys of lone parents who, in pursuit of brighter futures for themselves and their families, have opted to shoulder the hefty load of commitments entailed in juggling HE participation with being sole childcarer, substantially eating into time with their children, and sometimes also having informed exiting former employment. Lone-mother students frequently describe feeling resentful that the self-sacrifices they perceive in taking proactive steps to improve their own lives and become economically self-sufficient, are not more recognised and rewarded by the Government. Given the 'risky business' that HE participation is seen to be for students with family responsibilities (Reay, 2003), and evidence that such students frequently fail to make the transition from FE to HE studies (Scott *et al.*, 2003), there is an identified need for further research into decisions and influencing factors amongst lone-parent students who do not apply for or accept HE places after making preliminary investigations or completing FE qualifications.

The recurrence of financial problems throughout lone-mother students' learner journeys affirm the validity of recommendations for a more generous, and better organised and directed system of financial support for students with family responsibilities (Brown, 2007). In particular, lone mothers' recommendations for improved financial provision advocate the need for increased coherence between the student financing system, and entitlement to lone parent means-tested benefits, to provide a more consistent income throughout the year. Lone mothers' narratives highlight the benefits such improved coherence would offer in terms of avoiding confusion and periods of increased financial hardship – particularly over the long university summer holiday.

Gingerbread has similarly highlighted 'an organisational mismatch between DWP, Jobcentre Plus and the Learning and Skills Council', affecting lone parents (2007f: 6). Subsequent sections of this chapter address the relevance to lone-parent students of elements of student financing and lone parent support respectively.

Lone parents and Higher Education funding

The key concern dominating lone-parent students' recommendations for improved financial support for their HE studies straddles the boundary between student funding and lone parent support in highlighting the extent of dissatisfaction at the perceived injustice of previous entitlement to university grants and Income Support, having been replaced by loans that must be repaid, as discussed more extensively in Chapter 5 (also Scott *et al.*, 2003: 9). The following insight identifies the link between financing, incentive to study, and course completion:

> *I think it would be better if the government gave grants to single parents returning to study and we didn't have to go and kind of 'prove' that we needed the help. I'm sure that it would encourage more people to attend and would also help students to stick with the course.* (Jennifer, age 44, four children aged 10–20, Year 3 BA Education Studies and History)

While the implications of the transition from grants and Income Support to repayable loans may have been dire, with Callender suggesting that it has grossly exacerbated poverty and debt for lone parents (2002); lone parents' recommendations that these changes should be reversed to restore previous access to grants and Income Support, and lessen their compulsory reliance on student loans, unfortunately seem unlikely to be realised. In this sense, lone mothers' experiences as HE learners are not unique, but are rather shared with all students, as individuals bear rocketing costs of undertaking a degree, deferred as debt to be repaid after completion. What stands lone parents apart is their particular vulnerability to managing financial changes borne by all, given a combination of factors, including their sole responsibility for meeting high household costs, and decreased ability to participate in paid work due to childcare constraints. In the inevitable situation that these shifts in student financing are not to be reversed for any group,

232

even lone parents as arguably one of the most vulnerable demographics, this informs the recommendation for additional safeguards to contribute toward remediating inequalities in negative effects.

Existing arrangements of repayment of student loans represent similar inequalities in effect rather than requirement for lone parent learners. As apparent from discussion of the constraints of sole childrearing responsibilities throughout this book, lone parents are disadvantaged by facing substantially different personal circumstances to other students, but not student loan repayment requirements, when they graduate (see Callender, 2001). This informs the recommendation made by lone parents, commentators and service providers alike that the group should be subject to a higher income threshold for commencement of student loan repayment (see Scott *et al.*, 2003: 9). Lone-mother students' learner trajectories evidence that in order to facilitate movement onto the first rung of the career ladder and a sufficiently firm grip to hold on there, lone parents need to be protected from the requirement to commence student loan repayments too early, or assisted by additional Tax Credit provision to cover their increased outgoings:

> *It would be very handy . . . [if] you didn't have to pay back your student loan till you started earning a salary of at least £25,000, and then only at a very low rate taking into consideration your kids etc.* (Maria, two children, Year 2 BA History and Archaeology)

Chapter 5 introduced how the financial hardship encountered by lone-parent students can often leave them reliant on applications to university Access to Learning Funds (ALF). Representing just one example among many, one lone mother explained how a generous grant from her university's Access Fund when her ex-partner withheld maintenance payments, ultimately facilitated continuation of her degree.

In 2001, the arrival of an enabling, imaginative new package' of government support for student parents, including the childcare grant and bursary scheme, was welcomed (Callender, 2001), whereby the Government allocate bursary funds for HE Institution's to distribute discretionally to individuals in particular financial need. Research on student parents' HE participation since has however recommended the need for more creative distribution of such funds (see Scott *et al.*, 2003: 9). Indeed, a key criticism levied by the NUS against universities in terms of supporting lone parents has been over failure to allocate bursary funds. When the lid was lifted on top-up fees in 2006, bursary funds were increased as a concession designed to offset negative effects of the changes. Given evidence that lone parents are one of the student groups in the greatest financial hardship, they would be expected to be a key bursary beneficiary group, and hence particularly affected by shortcomings in distribution. In 2007 the NUS highlighted £25 million earmarked bursary funding to have gone unallocated to the poorest students by universities. Both the deficit in bursary allocation, and lone parents' documented negative experiences of application procedure as outlined in Chapter 5, indicate the need for substantial overhaul of bursary allocation procedure, including additional guidelines and training for administering staff. Without compromising the rigour of the process, it should be ensured that applicants are guaranteed privacy for communication of personal information, and recognition that it is not always possible or safe for non-resident parents to be contacted to provide maintenance verification. Administration of the allocation process should acknowledge more consistently and sensitively that it is often a demeaning process for applicants to have to ask for money in this way.

Lone parents' experiences of applying to their universities' Access to Learning Funds may well be shared by other financially vulnerable student groups forced to resort to such sources of support. In addition to financial support recommendations focusing specifically on the unique needs of lone parents, the findings of this research suggest further areas for improved provision informed by demographic characteristics of the lone mothers researched, and hence also relevant to these wider groups. These include the need for increased financial support for mature and part-time students, and for all students with dependants.

Some lone mothers recommend that more financial support should be available to enable mature students who already have a degree but are on a low income a second chance at education to retrain in a new area. This is a worthy goal, particularly given evidence presented in Chapter 3 as well as later in this chapter that lone parents are frequently over-represented amongst those students who had unsatisfactory experiences of initial education and may have been steered in the direction of particular low-status post-compulsory routes. However, the prospect of extending provision to repeat participation in Higher Education seems unlikely to be realised in the context of cuts to support for initial participation. In addition to this request, researching lone mothers'

HE participation informs recommendations for increases to mature student bursaries and Dependant's Allowance, improved childcare assistance, and increased disabled student support. Scott *et al.* have suggested childcare issues to be in need of more central integration into governmental WP strategy (2003: 9). Other lone mothers recommend the need for wider provision of Research Council funding for postgraduate studies. While postgraduate qualifications are indicated to be increasingly central to employability in the context of progressively competitive job markets and highly qualified populations, this recommendation, like others, may be seen as unlikely to be realised in light of significant recent cuts to Research Council funding.

Lone mothers studying part-time in Higher Education highlight the need for increased financial assistance, including with meeting the cost of childcare, and access to student loans. The importance to access of inequalities in financial assistance for part-time students has been acknowledged and addressed in the extension of eligibility for student loans to part-time students. However, part-time students are disadvantaged by the commencement of repayment liability three and a half years after borrowing, regardless of full-time or part-time student status, meaning that while the majority of full-time students will have completed their degree and be seeking employment by the time their student loan begins to accrue high levels of interest, the average part-time student will only be halfway through their studies. This inequality may intersect particularly detrimentally with the increased aversion to financial risk and debt documented amongst disadvantaged students, as discussed in Chapter 5 as well as earlier in this chapter.

While the above discussed issues around financial support address how aspects of student funding affect lone parents, the remainder of this chapter addresses how the group are affected by their entitlement to welfare support determinate on their status as lone parents, rather than as adult learners.

Lone-parent benefit entitlement

The narratives of lone-mother HE students provide insight into the centrality of adequate financial support to meeting essential needs for staples, including the cost of housing and food. The stories of these learners further illuminate that increasing recognition and support for lone-parent students' circumstances from the centralised welfare bureaucracy has the potential to greatly assist individuals' ability to successfully negotiate Higher Education and pave the way for their families' future financial independence and security.

One key recurring recommendation around lone-parent welfare entitlement iterated by lone-mother HE students, focuses on child maintenance disregard. While child maintenance was disregarded as income under the Tax Credits regime experienced by participants in this research, it was not disregarded for claimants on Income Support. This strategic differentiation contributes to the agenda of incentivising employment for lone parents. But the fact that child maintenance was not disregarded for Income Support claimants was felt to be inequitable and disincentivising by lone mothers in this research who were studying in Higher Education while on Income Support. Some lone mothers were sometimes also working under 16 hours per week, which was the then threshold for Working Families Tax credit entitlement, as the following indicates:

> For those of us that have a chance at maintenance payments, these are also undermined due to the fact that it is taken pound for pound out of any benefits that we are claiming – there is never any extra leeway to get ahead of the game financially. Why can't the government recognize that we are getting off our butts and trying to make our lives better? Could we not be re-categorized and paid any benefits on an educational wage basis that would not interfere with maintenance for our children's benefit and allow us to sustain things like mortgages, etc. (Denise, age 35, one child aged 9, Year 2 BA English)

While policy was subsequently reviewed to provide partial disregard of child maintenance on Income Support, this was once again thrown into uncertainty by the major overhaul constituted by the 2011 Welfare Reform Bill.

Chapter 4 introduced the importance of juggling participation in paid work alongside family and studies for many lone-parent students, while Chapter 5 detailed that for many this balance is seen as essential, with paid work and associated entitlement to Working Families Tax Credit providing the financial means to participate in Higher Education for many. This link is explicated clearly by many lone mothers, for example:

> *Tax credits are my lifeline. Without them I could not work part time, bring up my son and study for the future* (Nicolette, age 47, one child aged 11, BA Humanities)

In 2005, Callender *et al.* suggested that a 2003 change in the law, making student parents with household incomes below £58,000 per annum eligible for Tax Credits should ease the transition from benefits to work or university for student parents (2005: 19). As with other elements of recommended change implicated in this work, the direction of current policy is now oriented away from such increased provision, with Tax Credit cuts set to squeeze entitlement for such middle-income families, including those headed by lone parents.

Alongside access to Tax Credits and child maintenance as major sources of financial support informing lone-parent students' resource levels, additional areas of recommendations for increased support provision were indicated. Some recommend the potential for increased support from Housing Benefit and Council Tax Benefit to aid lone parents' HE participation:

> *It would be very handy to have either your rent paid for the terms weeks that you attend college, or your council tax bill waived for the months that you attend college.* (Maria, two children, Year 2 BA History and Archaeology)

For others, being awarded Disability Living Allowance (DLA) is cited as providing essential additional financial assistance. Demonstrating the negative implications of failing to secure adequate financial support, one lone mother lamented that if social services had provided greater assistance, including the respite care she had requested for her autistic son, this would have enabled her to complete her HE course and commence work as a social worker. Unable to secure this help, she had instead exited her course early without completing.

The recurrence of calls for increased childcare support to aid lone-parent students reinforces existing findings (Scott *et al.*, 2003: 9; Wisker, 1996: 8; Leonard, 1994: 174–175). Such key recommendations include increased financial assistance with meeting the cost of term-time and school holiday childcare, as well as assistance paying family members to care for children. Contemporary childcare funding policy developments will inevitably impact substantially upon those lone parents who participate in Higher Education. While the extension of childcare support to lone parents who undertake so-called 'mini-jobs' of under 16 hours per week may improve opportunities for some lone parents to participate in university and paid work simultaneously; overall reductions in levels of childcare support are projected to impact negatively. As highlighted in Chapter 5, for some families recent cuts in childcare support are estimated to represent up to a tenfold increase in costs (Family Action, 2011).

In addition to recommendations around childcare support, lone-mother HE students suggest that the UK Government or children's schools should fund the cost of school trips for children of students. This complements existing recommendations for increased provision of passported services, including free access to leisure facilities for children of students (Scott *et al.*, 2003: 9). Such provision addresses the problem highlighted in Chapter 6 of providing satisfactory and affordable structured school-holiday activity for older children. In 2009 the previous UK government introduced free swimming for all children aged under 16, providing, alongside the explicit aim of increasing fitness levels, valuable holiday entertainment for older children whose parents are at work or studying. The scheme, however, ended in 2010, assessed as not being good value.

While discussion so far outlines several areas in which lone parents and commentators recommend that government support for HE participation could be extended for the group, the major area of concern is Income Support entitlement. The migration of financing lone parents' HE participation from grants and Income Support to repayable student loans has been discussed above, and in more depth in Chapter 5. Alongside this core change in entitlement for lone-parent students studying full time in Higher Education, successive changes to lone parent welfare legislation aimed at mobilising lone parents into paid employment, have, as a by-product, impacted heavily on the terms of lone parent's HE participation. In 2008 the then government decreased the age of its youngest child at which lone parents were required to be available for work from 16 to 12 years old. This was based on recommendations in the Freud report, *Reducing Dependency, Increasing Opportunity: Options for the Future of Welfare to Work* (2007). Introduction of increased lone parent work requirement has been justified by comparisons with policy in a number of European countries, including Australia, the Netherlands, France and Germany (DWP, 2007: 40). The

UK previously stood out as one of the only European countries not compelling lone parents to seek employment. But leaning too heavily on insights from cross-cultural comparison is warned against in the UK context, given a markedly divergent lone parent profile. British lone parents are significantly younger, more disadvantaged, less qualified, and have lower employment rates than lone parents in other European countries (Klett-Davies, 2007).

NUS have acknowledged the vital resource that Income Support entitlement represents for lone-parent students, including highlighting the issue of financial support over university holiday periods (2009: 51). Requiring unemployed lone parents to be available for work, and hence migrating them from Income Support onto Job Seeker's Allowance has the additional consequence of disentitling lone-parent HE students whose children are over the threshold age from claiming Income Support and passported benefits including Housing Benefit, Council Tax Credit and children's free school meals, over the long university summer holiday. For this period from July–September inclusive, amounting to a quarter of the entire year, without entitlement to lone-parent benefits, lone-parent students are left without income to sustain their families, given that student financing is not designed to cover vacation periods. Here, as in other ways highlighted throughout this book, lone-parent students fall victim to their deviation from the assumed 'Bachelor Boy' model of HE studentship, given that, compared to younger traditional students, they are both impeded by their sole childcare commitments from taking on temporary employment, and unlikely to return from term-time student digs to the parental home. Hence they are left with several months of continuing rent and household costs, but no source from which to fund these. Some lone-parent students are entitled to claim Job Seeker's Allowance over the summer holiday, subject to individual assessment (Directgov, 2011), but this brings with it requirements around employment availability.

The NUS are particularly concerned about the effect of successive policy changes upon lone parents caught by shifting goal posts during their HE learner journeys. But the implications are also grave for lone parents considering entering Higher Education, who may be deterred by the increasing financial challenges. Excluding lone-parent Higher Education students from unemployment benefits because as students they are not deemed available for work, implicitly refuses to acknowledge the role of Higher Education as an instrument of future employability, career progression, and family economic self-sufficiency for lone parents. Advocacy groups including the NUS and Gingerbread have lobbied parliament during successive phases of welfare reform to add clauses to incoming policy, explicitly acknowledging that lone parents studying in Higher Education are fulfilling the criterion of taking active steps toward employment, but this has been largely unacquiesced. NUS's 2009 report recommended that 'DWP should restore lone parents' entitlement to access benefits whilst studying, without the requirement to be "available for work"' (2009: 54), but in the context of continuing trends, such a reverse in policy appears unlikely to be realised in the foreseeable future.

Lone parents, ideology, and paid work

It is argued that the UK experienced a shift in consciousness away from the traditional male breadwinner model over the decades of the late 20th and early 21st centuries, represented at the levels of both policy and culture. Under a breadwinner model, the primary role of mothers is seen as childrearing, informing the expectation that mothers will be financially supported either by a male breadwinner or, failing this, that the state will take on the role of breadwinner (Gottfried and O'Reilly, 2002; Crompton, 1999). In the process of the move toward an adult-citizen-worker model, whereby all able adults, including lone parents, are expected to be labour market active, it is suggested that contradictions have opened up in government policy between this new ideology and the previous breadwinner model (Land, 2007). This enhances understanding of some of the complex and contradictory situations that lone-parent students describe negotiating, caught in inconsistencies between various elements of financial support, and unsure of their expected role as both primary childcarers and breadwinners. Such ideological inconsistencies contribute, for example, to understanding the stress caused to lone parents by being subjected to increasing work requirements, but in the context of the highest cost childcare in the OECD that implicitly continues to assume care for children to be the unpaid responsibility of mothers. Since the 2010 regime change in the UK, incoming family welfare policy can be seen as representing a u-turn in reasserting a breadwinner model, through financially disincentivising employment by second earners in families, the majority of whom are women (Bell and Strelitz, 2011). However, while a conservative agenda may seek to reassert the primary role of married or partnered women as childcarers, it does not correspondingly extend to a socialist model of state as provider for partnerless parents. While contemporary policy incentivises second earners in couples to remain outside paid employment, it simultaneously extends the requirement for lone parents to enter the labour force. As well as through formal requirement, this is achieved by further disincentivising the alternative of welfare dependency. As partnerless parents in family welfare policy, as with the 'Bachelor Boy' model in Higher Education, lone-parent students find themselves token deviations from the implicit legitimate norm. Being neither male breadwinner, free from childcare constraints, nor female childcarer financially supported by a working partner, lone mothers deviate from implicit gendered expectations enshrined in policy.

Since the late 1990s, the UK Labour and Coalition governments alike have seen increasing parents' participation in paid work as central to achieving their commitments in tackling child poverty (see Child Poverty Strategy, 2011; Freud, 2007: 37). Children of lone parents are at particular risk of poverty, facing twice the risk of income poverty compared to two-parent families (Child Poverty Action Group, 2011). In *In Work, Better Off: Next Steps to Full Employment*, the Government pledged that 'a new social contract for lone parents will put tackling child poverty at the heart of our welfare system' (Department for Work and Pensions, 2007b: 7). But the effectiveness of paid work as a route out of poverty is evidenced to be unequal across different groups in society (Platt, 2007), and lone mothers' trajectories in this research support criticism from academic and policy commentators that successive policy developments are in fact responsible for increasing financial hardship and poverty for lone parent families (see Scott *et al.*, 2003).

Nevertheless, in their response to the Freud Report, Gingerbread (2007e) suggest that 'lone parent employment is one of the undoubted success stories of this [Labour] Government, the rate having risen 11 percentage points between 1997 and 2007, to 56.5 per cent.' Although not fully clear because of the documented lack of statistical data on student parents in Higher Education (NUS, 2007: 9), the relationship between increasing education and skills levels through the widening participation agenda in Higher Education, and improved lone parent employment should not be underestimated. But in the context of lone parent policy by successive governments accused of being shortsightedly oriented toward quick-fix lone-parent employment solutions with minimal resource cost (as previously discussed), it is perhaps small wonder

241

that the long haul of supporting university participation and its entry through Further Education (with its high returns yielded from heavy costs realised only in the long term), represents deferred gratification too unattractive for governments oriented to achieving short-term, measurable solutions to social problems. This, however, opens up the inherent contradictions between short-term and long-term solutions to lone parents' welfare dependency (Polakow *et al.*, 2004). Gingerbread have suggested that government programmes 'have not been very good at encouraging sustained employment' (2007c:1), and that the NDLP financing of lone parents' participation in learning only up to NVQ Level 2 (A-level equivalent) is discriminatory in implying that this is a sufficiently high level for lone parents (2007e: 8).

Gingerbread have highlighted the importance of 'employment retention/advancement' and 'contracting for sustainability' (2007c: 5), drawing attention to the recommendations for creating sustained employment in the 2006 Leitch Report, *Prosperity for All in the Global Economy: World Class Skills* (Gingerbread, 2007e: 10). By 2007, the lone-parent employment rate had begun to stall (Gingerbread, 2007c: 2), and while entering work at the same rate as the general population, lone parents are more likely to exit employment than partnered mothers (Gingerbread, 2007e: 2), and twice as likely to exit work as employees generally (CESI, 2007), hence being at high risk of ending up back on benefits. This indicates the impact of absence of parenting support at home upon ability to manage work, and informs the need for provision of a robust framework of childcare and financial support. The high exiting of jobs by lone parents further indicates failures to match individuals with jobs suitable to their circumstances, supporting charges of low-investment quick-fix solutions aimed at matching lone parents with any available job.

That in the UK parents of children over six currently have no right to request flexible working (Gingerbread, 2007e: 6), provides further rationale for lone parents to seek graduate jobs that frequently offer increased flexibility and autonomy around working hours, more suited to their sole childcare burden. The in-depth narratives provided by lone-mother HE students offer valuable evidence on factors assisting and hindering UK lone parents in increasing their levels of education and skills through HE participation. This is particularly significant in the international context, in which the UK continues to spend less than many other European countries on addressing the gap between the qualification levels of lone and partnered mothers, despite the presence of a larger gap than in many other countries (Gingerbread, 2007e: 3).

From a sociological perspective, increasing lone parents' participation in paid work and tackling welfare dependency should be far from the only, or even the primary, rationale for supporting the group's university participation. Valuable justifications for enfranchising lone parents through facilitating HE learning hinge on discourses of social justice, lifelong learning, life chances, social inclusion and mobility, and equality of opportunity. There are limiting implications of restricting the scope of justification to instrumental employment-oriented aims. Such focus inevitably leads toward targeting provision of learning opportunities to the vocationally oriented routes that have been problematised in this book as limiting lone parents' opportunities, both to experience education in its fullness, and to maximise their personal gains from participation. The narratives provided by lone mothers in this research indicate that many want to improve their level of education in preparation for entering the labour market at higher levels, but that they are not necessarily always ready to take this next step immediately (Gingerbread, 2007e: 18); this is particularly the case for those with younger children. Recognition that not everyone who wants to learn necessarily wants to return to work, embodies the lifelong learning model, in contrast to dominant skills-for-work policy. But presenting the case for allocation of resources frequently requires recourse to pragmatic rather than principled justifications, and it is to these ends that the instrumental role of Higher Education participation in supporting lone parents' economic independence is emphasised.

The identified necessity to 'make work pay' bolsters the case for facilitating lone parents' HE participation, increasing their prospects of entering the labour market at a level offering reasonable remuneration for their labour, childcare costs, and sacrifice of absence from their children. Evidence from this research indicates the sophisticated cost-benefit evaluations determining lone parents' decisions around whether it is worth being away from their children in work or education. Callender has warned that if government policy does not provide adequate support for university participation by lone parents, we may see them engaging with HE in decreasing numbers, undermining the widening participation agenda (2001).

The insights provided by lone-mother HE learners indicate a number of key areas for additional research. While the rich longitudinal narratives provide valuable in-depth insight into experiences, an identified need remains for this to be complemented by reliable large-scale statistical data. This is needed to bolster the case for acknowledging the significance of relevant intersecting biographical factors, and provide transparency around lone parents' concrete experiences that policy makers will be forced to recognise as evidence in support of improved provision. The NUS and NIACE have highlighted that the case for monitoring social characteristics within student populations has been won in relation to variables, including ethnicity and gender, and that HESA and the LSC have collected robust, high quality data, facilitating targeted funding and policy to address the needs of underrepresented groups. NUS suggest that with regard to lone parents, the absence of such data hinders assessment of the relative dedication of resources (2007b: 11).

Age emerged as being perceived as particularly significant by lone-parent students, indicating the value of more systematic research on employment rates and job-seeking experiences of lone-parent graduates in different age groups. Given documented lower completion rates of mature and working-class students, and the relevance to lone parents of factors evidenced to centrally inform course withdrawal, including the needs of dependants, employment demands, workload, and financial difficulty (Yorke, 2004), there is an identified need for more systematic investigation of catalysts for non-completion by lone-parent students. This is further implied by trajectories of exiting HE courses early due to problems juggling time and finances as lone parent learners.

Both the longitudinal research perspective and the different stages of HE learner journeys at which lone mothers participated in the research facilitate insight into HE outcomes for lone parents, as some graduated from their studies and entered the job market. This new stage of individuals' journeys exposes a new set of concerns around securing a job offering sufficient remuneration and the flexibility necessary to manage childcare alone. Evidence from the US suggests that 'workers who enter jobs in higher wage sectors of the economy ... are more likely to sustain and advance in their jobs' (Gingerbread, 2007e: 10), while the Centre for Economic and Social Inclusion (CESI) have highlighted that employment engagement for lone parents is associated with higher qualifications, while persistent welfare dependency is associated with a deficit of qualifications (2007). This informs the need for further research on employment outcomes of university participation for lone-parent students to contribute to understanding of the long-term benefits of investing in Higher Education for lone parents. It would however be further valuable to investigate the extent to which the identified problem of lack of suitable jobs leading to low employment rates of British lone parents (Jenkins and Symons, 2001: 121) is experienced by those graduating from Higher Education, and whether the identified constraints placed by family responsibilities upon graduate employment 'choices' (Edwards, 1993:147) are significant in returning lone parents to semi–professional employment after HE completion (Egerton, 2000: 7). BME graduates are evidenced to have both lower employment rates and average incomes after HE completion compared to white graduates (AGCAS, 2008; Li, Devine and Heath, 2008), and such inequalities may be anticipated to extend to WP students more broadly, including lone parents.

This book has documented both the temporary transitional changes experienced by lone mothers as they pass through the process of university participation, and deeper permanent facets of change to both life chances and identity. Pascall and Cox unearthed evidence of deep, permanent change (1993: 121) when they revisited mature students after HE completion (1993: 120). Further investigation would be valuable of the longer-term impact of HE participation upon lone parents as a distinct group.

The insights contributed to this book by lone parents negotiating the 'Bachelor Boy's' world of Higher Education convey the complex inter-sectionality of multiple factors in determining individuals' experiences and ultimately 'success' in negotiating a system that often appears stacked against them, in being designed for others who do not share their load of conflicting roles and responsibilities. In doing so, it sheds light on the interplay of individual agency, informal support structures, and access to formal support, in informing eventual outcomes as lone parents attempt to learn to juggle the competing demands upon their time and material resources. Policy cannot legislate for individual agency or informal support, and it would be a deficient strategy for informing opportunity and life chances that consigned responsibility for outcomes to such serendipity. Recent research by the Joseph Rowntree Foundation highlights that individuals' experiences are informed by the dual causation of both informal processes, and formal structures of provision (JRF, 2011: 1). This book has aimed to contribute lone-mother HE students' own stories and priorities to asserting the responsibility of policy makers to support social equity for lone parents through

245

facilitating HE participation. The positive effects of such investment are demonstrated to ripple out beyond intrinsic and instrumental gains to lone parents' as immediate beneficiaries. These extend to potential intergenerational benefits for the half of all UK children who now spend part of their childhood in a lone parent family, and to society at large in fostering social inclusion and attacking the symptoms of exclusion and welfare dependency. The narratives contributed to this research demonstrate that when they are supported with the resources to realise their potential through HE participation, many lone-parent learners are willing to put in the hard work to make long-term improvements to the lives of themselves and their children, and are further able to realise their ability and will to contribute valuably to society. This process of self-actualisation, when facilitated, unites intrinsic and instrumental outcomes in terms of personal and professional development, radically altering lone parents' lived experiences both as parents in the private world of the family, and citizens in the public spheres of education and work.

References

AGCAS (2008) *What Happens Next? A Report on Ethnicity and the First Destinations of Graduates 2006* [online] http://www.agcas.org.uk/agcas_resources/49-What-Happens-Next-A-Report-on-Ethnicity-and-the-First-Destinations-of-Graduates [accessed 27 May 2012].

Aimhigher (2007) *About Aimhigher*, [online] http://www.aimhigher.ac.uk/practitioner/programme_information/about_aimhigher.cfm [accessed 27 May 2012].

Arendt, H. (1958) *The Human Condition*. Chicago: Chicago University Press.

Asda Magazine (2006) September.

Althaus, F. (1996) 'Fathers in single-parent households are increasingly likely to be young, never married and low income', *Family Planning Perspectives*, 28(6): 285–286.

Baker, S. (2005) 'Like a Fish in Water: Aspects of the Contemporary UK Higher Education System', Unpublished PhD thesis, University of Wales.

Barnes, C. and Mercer, G. (2009) *Exploring Disability*. Cambridge: Polity.

Bawden, A. (2006) 'Study pays off for UK graduates, report shows', *The Guardian*, 12 September [online] http://education.guardian.co.uk/students/graduation/story/0,,1870488,00.html [accessed 27 May 2012].

BBC News 24 (2007a) 'Ask the expert: My ex's debts' [online] http://news.bbc.co.uk/1/hi/business/3757265.stm [accessed 27 May 2012].

BBC Radio 4 (2007b) 'I can't get out of debt' [online] http://www.bbc.co.uk/radio4/hometruths/indebt.shtml [accessed 27 May 2012].

Beckett, A. (2006) 'Going cheap', *The Guardian* [online] http://www.guardian.co.uk/g2/story/0,,1719754,00.html [accessed 27 May 2012].

Bell, K. and Strelitz, J. (2011). *Decent Childhoods: Reframing the Fight to End Child Poverty* [online] http://www.decentchildhoods.org.uk/wp-content/uploads/Decent_Childhoods_-_final11.pdf [accessed 30 May 2012].

Bonnet, A. and Meredith-Lobay, M. (2004) 'Graduate Tutors Committee: What is it?', *Gown Magazine*, Issue 1, Michaelmas: 28–30.

Bostock, S. (1998) 'Constructivism in mass higher education: A case study', *British Journal of Educational Technology* 29(3): 25–240.

Bradshaw, J. and Millar, J. (1991) *Lone Parent Families in the UK*. London: Department of Social Security, HMSO Docs / DSS-RR 6.

Brennan, J., Mills, J., Shah, T. and Woodley, A. (1999) *Part-time Students and Employment: Report of a Survey of Students, Graduates and Diplomats*. London: DfEE/HEQE/QSE.

Brine, J. and Waller, R. (2004) 'Working-class women on an Access course: Risk, opportunity and (re)constructing identities', *Gender and Education*, 16(1): 97–113.

Brown, R. (2007) 'Participation problems persist', *The Guardian*, 26 June [online] http://education.guardian.co.uk/higher/comment/story/0,,2110973,00.html [accessed 27 May 2012].

Burke, P. and McManus, J. (2010) *Art for a Few: Exclusion and Misrecognition in Art and Design Higher Education Admissions*. London: National Arts Learning Network.

Burns, A. and Scott, C. (1993) 'Career trajectories of single and married mothers who complete tertiary study as mature age students', *Education and Society*, 11: 39–50.

Byrne, M. and Flood, B. (2005). 'A study of accounting students' motives, expectations and preparedness for Higher Education', *Journal of Further and Higher Education*, 29(2): 111–124.

Callender, C. and Kemp, M. (2000) *Changing Student Finances: Income, Expenditure and the Take-up of Student Loans among Full time and Part-time Higher Education Students in 1998–99*, DfEE Research Report, 213. London: DfEE.

Callender, C. (2001) 'Thwarted ambitions'. *The Guardian*. [online].

http://education.guardian.co.uk/higher/story/0,,430434,00. html [accessed 27 May 2012].

Callender, C. (2002) 'The costs of widening participation: Contradictions in New Labour's student funding policies', *Social Policy and Society*, 1(2): 83–94.

Callender, C., Wilkinson, D., MacKinnon, K. and Vegeris, S. (2005) *Research Report on Higher and Further Education Students' Income, Expenditure and Debt in Scotland. 2004–2005* [online] http://www.scotland.gov.uk/Publications/2005/10/26105054/50552 [accessed 27 May 2008] Policy Studies Institute.

Cappleman-Morgan, J. (2005) 'Obstacle courses? Mature students' experiences of combining higher education with caring responsibilities', C-SAP PROJECT 2004–5. [online] http://www.c-sap.bham.ac.uk/media/com_projectlog/docs/PG_04_16.pdf [accessed 27 May 2008]

Carlisle, D. (2005) 'Caring to learn? Getting young mothers back into education', *Community Practitioner*, 78(10): 347–348.

CESI (Centre for Economic and Social Inclusion) (2007) Gingerbread Lone parents and employment seminar, 19 September.

Cha, Y. (2011) 'Reinforcing separate spheres: The effect of spousal overwork on men's and women's employment in dual-earner households', *American Sociological Review*, 75(2): 303–329.

Child Poverty Action Group (2011) 'Risk of income poverty by household type, 2009/10', *What is poverty?* [online] http://www.cpag.org.uk/povertyfacts/#impact [accessed 27 May 2012].

Christie, H., Munro, M., and Wager, F. (2005) 'Day students in higher education: Widening access students and successful transitions to university life', *International Studies in the Sociology of Education*, 15(1): 3–30.

Clance, P.R. (1985) *The Impostor Phenomenon: When Success Makes You Feel Like a Fake.* Toronto: Bantam.

Closer Magazine (2006) 'Guilty mums,' 16–22 September.

Connor, H., and Dewson, S., with Tyers, C., Eccles, J., Regan., and Aston, J., (2001) *Social Class and Higher Education: Issues Affecting Decisions on Participation by Lower Social Class Groups.* London: Institute for Employment Studies.

Crompton, R. (1999) 'The decline of the male breadwinner: Explanations and interpretations', in Crompton, R. (ed.) *Restructuring Gender Relations and Employment: The Decline of the Male Breadwinner.*

Oxford: Oxford University Press: 1–26.

Crompton, R. and Harris, F. (1999) 'Employment, careers, and families: The significance of choice and constraint in women's lives', in Crompton, R. (ed.) *Restructuring Gender Relations and Employment: The Decline of the Male Breadwinner*. Oxford: Oxford University Press: 128–149.

Crossan, B., Field, J., Gallacher, J. and Merrill, B. (2003) 'Understanding participation in learning for non-traditional adult learners: Learning careers and the construction of learning identities', *British Journal of Sociology of Education*, 24(1): 55–67.

Davies, S., Lubelska, C., and Quinn, J. (eds.) *Changing the Subject: Women in Higher Education*. London: Taylor and Francis.

Deem, R. (1986) *All Work and No Play? A Study of Women and Leisure*. Milton Keynes: Open U.P.

Deer, C. (2005) 'Higher education access and expansion: The French experience,' *Higher Education Quarterly*, 59(3): 230–41.

DeParle, J. (2004) *American Dream: Three Women, Ten Kids, and a Nation's Drive to End Welfare*. New York: Penguin.

Department for Education and Employment (1997) The Dearing Report – National Committee of Inquiry into Higher Education, *Higher Education in the Learning Society*. London: Department for Education and employment [online] http://www.leeds.ac.uk/educol/ncihe/ [accessed 27 May 2012].

Department for Education and Skills (2003) *The Future of Higher Education* [online] http://www.bis.gov.uk/assets/biscore/corporate/migratedd/publications/f/future_of_he.pdf [accessed 27 May 2012].

Department for Work and Pensions (2007a) *Ready for Work: Full Employment in our Generation*. London: The Stationery Office [online] http://www.dwp.gov.uk/welfarereform/readyforwork/readyforwork.pdf [accessed 27 May 2012].

Department for Work and Pensions (2007b) *In Work, Better Off: Next Steps to Full Employment*. London: The Stationery Office [online]

Department for Work and Pensions and Department for Education (2011) *A New Approach to Child Poverty: Tackling the Causes of Disadvantage and Transforming Families' Lives* [online] https://www.education.gov.uk/publications/eOrderingDownload/CM-8061.pdf [accessed 27 May 2012].

Dew, J. (2009) 'Has the marital time cost of parenting changed over time?', *Social Forces*, 88(2): 519–541.

Directgov (2011) *Benefits for Higher Education Students with Low Incomes* [online] http://www.direct.gov.uk/en/MoneyTaxAndBenefits/BenefitsTaxCreditsAndOtherSupport/On_a_low_income/DG_10034876 [accessed 27 May 2012].

Duckworth, K. (2005) 'Effects of mothers' education on parenting: An investigation across three generations', *London Review of Education*, 3(3): 239–264.

Duncan, S. and Edwards R. (1999) *Lone Mothers, Paid Work and Gendered Moral Rationalities*. Basingstoke: Macmillan.

Eccles, J. S. and Daris-Kean, P. E. (2005) 'Influences of parents' education on their children's educational attainments: The role of parent and child perceptions', *London Review of Education*, 3(3): 191–204.

Edwards, R. (1993) *Mature Women Students: Separating or Connecting Family and Education*. London: Taylor and Francis.

Egerton, M. (2000) 'Monitoring contemporary student flows and characteristics: Secondary analyses using the labour force survey and the general household survey', *Journal of the Royal Statistical Society*, B, 163, Part 1: 63–80.

Equality Challenge Unit (2007) Plenary session. 'Gendered choices and transitions: Part-time pathways, full-time lives', London: Birkbeck College, 18 May.

Family Action (2011) *Welfare that Works Better – 10 Recommendations for Improving the Universal Credit* [online] http://www.family-action.org.uk/section.aspx?id=13397 [accessed 27 May 2012].

Fawcett Society (2007) *Women and Debt*, Report. [online] http://www.fawcettsociety.org.uk/documents/Women%20and%20debt.pdf [accessed 27 May 2012].

Ford, R. (1996) *Childcare in the Balance: How Lone Parents Make Decisions about Work*. London: Policy Studies Institute.

Freud, D. (2007) *Reducing Dependency, Increasing Opportunity: Options for The Future of Welfare to Work*. An Independent Report to the Department for Work and Pensions, Corporate Document Services. [online] http://www.dwp.gov.uk/docs/welfarereview.pdf [accessed 27 May 2012].

Gallagher, A., Richards, N. and Locke, M. (1993) *Mature Students in Higher Education: How Institutions can Learn from Experience*. University of East London.

Garfinkel, H. (1967) *Studies in Ethnomethodology*. London: Routledge and Kegan Paul.

Gilbert, L.A., and Holahan, C.K. (1982) 'Conflicts between student/professional, parental and self-development roles: A comparison of high and low effective copers', *Human Relations*, 8(35): 635–48.

Gingerbread (2006) *Money for Higher Education Students: A Guide for Lone Parents*. London: Gingerbread [online] http://www.gingerbread.org.uk/information-and-advice/documents/moneyforhighered.pdf [accessed 20 March 2008]

Gingerbread (2007a) Keynote address. 'Lone parents, education and training: Facilitating access and participation', 20 July, University of Sussex.

Gingerbread (2007b) Lone parents and employment seminar, 19 September.

Gingerbread (2007c) Seminar briefing, Lone parents and employment seminar, 19 September.

Gingerbread (2007d) *One Parent Families Today: The Facts*. London: One Parent Families/Gingerbread.

Gingerbread/One Parent Families (2007e) 'Reducing dependency, increasing opportunity: Options for the future of welfare to work', *A Response to David Freud's Review from One Parent Families*. London: One Parent Families.

Gingerbread/One Parent Families (2007f) *In work better off response*. London: Gingerbread/One Parent Families.

Gingerbread (2012) 'Statistics: Work and childcare' [online] http://www.gingerbread.org.uk/content.aspx?CategoryID=365&ArticleID=267 [accessed 30 January 2012].

Goffman, E. (1963) *Stigma: Notes on the Management of Spoiled Identity*. London: Prentice-Hall.

Gottfried, H. and O'Reilly, J. (2002) 'Reregulating breadwinner: The weakness of a strong male breadwinner model', *Social Politics. International Studies in Gender, State and Society* (9): 29–59.

Greif, G.L. (1992) 'Lone fathers in the United States: An overview and practice implications', *British Journal of Social Work*, 22: 565–574.

Gregg, P. (2007) Gingerbread lone parents and employment seminar, 19 September.

Hands, A., Mackay, J., Ormiston-Smith, N., Perryman, S. and Wright-Anderson, P. (2007) *Staying the Course: The Retention of Students in Higher Education*. National Audit Office Report. London: The Stationery Office.

Haskey, J. (2005) *Living Arrangements in Contemporary Britain: Having a Partner Who Usually Lives Elsewhere; Living Apart Together.* London: Office for National Statistics, and University of Oxford.

Hencke, D. (2006) 11/09/06 'Kelly helps women juggle work and family', *The Guardian*, 11 September [online]. http://money. guardian.co.uk/print/0,,329573532-121284,00.html [accessed 27 May 2012].

HESA (2012) 'Number of mature students with SEC 1–7 by gender, mode, domicile and grouped SEC, 2010/2011'. Date provided on request.

Hinton-Smith, J. T. (2007a) Lone parents, education and training: Facilitating access and participation workshop, 20 July, University of Sussex.

Hinton-Smith, J. T. (2007b) *Lone Parents as Higher Education Students, University Life Uncovered.* Higher Education Academy (HEA) Social Policy and Social Work (SWAP) Network Monograph series.

HM Government (2011) *Opening Doors, Breaking Barriers: A Strategy for Social Mobility.* [online] http://www.dpm.cabinetoffice.gov. uk/sites/default/files_dpm/resources/opening-doors-breaking-barriers.pdf [accessed 27 May 2012]

Hochschild, A. (1983) *The Managed Heart: Commercialization of Human Feeling.* Berkeley: University of California Press.

Horne, M. and Hardie, C. (2002) 'From welfare to higher education: A study of lone-parent students at Queen Margaret University College', *Edinburgh Journal of Adult and Continuing Education*, 8(1): 60–72.

Hussey, T. and Smith, P. (2010) 'Transitions in higher education', *Innovations in Education and Teaching International*, 47(2):155–164.

Hyatt, J., and Parry-Crooke, G. (1990) *Barriers to Work: A Study of Lone Parents' Training and Employment Needs.* London: National Council for One Parent Families.

Hyde, S. (2007) 'An absence of gender in the workplace learning agenda? – Reflections on a life history project with workplace learners', Gendered Choices and Transitions: Part-Time Pathways, Full-Time Lives. London: Birkbeck College, 18 May.

Jackson, S. (2004) *Differently Academic? Developing Lifelong Learning for Women In Higher Education.* Netherlands: Kluwer.

Jacobs, J.A. and Gerson, K. (2004) *The Time Divide: Work, Family and Gender Inequality*. Cambridge, MA: Harvard University Press.

Jarvis, C.A. (2003) 'Desirable reading: The relationship between women students' lives and their reading practices', *Adult Education Quarterly*, 53(4): 261–276.

Jenkins, S.P., and Symons, E. J. (2001) 'Childcare costs and lone mothers' employment rates,' *The Manchester School*, 69(2): March.

Jones, K. (2006) 'Valuing diversity and widening participation: The experiences of Access to Social Work students in further and higher education', *Social Work Education*, 25(5): 485–500.

de Jonghe, E. 'The student and mass higher education', *Higher Education*, 2(2): 243–251.

Joshi, H. (1998) 'The opportunity costs of childbearing: More than mothers' business', *Journal of Population Economics* 11(2):161–183.

Kendall, L. (1999) 'Recontextualizing "cyberspace": Methodological considerations for on-line research', in Jones, S. (ed.) *Doing Internet Research: Critical Issues and Methods for Examining the Net*. London: Sage: 57–75.

Kiernan, K., Land, H., and Lewis, J. (1998) *Lone Motherhood in Twentieth-Century Britain: From Footnote to Front Page*. Oxford: Oxford University Press.

Kingston, P. (2006) 'The changing face of success', *The Guardian*, 1 August [online] http://education.guardian.co.uk/higher/news/story/0,,1834155,00.html [accessed 27 May 2012].

Klett-Davies, M. (2007) *Going It Alone? Lone Motherhood in Late Modernity*. Aldershot: Ashgate.

Knox, H., (2005) 'Making the transition from further to higher education: The impact of a preparatory module on retention, progression and performance,' *Journal of Further and Higher Education*, 29(2): 103–110.

Komulainen, K. (2000) 'The past is difference – the difference is past', *Gender and Education*, 12(4): 449–462.

Labour Force Survey (2009) [online] http://www.esds.ac.uk/government/lfs/ [accessed 27 May 2012].

Laing, C., Chao, K.M., and Robinson, A. (2005) 'Managing the expectations of non-traditional students: a process of negotiation,' *Journal of Further and Higher Education*, 29(2): 169–179.

Land, H. (2007) Keynote address, 'Sinners, scroungers, saints: Lone mothers, past and present', The Women's Library, London Metropolitan University.

Land, H., and Lewis, J. (1998) 'The problem of lone parenthood in the British context', in Ford, R. and Millar, J. (eds.) *Private Lives and Public Responses*. London: Policy Studies Institute: 141–153.

Layer, G. (2006) 'Part-time – but not forgotten: Policy-makers and the media are working with an outmoded image of life in higher education', *Adults Learning*, 17(5): 16–17.

Leitch, S. (2006) *Prosperity for All in the Global Economy: World Class Skills.* London: HM Treasury.

Leonard, M. (1994) 'Mature women and access to HE', in Davies, S., Lubelska, C., and Quinn, J. (eds.) *Changing the Subject: Women in Higher Education.* London: Taylor and Francis: 163–177.

Li, Y., Devine, F. and Heath, A. (2008) *Equality Group Inequalities in Education, Employment and Earning: A Research Review and Analysis of Trends over Time.* Equality and Human Rights Commission Research Report No. 10. Manchester: EHRC.

Lipman, E. L., and Boyle, M. H. (2005) 'Social support and education groups for single mothers: A randomized controlled trial of a community-based program', *Canadian Medical Association Journal*, 173(12): 1451–1456.

Lipsett, A. (2007a) 'Students get OU satisfaction'. *The Guardian*, 12 September [online] http://education.guardian.co.uk/students/news/story/0,,2167365,00.html [accessed 27 May 2012]

Lipsett, A. (2007b) '20% of new students dropping out, says report,' *The Guardian* 26 July [online] http://education.guardian.co.uk/higher/news/story/0,,2134548,00.html [accessed 27 May 2012].

Lowry, S. (1980) *The Guilt Cage: Housewives and a Decade of Liberation.* London: Elm Tree.

Mann, C. and Stewart, F. (2000) *Internet Communication and Qualitative Research: A Handbook for Researching Online.* London: Sage.

May, V. (2004) 'Meanings of lone motherhood within a broader family context,' *The Sociological Review*, 52(3): 390–403.

McShand, D. 2004 *Dropping in or Dropping Out? A Study of Students who Withdrew During the 2002/2003 Academic Year* [online] http://www.wmin.ac.uk/pdf/DIDOReport%202002_3.pdf [accessed 27 May 2012] Educational Initiative Centre, University of Westminster.

Medhurst, P. (2007) 'Families and part-time study: Allies or otherwise', Gendered Choices and Transitions: Part-Time Pathways, Full-Time Lives. London: Birkbeck College, 18 May.

Meikle, J. (2006) 'Universities push for support for part-timers', *The Guardian*, 26 October [online] http://education.guardian.co.uk/ students/finance/story/0,,1931277,00.html 24 [accessed 27 May 2012].

Mental Health Foundation (2011) 'Statistics on mental health' [online] http://www.mentalhealth.org.uk/help-information/mental-health-statistics/ [accessed 27 May 2012].

Meredith-Lobay, M. (2004) 'Student parents', *Gown Magazine*, Issue 1, Michaelmas: 17–18.

Merrill, B. (1999) *Gender, Change and Identity: Mature Women Students in Universities.* Aldershot: Ashgate.

Millar, J., and Rowlingson, K. (2001) *Lone Parents, Employment and Social Policy: Cross-National Comparisons.* Bristol: Policy Press.

Mirza, H. (2007) 'The (in)visible journey: Black women's life-long lessons in Higher Education', Keynote address. Gendered Choices and Transitions: Part-Time Pathways, Full-Time Lives. London: Birkbeck College, 18 May.

Moorhead, R., Douglas, G., and Sefton, M. (2004) *The Advice Needs of Lone Parents.* Cardiff University.

Moreau, M.P., and Leathwood C. (2006) 'Balancing paid work and studies: Working (-class) students in higher education', *Studies in Higher Education*, 31(10): 23–42.

Murphy, H. and Roopchand, N. (2003) 'Intrinsic motivation and self-esteem in traditional and mature students at a post-1992 university in the north-east of England', *Educational Studies*, 29(2–3): 243–259.

Naidoo, R. and Callender, C. (2000) 'Towards a more inclusive system of HE? Contemporary policy reform in higher education', *Social Policy Review*, 12: 224–249.

Nelson, J.R., Niemann, J., and Van Stone, N. (1994) 'Poor single-mother college students' views on the effect of some primary sociological and psychological belief factors on their academic success', *Journal of Higher Education*, 65: 571–581.

NUS (2007a) *Lone Parents and Reforms To Benefit Entitlement*, Letter to John Denham, Secretary of State for Universities. London: NUS.

NUS (2007b) *Student Parents' Project: Literature Review* (Draft). London: NUS.

NUS (2009) *Meet the Parents: The Experience of Students with Children in Further and Higher Education.* London: NUS [online] http://www.

nus.org.uk/PageFiles/5386/NUS_SP_report_web.pdf [accessed 27 May 2012]

NUS and CIB (2011) *Working Towards Your Future: Making the Most of Your Time in Higher Education*. London: CBI [online] http://www.nus.org.uk/Global/CBI_NUS_Employability%20report_May%202011.pdf [accessed 27 May 2012].

Office for Fair Access (OFFA) (2010) *Targeted Outreach is the Key to Widening Access at Highly Selective Universities* [online] http://www.offa.org.uk/press-releases/targeted-outreach-is-the-key-to-widening-access-at-highly-selective-universities-says-offa/ [accessed 27 May 2012].

Oliver, M. (1996) *Understanding Disability: From Theory to Practice*. London: Macmillan.

Open University Senate (2010) 'Minutes of the meeting of the Senate held on Wednesday 13 October 2010.' [online] http://www.open.ac.uk/foi/pics/d126249.pdf [accessed 27 May 2012].

Panel on Fair Access to the Professions (2009) *Unleashing Aspiration: The Final Report of the Panel on Fair Access to the Professions*. London: The Cabinet Office [online] http://www.bis.gov.uk/assets/biscore/corporate/migratedd/publications/p/panel-fair-access-to-professions-final-report-21july09.pdf [accessed 27 May 2012].

Parr, J. (2000) *Identity and Education: The Links for Mature Women Students*. Aldershot: Ashgate.

Pascall, G. and Cox, R. (1993) *Women Returning To Higher Education*. Buckingham: The Society for Research into Higher Education and the Open University Press.

Platt, L. (2007) *Poverty and Ethnicity in the UK*. York: Joseph Rowntree Foundation.

Polakow, V., Butler, S. S., Stormer Deprez, L. and Kahn, P. (eds) (2004) *Shut Out: Low-Income Mothers and Higher Education in Post-Welfare America*. Albany: State University of New York Press.

Policy Research Institute, Leeds Metropolitan University (2007) *Towards Skills For Jobs: What Works in Tackling Worklessness? Rapid Review of Evidence*. Coventry: Learning and Skills Council.

Prangley, E., Targeted Student Finance Team, DIUS (2007) Personal correspondence. 25 March.

Preece, J., Woodrow, M. and Weatherald, C. (eds.) (1998) *Beyond the Boundaries: Exploring the Potential of Widened Participation in Higher Education*. Leicester: NIACE.

Procter, I. and Padfield, M. (1998) *Young Adult Women, Work and Family: Living a Contradiction.* London: Mansell.

Quinn, J. and Allen, K. (2010) 'Who fits in the creative world?', 10 December, London Metropolitan University.

Ramsey, A. (2008) *Graduate Earnings: An Econometric Analysis of Returns, Inequality and Deprivation Across the UK*, Belfast: Department for Employment and Learning.

Reay, D. (2003) 'A risky business? Mature working-class women students and access to higher education', *Gender and Education*, 15(3): 301–317.

Rentoul, J. (2007) 'The Campbell years', *The Independent on Sunday*, *New Review*, 1 July: 22–26.

Rich, A. (1985) 'Taking women students seriously', in Culley, M., and Portuges, C. (eds.) *Gendered Subjects: The Dynamics of Feminist Teaching.* London: Routledge and Kegan Paul.

Scott, C., Burns, A. and Cooney, G. (1996) 'Reasons for discontinuing study: The case of mature age female students with children', *Higher Education*, 31(2): 233–253.

Scott, C., Burns, A. and Cooney, G. (1998) 'Motivation for return to study as a predictor of completion of degree amongst female mature students with children', *Higher Education*, 35(2): 221–239.

Scott, G., Frondigoun, E., Gillespie, M. and White, A. (2003) *Making Ends Meet: An Exploration of Parent Student Poverty, Family Finances and Institutional support.* Glasgow: Scottish Poverty Information Unit.

Scott, S. (2007) *Shyness and Society: The Illusion of Competence.* Basingstoke: Palgrave.

Shakespeare, T.W. (2006) *Disability Rights and Wrongs.* London: Routledge.

Shakespeare, T.W. and Watson, N. (2002) 'The social model of disability: An outmoded ideology', *Research in Social Science and Disability*, 2: 21–28.

Shaw, M. and Woolhead, G. (2006) 'Supporting young mothers into education, employment and training: Assessing progress towards the target', *Health and Social Care in the Community*, 14(2): 177–184.

Shepherd, J. (2006) 'Shocked, puzzled and annoyed', *The Guardian*, 18 Sept. [online] http://education.guardian.co.uk/higher/news/story/0,,2171189,00.html [accessed 27 May 2012].

Skeggs, B. (1997) *Formations of Class and Gender: Becoming Respectable*. London: Sage.

Skills and Enterprise Network (2001) *Labour Market Quarterly Report*. Sheffield: Skills and Enterprise Network.

Smith, G., Research and Development Officer, NUS (2007) Personal correspondence. 20 March.

Smithers, R. (2004) 'Learn for joy not just jobs says new minister', *The Guardian*, 24 Sept. [online] http://education.guardian. co.uk/higher/news/story/0,,1311628,00.html [accessed 27 May 2012].

Sobotka, T. (2006) 'In pursuit of higher education, do we postpone parenthood too long?', *Gender Medicine*, 3(30): 183–186.

SPAN (Single Parent Action Network) (2007) Gingerbread lone parents and employment seminar, 19 September.

Spender, D. (ed.) (1981) *Men's Studies Modified: The Impact of Feminism on the Academic Disciplines*. Oxford: Pergamon.

Spender, D. (1982) *Invisible Women: The Schooling Scandal*. London: Writers and Readers.

Sudweeks, F. and Simoff, S. J. (1999) 'Complementary exploration data analysis: The reconciliation of quantitative and qualitative principles', in Jones, C. (ed.) *Doing Internet Research: Critical Issues and Methods for Examining the Net*, 29–57, London: Sage.

Sutherland, J.-A. (2010) 'Mothering, Guilt and Shame', *Sociology Compass*, 4: 310–321.

Taylor, Y. (2007) 'Going up without going away? Working-class women in Higher Education', *Youth and Policy*, No. 94: 35–50.

Taylor-Gooby, P. and Stoker, G. (2011) 'The Coalition Programme: A New Vision for Britain or Politics as Usual?', *The Political Quarterly*, 82(1): 4–15.

Unistats (2011) [online] http://unistats.direct.gov.uk/ [accessed 27 May 2012].

Wain, K. (2000) 'The learning society: Postmodern politics,' *International Journal of Lifelong Education*, 19: 36–53.

Waldman, A. (2009) *Bad Mother: A Chronicle of Maternal Crimes, Minor Calamities, and Occasional Moments of Grace*. New York: Doubleday.

Wall, G. 2010 'Mothers' experiences with intensive parenting and brain development discourse', *Women's Studies International Forum*, 33(3):253–263.

Walsh, J. (2007) 'Equality and diversity in British workplaces: The 2004 workplace employment relations survey', *Industrial Relations Journal* 38(4): 303–319.

Ward, L. (2005a) Women making slow progress in pay fight', *The Guardian*, 18 May [online] http://money.guardian.co.uk/print/0,3858,5195930-110400,00.html [accessed 27 May 2012].

Ward, L. (2005b) 'Childcare burden falls on family', *The Guardian*, 20 May [online] http://www.guardian.co.uk/print/0,3858,5148213-103690,00.html [accessed 27 May 2012].

Watson, D. (2007) Keynote address, Centre for Higher Education and Equity Research (CHEER) launch, University of Sussex, 15 November 2007.

Weil, S. (1986) 'Non-traditional learners within traditional higher education: Discovery and disappointment', *Studies in Higher Education*, 11(3): 219–235.

Weiner, G. (2002) 'Review: Mortimore, P. *Understanding Pedagogy and its Impact on Learning*', *British Educational Research Journal*, 28(6): 905–907.

Welfare Reform Bill (2011) [online] http://www.publications.parliament.uk/pa/cm201011/cmbills/154/11154.i-v.html [accessed 27 May 2012].

Wilcox, P., Winn, S., Fyvie-Gauld, M. (2005) '"It was nothing to do with the university, it was just the people": The role of social support in the first-year experience of higher education', *Studies in Higher Education*, 30(6): 707–722.

Willis, P. (1977) *Learning to Labour: How Working Class Kids get Working Class Jobs*. Farnborough: Saxon House.

Wilkinson, R. and Pickett, K. (2011) *The Spirit Level*. London: Penguin.

Wintour, P. (2007) 'No. 10 backs plan to force lone parents back to work', *The Guardian*, 12 February [online] http://money.guardian.co.uk/news_/story/0,,2011049,00.html [accessed 27 May 2012].

Wisker, G. (1996) *Empowering Women in Higher Education*. London: Kogan Page.

Women in the European Union 'Women, Work and Employment in Europe, 2.4. The sexual division of domestic labour, 2.4.1. The attribution of domestic responsibilities to women' [online] http://www.helsinki.fi/science/xantippa/wee/weetext/wee224.html [accessed 27 May 2012].

Woodfield, R. (2000) *Women, Work and Computing*. Cambridge: Cambridge University Press.

Woodfield, R. (2002) *Student Perceptions of the First Year Experience of University 2000–2001 – Results from a Qualitative Email Survey*, Final Report to University of Sussex Student Services Division: 1–169.

Woodfield, R., Earl-Novell, S., and Solomon, L. (2005) 'Gender and mode of assessment at university: Should we assume female students are better suited to coursework and males to unseen examinations?', *Assessment and Evaluation in Higher Education*, 30(1): 33–48.

Woodfield, R. and Earl-Novell, L. (2006) 'An assessment of the extent to which subject variation between the arts and sciences in relation to the award of first class degree can explain the 'Gender Gap', *British Journal of Sociology of Education*, 27(3): 355–372.

Woodfield, R. (2007) *What Women Want from Work: Gender and Occupational Choice in the Twenty-First Century*. Basingstoke: Palgrave MacMillan.

Woodley, A. and Wilson, J. (2002) 'British higher education and its older clients', *Higher Education*, 44: 329–347.

Work directions (2007) Gingerbread lone parents and employment seminar, 19 September.

Working Links (2007) Gingerbread lone parents and employment seminar, 19 September.

Yorke, M. (1999) *Leaving Early: Non-completion in Higher Education*. London: Falmer.

Yorke, M. (2001) 'Outside benchmark expectations? Variation in non-completion rates in English higher education', *Journal of Higher Education Policy and Management*, 23(2): 147–158.

Yorke, M. and Longden, B. (2004) *Retention and Student Success in Higher Education*. Maidenhead: Open University Press.

Young, M. and Willmott, P. (1957, 1969) *Family and Kinship in East London*. London: Penguin.

Zachry, E. M. (2005) 'Getting my education: Teen mothers' experiences in school before and after motherhood', *Teacher's College Record*, 107(12): 2566–2598.

Zepke, N. (2005) Diversity, adult education and the future: a tentative exploration, *International Journal of Lifelong education*, 24(2): 165–178.

Index

rescheduling 69
Research Council Funding: postgraduates
234–5
residential summer schools 128
retention 153, 220, 242; rates worldwide
14, *see also* withdrawal
Rich, Adrienne: woman centred
university 220
risk 95, 161, 162, 231; aversion 20
role conflict: guilt 81–6
role models 48, 182, 189, 208; positive 52
role-identities 75
rules: bending 156

Save the Children 11
savings 94
Scandinavia 135
school: experience of 27, 37
school holidays 6; activities 238; study
63–5
school hours: university timetable 222
school meals: free 96
schooling: negative experiences 219
Scott, C. 116, 134, 191, 234
Scottish Child Poverty Action Group 16
self: care of 78; impact of education on
199
self-confidence 51, 80
self-directed study 161
self-discipline 60, 159
self-doubt 198
self-esteem 35, 49, 179, 191–7, 219
self-help groups 219
self-identity: crisis 201
self-improvement 40
self-respect 43
siblings 36
Single Parents' Action Network (SPAN)
123
sleep: lacking 80
social class 3, 30, 95, 156, 198, 200; debt
110–11; effects of 148–9; identity 161;
informal childcare 129, 134; mixed 32;
transition to HE 163, *see also* working
class
social experience 79

social housing 119
social identity 198
social inclusion 5, 243; lifelong learning
11, 12
social inequality 215
social issues: changing views 182
social justice 243
social life 79–80, 139, 170; effect of
children's age 173–4
social mobility 33, 217
social networking 172
social science 45
social stigma: lone motherhood 53, 192
social values 189
social work 46
socialising 124–5
socioeconomic status 190
spoiled identity 198
stereotypes 187, 190; gender roles 47
stigma 53, 192, 198
stress 57, 70, 76, 81, 111, 167–9; multiple
roles 59; transition to HE 164
strugglers 203
Student Finance Policy Division 212
student finance system: streamlining 213
student finances: positive effects of 120–1
student financing 15–17; lone parents
102–7
student focused approach 155
student identity 194
student loans 11, 103, 207; eligibility 112;
part-time repayment problems 235;
repayment 232
Student Loans Company 112
student status 28
student support system 101; Benefits
Agency 16
Student Welfare 213
students (part-time) 57–9; disadvantages
235; learner identity 67; loans 207
studying: managing with family and
employment 69–81; school holidays
63–5; support groups 219; time 60–5,
196
subject choice: gender 36
support networks 49, 92